Clive Davis is universally regarded as the most important figure in the revolution in the record industry, which began in the 1960s with the full emergence of rock music as a vital and valid cultural medium. *Clive* is the highly personal story of this most celebrated and discussed executive in the record business.

It focuses on the Davis years at Columbia Records, from his joining the CBS legal department in 1960 through his much publicized termination in 1973. When, in 1965, the relatively unknown Davis was made Chief Administrative Officer of Columbia, this appointment shocked the industry. But Davis plunged in immediately in this new capacity to work on Columbia's crucial marketing and creative problems and commenced the task of reinvigorating a traditionally establishment company through the signing and promoting of pioneering rock artists whose eventual success would make Columbia foremost in the industry in terms both of earnings and prestige.

In his book Davis discusses the careers of Bob Dylan, Simon and Garfunkel, and Barbra Streisand and covers his relations with the various artists he signed and guided, with heavy concentration on popular and contemporary rock performers (including Donovan, Janis Joplin, Chicago, Santana,

Blood, Sweat & Tears, Laura Nyro, Johnny Winter, Edgar Winter, The Mahavishnu Orchestra, Loggins & Messina, and Billy Joel). He also details what he calls "the heaviest talent-raiding campaign ever conducted in the history of the music business," involving the acquisitions of such artists as Neil Diamond, Liza Minnelli, and Pink Floyd.

And various other aspects of the record business fall within Davis' scope: the hotly contested negotiating battles with other companies; the bitter struggle to launch hit singles; the use of independent producers; the criteria for auditioning new artists; the precise structuring of advertisement and promotion campaigns; career planning and relations with Columbia's middle-of-the-road artists (among them Andy Williams and Johnny Mathis), classical artists (Leonard Bernstein, Vladimir Horowitz), and country-and-western artists (Johnny Cash); and the "considerable grip of office politics."

Clive Davis undertook to write this book not as personal vindication of his controversial firing, but to create the fullest work possible on the intricacies of the fastest growing entertainment industry in this country. And he has succeeded brilliantly. *Clive* is not only utterly absorbing in its many stories concerning some of the most famous and accomplished musical artists of our time, but it is also a primer and bible of a business whose inner workings heretofore have never been explained to the enormous public that it daily entertains and edifies.

# CLIVE

## INSIDE THE RECORD BUSINESS

# CLIVE
## INSIDE THE RECORD BUSINESS

## by Clive Davis
### with James Willwerth

WILLIAM MORROW & COMPANY, INC.
NEW YORK    1975

*Printed in the United States of America.*

*Published simultaneously in Canada by*
*George J. McLeod Limited, Toronto.*

2 3 4 5   78 77 76 75

*Book design by Helen Roberts*

**Library of Congress Cataloging in Publication Data**

Davis, Clive.
　　Clive: inside the record business.

　　1. Davis, Clive.　2. Phonorecords—Industry and trade—United States.
3. Music, Popular (Songs, etc.)—United States.　I. Willwerth, James, joint author.　II. Title.
ML429.D36A3　　338.4′7′7899120924 [B]　　74-12246
ISBN 0-688-02872-1

*This book is dedicated to my parents,*
*Flo  and  Joe,*
*who live on inside me every day of my life.*

## Acknowledgments

None of this could have been written without my wife, Janet, who steadfastly shared the joys and sorrows; Fred, Lauren, Jeanette, Seena, Jerry, Jo, and Harry, who were always there when I needed them; those treasured friends who became family —they know who they are; Jim Willwerth, for provoking, stimulating, and then sharing the contents; Helen Merrill, for her encouragement; and Jim Landis, for his standards and his support.

# CLIVE
## INSIDE THE RECORD BUSINESS

# One

1 ═══════════════════════════════

I sensed change. I don't know, even now, precisely how I knew; I didn't know *what* I knew. But I felt movement. And as my sense of it grew, and my ability to evaluate it grew, I felt direction. For music was changing radically. And though this sense at first emerged timidly, after a short period of time it was rare for me to question it.

I am not, as the above might suggest, a seer or prophet. For close to eight years I was chief operating officer of Columbia Records. It was a period of constant cultural and musical change throughout America and England, also a time of enormous excitement within the music industry. In that context I was a businessman involved in music—who happened to lean heavily toward creative matters. Nothing more. For when I started in music, I had no particular *ear*. And I surely—at that time—felt no urgent kinship with what would later be called "rock consciousness."

Men in the music business, moreover, do not easily make futuristic judgments. Nor, in the strictest sense, are they expected to "discover" artists. They are paid to *recognize* talent and then to turn this resource into profit. The quest for artistic excellence, and sometimes for showmanship or virtuosity is, bluntly stated, a search for profit. This is somewhat camouflaged by music's emotional lure, its compelling excitement, the industry's glamour, and the challenge of "breaking out" new talent; for these tend to make the music business a romantic place. And it is often true that an artist pursues his artistic vision with considerable purity; or an executive can convince himself he's playing a marvelous game and getting paid for it.

Yet any company's accountants, or, in the impersonal world of big business, corporate management, can shock happy executives back to reality in a hurry; they want profits, more and more every year. I do not mean to suggest a mean-spirited grope for it. The problem is more subtle. For artists' careers sometimes take years to build, backed by investments of hundreds of thousands of dollars. And artists can be fragile, demonic creatures quite unconcerned with corporate cash flow. Except when it affects them personally. And public tastes change, sometimes very fast.

A record executive's job, therefore, is to spot emerging artists, nurture them (the right manager, booking agency, producer) and then launch, merchandise and showcase them. He must know the ingredients of musical excitement and be able to feel the potential for commercial success. It is dangerous to be too progressive or too far ahead of your time—but it is far more disastrous to lag behind it. The difference can be as subtle as defining what is coming . . . and what is *arriving*. When an artist (an industry term universally applied to all performers, incidentally, without any judgment, as such, about art) or a musical trend has arrived, you must be fully in place. Errors in judgment can cost millions of dollars, careers, prestige . . . and points on the stock market.

So this story must begin with the Bottom Line. *(i.e., the profit)*

# 2

When I became Administrative Vice-President of Columbia Records in 1965, at that time the company's number two position, Columbia seemed on the verge of serious financial trouble. Broadway cast albums, a traditional financial backbone, were declining with shocking speed. Mitch Miller's Sing Along albums, worth millions in the early sixties, had faded. Johnny Mathis, long one of America's most popular vocalists, had left the company, moving to Mercury Records for more than double the royalty. And classical music was now barely breaking even; "warhorse" recordings—sure-fire best sellers like Beethoven's Ninth Symphony or Bach's B Minor Mass—were if anything overrecorded. They could not be expected to generate any new volume of sales.

We were overstocked as well with traditional Christmas albums. And worst of all, recording costs for all kinds of music were rising dramatically.

Columbia had enjoyed a well-deserved reputation as one of the major record labels. Yet few outside the company knew the financial realities of the situation. Columbia was perilously close to being a marginal operation. The pre-tax profits were less than 5 percent of sales, hovering around five million dollars a year—hardly enough to cover the cost of a few large new record deals. Like most sizable corporations, Columbia's parent company, CBS, hid these problems by refusing to divulge its various divisions' profit and loss figures. Yet the bookkeeping ability to hide Columbia's Bottom Line from public view did nothing to soften the fact that I had walked into a potential financial crisis of considerable urgency.

In addition to problems caused by the loss of Broadway and Sing Along best sellers, and Mathis's departure, Columbia was scheduled soon to renegotiate the contracts of its three most important remaining artists: Bob Dylan, Barbra Streisand and Andy Williams. These contracts would expire at the same time, and it was clear that the artists' managers planned a confrontation. The managers for Streisand and Williams even discussed joining forces to increase their jawboning power, and all three artists were ready to shop around if Columbia balked at their demands.

Let me push a little deeper. Columbia had coasted nicely through the previous decade with a solid middle-of-the-road (MOR) format, aided during the late fifties and early sixties by the immense popularity of the Broadway cast albums it recorded. *My Fair Lady,* for example, sold more than five million albums, *South Pacific* more than two million albums and *Camelot* almost as much. Equally important, the company had a solid stable of gifted MOR artists—Ray Conniff, Doris Day, Percy Faith, Tony Bennett, Streisand, Williams, Jerry Vale, Robert Goulet—all of whom could record compositions from the same musicals. In fact, it was written into their contracts that they *had* to record them. So we had it both ways. Rodgers and Hammerstein and Lerner and Loewe wrote successful musicals, and Columbia acquired the original cast-album rights; then Williams, Streisand, Percy Faith and others recorded the songs again.

And then we had Mitch Miller. He had produced a tremendous succession of eleven gold albums in a row, adding considerably to Columbia's coffers. He was also an extraordinarily capable head of Columbia's Artist and Repertoire department (A&R) until the Sing Along millions allowed him to retire. Unfortunately, he was *also* opposed to rock music. He'd quit the A&R department several years before I entered the executive offices—but he'd succeeded in establishing a middle-of-the-road mentality among the company's A&R men, who are also called producers. They simply did not have an ear for rock; they felt threatened by it. In some ways, this was the most serious problem of all. The A&R department signs and produces the talent which makes the money. And here was Miller saying rock wouldn't last. He didn't like it, either. Miller and most of Columbia's executives felt fat and happy and had no reason to change their ways.

Still, it came down to a business decision. It didn't matter whether Miller was right or wrong about the aesthetics of rock; nor did it matter that the Company's President, Goddard Lieberson, had brought the best of Broadway and classical talent to Columbia. It was a sales crisis. After eleven gold albums, Miller dropped suddenly to sales of five hundred thousand, then three hundred thousand, *then to seventy-five thousand albums.* "Oh my God," everyone was saying. "After eleven gold albums, we aren't getting anything more. The concept is played out!"

And suddenly Broadway cast albums began dropping from the charts like wounded angels. *Mame* was the first example. It ran for years. Nightclub entertainers sang its title song all over the country—it was a big hit musical. Yet the original cast album sold only three hundred thousand copies. This was eventually followed by *Cabaret,* another immensely popular show; the cast album sold fewer than two hundred and fifty thousand copies.

I was taken aback. I couldn't understand it. We'd produced albums for two big, successful shows—rights bought by investing heavily in the shows themselves—and they weren't selling. Something was terribly wrong. The contrast between sales of these and earlier Broadway musicals was staggering. A few years earlier, *Flower Drum Song* had been nowhere near as successful a show as *Mame.* Yet its cast album easily sold six hundred thousand units.

And *Cabaret* was as popular as *Camelot* had been earlier . . . yet *Camelot* sold one and a half million.

A select few Broadway musicals were making it as albums—*Hello, Dolly!* and *Fiddler on the Roof,* both on RCA, as it happened—but it was suddenly clear that shows with good writing and arrangements could no longer be counted on to sell albums. The public's taste was changing—and fast.

Radio programming was part of the problem. At *Flower Drum Song*'s peak, Pat Suzuki's version of "I Enjoy Being a Girl" was played throughout the country on Top Forty stations (stations that play the top hits of the day); other MOR artists recorded it and got substantial air time. So the AM radio audience, the industry's most dependable consumer group, was massively exposed—and presumably turned on—to *Flower Drum*. And to its predecessors.

Rock music—Elvis Presley, Bill Haley & the Comets, Chuck Berry—wasn't the music of the masses. Not yet.

But by 1965, Top Forty air time had given way to Peter, Paul & Mary, Bob Dylan, Joan Baez and The Beatles. Until the arrival of *Hair,* Broadway writers had clearly not been in tune with the public's changing taste. We could no longer duplicate the sales successes of *South Pacific, My Fair Lady* or *Camelot.* The most popular radio stations didn't play their songs. A musical had to have a hit single—Louis Armstrong's "Hello, Dolly!" for example—to push its album into significant sales figures. Even then, the likes of Armstrong faced stiff competition on the charts against the growing proliferation of pop groups.

It was as if Columbia had collected a vast vault of gold and then the country disavowed the gold standard. The new legal tender was . . . Diamonds? Social protest? Flowers? I didn't know. I only knew that I had to replenish the company's fast-disappearing sales volume; better yet, get us off the frightening plateau of marginal sales profits.

But how?

The vague answer was rock—"contemporary" music. Unfortunately, mine was a minority—and unpopular—view. At this point, as Columbia's newly appointed Administrative Vice-President, I was a former corporate lawyer with no musical credentials. My case for making major investments in the contemporary scene was not strengthened by this; or by the cloudiness of my vision. I knew only that music was *changing*, not how; and I was ill-equipped to argue about it. I had no A&R training, no claim to having "ears." And I was an unexpected—some said dumbfounding—entry in the company's executive sweepstakes, catapulted during a corporate shake-up into a top position over the heads of considerably more experienced marketing and music people.

Columbia's contemporary roster was limited at the time to Bob Dylan, The Byrds, Simon & Garfunkel and Paul Revere & The Raiders—who, ironically, were then selling the most of the four. Paul Revere, flatly, was the closest we came to "rock 'n roll" . . . music alien to the company in the aftermath of Mitch Miller's famous "It won't last" statements. Dylan by now was extremely well known, having come a considerable distance since being nicknamed "Hammond's Folly" by corridor gossips (because John Hammond, by far the company's strongest talent discoverer, had signed him but hadn't immediately found commercial success with his sound). Dylan's prestige was enormous but his record sales oddly were good, rather than great. "Like a Rolling Stone" was his only major single by that time; most of his songs were hits for other artists.

Simon & Garfunkel, meanwhile, had just created a stir with their single "The Sound of Silence" and they were reuniting to record an album based on that hit. It would be more than a year before *The Graduate* and "Mrs. Robinson" made them household names. The Byrds were among the vanguard of artists combining folk music and rock—a quality group. But at Columbia, they were the exception rather than the rule. The one executive who seemed to feel the change coming was Billy James, a writer, publicist and creative spirit who roamed the West Coast listening to artists and issuing clarion—and unheeded—calls that times were indeed changing. Few of Columbia's A&R men lived in the world of Top Forty or understood the emerging world of contemporary music. The company's creative makeup was predominantly, stubbornly middle-of-the-road.

All this led—eventually—to the 1967 Monterey Pop Festival, to what came to be a tidal wave of new music and, by no coincidence, to a happy explosion on Columbia's Bottom Line, jumping sales profits from five to more than fifty million dollars a year by the time I was fired in 1973. I had sensed change; or, to be more precise, I had sensed that Columbia had no choice but to change or suffer.

# 3

I'm from Brooklyn, and I'm competitive. I can also be zealous, hardworking, brittle, exuberant and affectionate. But basically Brooklyn left me with a slightly flinty edge, an acute sense of my surroundings and the idea that dignity and fairness must be joined with a clear definition of one's own standards. Enthusiasm is useful . . . *if* it is combined with a hard—occasionally brutal—willingness to follow your ideas, heed your intuitive voice, yet to avoid leaning toward your sense of trust *too* much.

I grew up in Brooklyn's Crown Heights section: Union Street off Eastern Parkway. We called this a middle-class neighborhood, which may have been stretching things a bit, but Crown Heights had a special sense of family prosperity about it. The terrain consisted mostly of one-family houses with occasional apartment buildings, and was about 80 percent Jewish, plus Italians and Irish. We had a warm, active household. My father was an incessant practical joker, a devoted family man with a winning smile and crinkly eyes, who constantly slapped people on the back and made friends wherever he went. His name was Herman, yet long before I was born he was nicknamed Joe, as in "Good Old Joe." He was *always* joking. My great-aunt once fell into open-mouthed sleep next to him in the movies; she woke up chewing on a cigar.

When we went to the Dodgers games on Sunday, my father bought bleacher seats but often took us to the grandstands after befriending a ticket taker. And when we went to get a shoeshine, he'd turn to me and say for the shine boy's benefit: "See, I *told* you we'd find him! No matter how far we had to walk, we'd find him!"

He worked in electrical contracting for a while, then went on the road to sell ties and shirts. He had a lot of technical skill and a salesman's knack. Yet he never really prospered, and underneath his good nature, some sadness showed.

My mother, Florence, grew up as the belle of her neighborhood: a dark-haired, gregarious, vivacious beauty. "Good Old Joe" was nine years older than she, and they were married against her family's wishes. Her family somehow sensed—rightly, as it turned out—that he wouldn't be able to support her in the style to which she was accustomed, for my mother's family was connected to Russeks, a prosperous New York department store. She was, in fact, the showcase daughter of her family, dressed in great style by my grandmother and periodically paraded up and down Williamsburg streets to show the neighbors how well the family was doing.

Nonetheless, Joe swept "Flo," as she was called, off her feet. And my mother managed to make an economically limited household seem like a modest palace. Her sense of style always enabled us to dress well and live better than we should have. And she remained so attractive and regal, despite living under financial restrictions she hadn't known until she married, that she always caused a stir when entering a room.

Outside my home, an important diversion was baseball—that is, the Dodgers. Ebbetts Field was eight blocks away, and I sat on its hard bleachers at least twenty-five times a season. My heroes were Dixie Walker, Whitlow Wyatt, Dolf Camilli . . . and later, Pete Reiser, Pee Wee Reese, Duke Snider and Carl Furillo. I knew their batting averages, earned runs and R.B.I.s by heart. Sometimes when I read record charts and sales figures now, I thank the Dodgers. Studying baseball statistics was excellent training.

Along with all other Dodger fans, I automatically hated the Yankees and the Giants. Duke Snider was automatically better than Willie Mays or Mickey Mantle. Pee Wee Reese *had* to be better than Phil Rizzuto. Even radio announcer Red Barber was in a different class from Mel Allen—no comparison at all. It was a time, too, of stickball and punchball, stoopball and boxball, hit the penny, triangle, touch tackle, ring-a-levio, Chinese handball, and of double features—Frankenstein and the Wolfman, Abbott and Costello and later Martin and Lewis at the Saturday matinees. Matters of importance were regularly discussed on selected doorsteps, or at Darren's candy store. Six or seven of us, hair chopped into crew cuts or combed into lumpy waves, might gather to discuss baseball, football, girls . . . even world events. The *Daily News* arrived at the Eastern Parkway newsstand at about 11 P.M., and we'd all line up to check the sports pages.

I liked music then, but it was certainly less important than baseball. This was the era of Martin Block's "Make Believe Ballroom," and the Battle of the Baritones. My stubborn streak surfaced here: I was so turned off by Sinatra's swooning fans that I took a minority position, favoring Crosby and Como. Not that I thought they were better; I didn't make qualitative judgments. I just didn't like all the screaming.

Kay Starr was the first singer I really noticed. She had a gutsy quality to her voice; it said *something* to me, though I didn't know what. Until then I'd been interested mostly in hit records, but I got *into* Kay Starr, particularly one of her hits called "Wheel of Fortune." I really liked Billy Eckstine's version of "My Foolish Heart" as well. Basically, I preferred blues and ballads; they conveyed levels of experience and emotion that I hadn't heard articulated. Other songs that mattered to me included Vera Lynn's version of "Again" and Edith Piaf's "La Vie en Rose."

Family life continued placidly. I was winning some attention for my schoolwork. My parents encouraged me—but they always added: "Book learning is great, but don't forget the value of common sense!" On Sundays we went to my father's parents' house in Brooklyn's Coney Island section, a dozen or more family members passing the day with laughter and storytelling, and paying traditional respect to "Zadie" and "Bubby."

I was mildly musical. In junior high school, I won a neighborhood talent contest; the reward was a chance to take singing lessons at a discount. I was about fourteen, and after that I sang occasionally at parties. Nothing fancy—someone would play the piano and I'd be asked to sing. I was a baritone; I usually stood by the piano and belted out "My Foolish Heart" or "If I Loved You." After that I sang in the choruses at various schools, and later in a choral group at New York University. It never occurred to me to go into music; I was an academic. The things I cared about were grades and student politics. In the third grade at P.S. 161 I could add six vertical and horizontal columns of numbers in very short order, and by the time I finished elementary school I could add these columns of numbers on sight. I used to showcase this talent for friends occasionally: good training for *Billboard*'s charts.

My musical tastes in high school and college moved over to Broadway. This was a problem; I couldn't always afford the shows, but one way or another I managed to see *Oklahoma, Carousel, Bloomer Girl, South Pacific, Song of Norway* and *Desert Song.* They were all . . . entertaining. I enjoyed them but there was no lasting effect. In some ways, *Carousel* was a breakthrough. The story line tugged at me. I walked out of the theater tremendously impressed that I'd been affected on so many different levels, musically *and* dramatically. Before that, I was affected mostly by a show's music—*Oklahoma*, for example—while wondering why the story lines were so weak. But *Carousel*'s "Soliloquy" really caught me . . . a beautiful, moving marriage of lyrics and melody.

Still, my "act" was schoolwork. I was your basic, garden-variety, ambitious, upwardly mobile, hardworking Jewish boy from Brooklyn. I was *bound*—and so were the kids around me—to go beyond my parents. It was simply the way things were. Our parents had worked hard, but we had to work harder; we had to become doctors and lawyers, professional people, scholars, business executives.

In elementary school and at Erasmus Hall High School, I kept my grades at the top of the class. I eventually received a full tuition scholarship to New York University. At NYU, I immediately ran for President of the freshman class, and won. During one campaign motorcade, my jokester father suddenly appeared in his *own* car, honking furiously at me. I was mortified and in my embarrassment pretended not to hear him. But Joe and Flo were enormously proud of my successes, literally glowing when a new honor was announced. Still, they never stopped talking about "common sense."

Then they died.

It was a sudden, shocking transition to adult life, coming right after my freshman year. My mother died overnight of a cerebral hemorrhage at forty-seven, a beautiful, selfless, warm woman taken long before her time. Dad was on the road selling ties when it happened. He was cut down by a heart attack eleven months later. He was fifty-seven. The sense of loss was . . . crushing. I was truly cut away from my past; and I think sometimes, now, how fulfilling it would have been to share my experiences at Columbia with them, how much they would have loved this.

But instead, at eighteen, I went to live with my sister Seena, her husband, Jerry Howard, and their infant daughter, Honey, in Bayside, Queens. Two of my mother's sisters, Jeanette and Dorothy, had moved nearby with their families, and so some family unit remained, however fractured. Bayside was a grassy suburb at the time, filling fast with World War II veterans and their wives and kids. I commuted to the campus in Greenwich Village by bus and subway, an hour each way every day, and partially to keep the emptiness left by my parents' passing at a distance, I plunged headlong into student politics and my studies. The result was to be a full-tuition scholarship to Harvard Law School.

I felt I should go to school outside of New York. I needed new challenges, new tests. There seemed little left at NYU; I had been elected President of the college's Student Council and President of my alumni class as well. My ego was a bit inflated after four years of prestigious student offices and top grades.

Harvard surely provided plenty of lumps. It was a classless society, severely competitive, overstuffed with aggressive students carrying top academic and social credentials. It was impossible *not* to feel insecure; my past successes meant *nothing*. I had a scholarship, but maintaining it required a B average, and I had to keep grinding away at the books. At Harvard you worked and worked . . . and worked more. It was a seven-day-a-week schedule; soon the work made me dislike law school intensely.

I then began to wonder whether I would *like* practicing law . . . a conflict which led me eventually to Columbia Records. I never really felt comfortable at Harvard. Most subjects were tedious; the idea seemed to be development of your thought processes, not your thoughts. A lifetime of this loomed dull and deadly.

However, Harvard taught me to work hard, and then some. And that is a plus, because it is a trait required in the record industry: the stamina to deal with constant, onrushing projects and problems. The school had six days of classes each week; on Sunday, you prepared for Monday's classes. Eventually that became my schedule at Columbia, with a difference: the work was fulfilling . . . and often fun.

My grades remained high. At the end of my freshman year I had an A— average and I was elected to the Board of Student Advisors, an honor society running the Moot Court competition. My musical interests during this time were still bound to Broadway. However, even that dropped off, because the musicals were 250 miles away. My head was also fully buried in books and student activities. I never got into rock at all—I thought Elvis Presley and Bill Haley were too gimmicky. Later I began to listen to The Kingston Trio. For a while the most important thing in my life was Adlai Stevenson's Presidential campaign. I did a lot of volunteer work for him and helped form "College Students for

Adlai Stevenson." I was a solid campus liberal—something I was later to tell Bob Dylan under somewhat embarrassing circumstances.

Music, however, was marginal in my life. The one inkling of interest—buried quite deeply, it now seems—came through a copyright course at Harvard. The class was required to read *Variety*, and I was tremendously taken with it. I just loved it, and after the course ended I *kept* reading. I'd read about the movies and what they were grossing, and then compare my taste to the public's. The paper was extremely comprehensive; the money side of movies was intriguing.

I'd always enjoyed charts and statistics, going back to my Dodgers days; and so I'd get the anniversary issue of *Variety* and compare the leading movie gross, *Gone with the Wind,* with other films. The paper's jargon, all the various handstands it did with the English language, never bothered me. It was the era of star-oriented movies; I was curious about their pulling power— how a Bette Davis movie fared against a Joan Crawford film, how they did against Humphrey Bogart or Lana Turner.

I spent considerable time at this. Eventually I turned as well to the music charts. It was an extension of the star syndrome: measuring how singers did against each other, watching their songs climb the Hit Parade. I was a reader of charts and statistics, and I found an excitement in them which is hard to explain, as if they represented a flow of *energy.*

I graduated from law school in 1956, entering the legal world with some uneasiness. I first joined a small New York firm, thinking this would take me out of the competitive rat race of big New York firms, which seemed to be an extension of Harvard. The going rate from top firms then was $4,500 a year, and this firm, Hale, Kay and Brennan, was willing to start me at that. I was extremely pleased. The firm had started in 1952, and had grown from three to ten men in just four years. Unfortunately, they lost their two largest clients a year and a half later through mergers with larger companies, forcing them to cut back three men. I stayed on for a while, but it was clear that the challenge of the work would not be the same and a lawyer's early years must be a time for concentrated learning. I decided to risk the discomforts of a larger firm for more challenging work. In 1958 I moved to Rosenman, Colin, Kaye, Petschek and Freund, a large prestigious firm of forty lawyers.

Rosenman was Sam Rosenman, counsel to Franklin Roosevelt and Harry Truman. Ralph Colin was counsel to William Paley and CBS. I was involved mostly in nonlitigation—estate planning, corporate and contract work. One of my responsibilities, for example, involved handling the estate of artist Lyonel Feininger, mostly holding the widow's hand through a series of estate tax evaluations, and then reevaluations, of Feininger's paintings. Another responsibility was to act as counsel for Columbia Artists Management, Inc., a large concert-touring operation principally for classical artists and Broadway musical road shows, corporately unconnected, incidentally, with Columbia Records.

For a while I enjoyed life at the Rosenman firm enormously. I became close friends with several of the younger associates, helped by the fact that we were all living the foxhole existence of learning a new profession under demanding and exacting standards set by the hardworking and often brilliant partners. You learned a lot . . . and you put in the hours. It wasn't officially talked about, but you knew that you were expected to produce fifty hours of billing a week—that meant two late nights a week, and often Saturdays in the office. I was used to work; I'd worked endlessly hard before. But it wasn't *exactly* the work which bothered me.

The firm was structured at that time to discourage initiative. Rosenman and Colin brought in most of the business. Practically everyone else was expected to service their accounts. You were not encouraged to bring in your own; I could see that I'd be *servicing* someone else the rest of my life. My life wouldn't change—just week after week of fifty or more billing hours.

I began to get depressed about this. Walking along Madison Avenue toward the firm one morning, I felt an overpowering sadness, as if a cold hand had passed over me. I felt like crying. I had some work to do that day—and I didn't want to do it. I began thinking this *couldn't* be me; this *isn't* me. I liked the men I was working with and greatly respected their intellect. But I wasn't expanding the way I felt I should expand. A law career at Rosenman seemed total submergence of what I was. It just wasn't me.

A few weeks earlier, I'd been offered another job. A Rosenman colleague named Harvey Schein had gone to CBS to become General Attorney for Columbia Records. It was a small department, two men in fact, and Schein would soon be alone. We'd known each other for about a year at Rosenman and he thought my experience with Columbia Artists Management would be useful. I was making $9,500 at Rosenman at the time, and he offered a salary raise to $11,000, holding out the possibility that I'd succeed him as the record division's chief counsel within the year.

It was something to consider, and I wrestled with the problem at length, particularly that morning on Madison Avenue. Money wasn't the question. The problem was whether I wanted to alter my career as much as this.

I went to see Ralph Colin, who sat on the CBS Board and knew CBS and Columbia Records better than anyone at the firm. I asked him how he felt about my taking the job.

Colin had been appraising my work; Columbia Artists Management happened to be his client. He said I was doing good work at Rosenman and he estimated I'd be considered for a partnership in about five years. He felt Columbia Records was growing . . . but he wondered if I'd *relate* to the music world—to him it was a lot of hype and finger-popping. He saw me mostly as a Harvard Graduate, an Ivy League kid unfamiliar with the record industry's Tin Pan Alley mannerisms.

Would I be happy there?

He didn't know that I'd grown up in Brooklyn, that I was comfortable with all sorts of people, and that I was growing more and more restive with life at his firm. Soon after that I took Schein's offer and went over to Columbia.

And I began reading *Variety* again.

# Two

## 1

When I joined Columbia Records in November, 1960, the company had two corporate lawyers: Harvey Schein and myself. Harvey, however, was traveling constantly overseas, preparing for his coming promotion as the International Division's operating head.

So my entry into this operation was no small jolt. I'd expected to get at least twelve months' experience as Assistant Counsel before taking over Harvey's job. But as soon as I got there I had to fill in as General Attorney a great deal of the time. I had to learn *everything* about the record business at once, and this meant working practically day and night for the first six months. I took courses in Antitrust, Unfair Competition, Patent, Trademark and Copyright Law at NYU night school. I spent long evenings plowing through thick volumes of statutes and legal background on the entertainment industries. And I spent even longer hours at my desk cramming in every piece of information I could find. But I didn't mind because I had to be ready. For soon I would have full responsibility for the office.

It almost didn't happen.

About the time Harvey was promoted, in the summer of 1961, CBS happened to undergo one of its periodic restructurings. Previously, each division's law department reported directly to the division president; now the lawyers were to report to CBS Chief

Counsel Tom Fisher. Fisher, it was reasoned, could review salaries and promotions more rationally. And the lawyers under him might in turn make better legal judgments, since they were not directly beholden to the division presidents.

Fine. Except that I was suddenly in competition with CBS's entire thirty-five-man legal department for Harvey Schein's job, a juicy one by corporate standards. And Fisher was said to feel that it should go to one of the corporation's more senior television lawyers.

I was pretty upset, and I made this known to Schein; for I'd come over from the Rosenman firm with the understanding that if my performance was satisfactory during the trial period—which it was—I'd be offered Schein's job when he moved over to the International Division.

By most standards, it was a minor corporate squabble; fortunately, Goddard Lieberson and his Executive Vice-President, Norman Adler, intervened and I was offered Schein's job. The story is hardly worth telling, in fact—except for its symbolism. We are often told that "circumstances" can interfere with life's best-laid plans . . . at least take us in unplanned directions. Yet few institutions are capable of manipulating an individual's life as much as a large corporation. For in corporate business, you must constantly *confront* your puppet status. The restructuring of CBS at this juncture was sensible enough, or so it seemed. Yet I clearly had no say in it, and when the effects of it reached down to touch me, I had no protection except the good will of my immediate superiors.

This time, I was lucky. In 1965, another restructuring would, nearly accidentally, raise me to the company's top administrative position—in effect, a walk-up to the Presidency. But a number of years later, changes in the corporation's hierarchy would contribute to my termination in 1973. The lesson, even in 1961, was obvious: hard work, talent, even vision—in the record industry or *any* business—isn't enough. Luck is the edge.

As General Attorney I quickly earned my spurs. The work load was growing fast, and I soon expanded the department to four lawyers. Our biggest problem during that period was a Federal Trade Commission suit against the Columbia Record Club for restraint of trade.

It was a complicated problem, and one that affected my career enormously. For the suit, in effect, threatened the heart of Columbia's vast mail-order operation, and I had to begin a crash course in company operations to build our case.

The Record Club had been started in 1955, and management soon realized it couldn't satisfy its customers with Columbia's catalog alone. So the company decided to bring in outside labels, making exclusive licensing arrangements with such companies as Mercury, Warner Bros., A&M, Kapp and Vanguard, and paying royalties for the right to distribute their records. It worked out nicely. Most of the other companies had concluded they couldn't run a mail-order business profitably by themselves; they were delighted to use us. The Record Club, in turn, was turning a nice profit and controlling something like 60 to 70 percent of the industry's mail-order business.

Unfortunately, RCA and Capitol, which had started clubs in 1958, concluded that it was illegal to distribute other companies' records. And at some point, the FTC came to the same conclusion and filed suit against us. We decided to fight.

As Columbia's counsel, I was the liaison between the company and my old firm, Rosenman, which handled the case. Researching the case required traveling across the country with two of Rosenman's most able partners, Asa Sokolow and Stuart Robinowitz, to interview heads of other companies, artists, managers, rack jobbers and record dealers—thus to build a case that we were not in fact restraining trade. The education was fantastic; we interviewed people at every level of the business.

The FTC had argued that we were restraining retail as well as mail-order competition, because the allied companies would ultimately become dependent on us. Since they couldn't finance their own clubs, they would be at our mercy. As the scenario went, we'd make so much money selling their records that soon we'd be stealing their artists as well.

We argued that this was overprotective, even ridiculous. The companies couldn't afford their own clubs; and they were making money from ours—hardly unfair competition. At the time the issue seemed quite important, for record club revenues totaled a large percentage of retail sales. The rack-jobbing explosion of the sixties (which was to bring records for the first time into discount department stores and supermarkets throughout the country) was only just under way. Mail orders were still the most convenient way for suburban and rural people to get records.

As it happened, this feeling was strongly shared by the other licensees, all of whom testified for us. Artists, music publishers and other record companies testified too. The artists were delighted to get their albums into untapped markets; the publishers of course got more copyright money when more records were sold. Only the retailers testified for the FTC. We were selling the records at large discounts and they saw this as a tremendous threat.

As a result, the Hearing Examiner dismissed the entire complaint. Part of the decision was later appealed, and eventually Columbia was forced to give up its exclusivity clauses. Still, no one seemed to catch up with Columbia's club. RCA at one point combined its mail-order operations with Book-of-the-Month Club, and then later with Reader's Digest. Neither of these moves worked, and the RCA club operates rather marginally now. Capitol eventually sold its club to the Longines Symphonette operation.

In any case, the rack-jobber explosion in discount stores and supermarkets, and the practice of discounting records in retail stores, eventually dwarfed club sales. Columbia's club still does well, but in the overall record market, it is not as important as it used to be.

# 2

I took to my new life happily. The legal work was fascinating and diverse. I worked on Broadway show contracts, and I liked this; and I began going to Broadway opening nights as well. I'd read *Billboard, Cashbox, Record World* and *Variety* and soon I got into nearly every one of the company's operating areas. I *liked* this work. Handling the marketing department's legal problems required that I learn about pricing strategies and other business problems. When artists' contracts were drawn up, I got to know the managers and occasionally the artists themselves. Columbia had been active in establishing foreign subsidiaries under Schein's leadership, and so the job involved going to London and Paris as well. It was challenging and exciting work.

I noticed that this was beginning to separate me from other CBS lawyers. Most operated as if the corporate business people were their "clients"—they didn't seem eager to learn a great deal about the business itself. It was a hands-off attitude, a nine-to-five attitude, and it made no sense to me. I couldn't practice law in a *vacuum*; it seemed foolish to be advising men without having a feel for their actual business problems. I soon began going to the industry's yearly conventions; this set a precedent. Soon after that lawyers from other record companies were beginning to show up at conventions too.

I threw myself into the business most of all because I loved it. Yet I had no idea where this would lead. Lieberson had gotten some idea of my skills when we traveled together; but I wasn't thinking *that* big. A good lawyer might easily climb the corporate hierarchy; but I was still a newcomer to the business, and—most important of all—a man without any background in marketing or music.

I was working hard and having fun. At that point, my goals were as cloudy to me as the title of next year's chart-busting album.

# 3

Columbia, in turn, was expanding. The company was divided into three parts: the domestic record business, the foreign record business and all nonrecord operations. Goddard Lieberson, a stylish, witty, deceptively mild-mannered executive who first made his name in the classical A&R department—and later through his work with Broadway original cast albums—sat at the top as President. Below him, Norman Adler, Executive Vice-President, controlled the Record Club, the Retail Marketing Division (sales, promotion, merchandising and advertising) and Manufacturing (record pressing, engineering, development) . A&R, a traditionally independent arm of the company, didn't report to Adler; the department worked directly with Lieberson.

A&R is any company's bread-and-butter operation. A good A&R man is expected to find new talent, nurture it, help each of the company's already signed artists to stay at the peak of their potential—perhaps reach beyond it—and finally to have an ear for coming, and passing, trends in music. A&R men can be as fragile and unpredictable as the artists themselves. A&R is the company's creative arm, and one thing is certain: a record company without a good A&R department will dry up in a hurry. For all these reasons, the A&R department seemed to many executives a near-magical source of power. *Everyone* wanted A&R to report to him. By contrast, Lieberson and others felt that the department should be separate from Marketing, reporting only to the company President.

Behind this structure lay the strategy of "creative tension." A&R people always assumed that they produced the best music, and that anything short of a chart-buster was the fault of the Marketing people. The Sales and Promotion departments, in turn, felt that poor sales meant a lack of talent among the A&R men— thus the healthy tension which theoretically leads to better work on all sides.

Adler, however, felt he deserved more responsibility. He'd been the company's General Attorney at one point, then the pioneering, imaginative head of the Record Club; now he wanted A&R reporting to him. The problem was further complicated by two men below him—two enormously capable Marketing Vice-Presidents named Bill Gallagher and Len Levy. Gallagher ran Columbia's Marketing Division; Levy had charge of Epic Records, Columbia's sister label (created primarily as a marketing and A&R device to avoid having the Columbia label get too swollen). Gallagher and Levy wanted power over their A&R departments as well.

It happened at this time, in 1964, that Columbia hired the Harvard Business School to study its organizational structure. Corporate CBS had been encouraging its divisions to expand and diversify because the board felt that television growth, being government-licensed, might be limited. In this connection, Columbia had acquired Fender Guitars and Creative Playthings, the educational toy company, and would soon buy Rogers Drums and Leslie Speakers. The Record Club was also expanding, and the domestic operation was becoming bigger. It was clear that all these amorphous groups could not report directly to Lieberson; it would simply be too much.

When the Harvard report came in, it suggested combining the Marketing and A&R operations. It isn't hard to imagine the below-surface turmoil this caused. Personally, I thought the Harvard people were wrong—but I was just an attorney and I had no say in the matter. It soon became clear that Lieberson was planning to juggle Columbia's entire organizational structure, and in his mind he was already fiddling and poking at an efficient model for the future. I didn't assume that I figured prominently in his plans, although I knew he was impressed with my work. I'd stood up well in various negotiations he'd witnessed and he was pleased with my work on the FTC suit.

But Lieberson had—reasonably enough—no sense of my interest in the creative areas. As far as he knew, I had none. We had never discussed creative matters; in fact, we had never really discussed music at all. He apparently thought that I handled myself well enough dealing with artists, managers and their lawyers. And it was clear that Lieberson liked lawyers, for he'd promoted Harvey Schein to head of the International Division, and he'd taken Norman Adler out of the General Attorney's chair. Neil Keating, the able head of the Record Club for the previous six years, was also a former General Attorney. Traditionally, lawyers did well at Columbia. Yet I did not think my career would be so affected by the reorganizations.

The company suddenly was in the subtle grip of considerable office politics when the A&R recommendations came down.

Below Adler, Vice-Presidents Gallagher and Levy suddenly developed pangs of considerable ambition. Gallagher's ambition carried the most weight. By any standards, he was already a giant in the record industry, a marketing man of substantial reputation who was instrumental in setting up Columbia's wholly owned distribution operation.

Gallagher, in fact, was sometimes called "The Pope" within the company. A stout, imperious man, he was capable of carefully plotted office politics when it suited him. While setting up Columbia's distribution operation, he had installed, promoted and granted favors to large numbers of people, who in turn became intensely loyal to him. He had a Vatican-like ability to secure loyalty from his followers, and as he dispensed grace—or took it away—his following grew and grew. Levy, in turn, ran a separate, smaller operation. He was doing his job extremely well, often working into the early hours of the morning, overseeing almost every sale to distributors, making sure nothing was lost. Both men wanted to go further within the company.

Adler, meanwhile, was planning *his* future. He was already responsible for a large number of operations and a great deal of money. Yet he had strong people doing well underneath him, and he felt that he could handle new challenges and more responsibility.

Lieberson, of course, was watching all this half-visible moving and shaking from the safety of his office. He knew that Norman Adler had little experience in A&R; what's more, he felt that Adler had only a limited feel for it.

Beyond that, Lieberson felt a need to guard *his* A&R prerogatives. He had risen to the Presidency by this route and considered parts of it his private preserve. He'd made up his mind early not to share it with Adler. But Gallagher was somewhat harder to put off, for he clearly wanted to rise further in the company. And, after Marketing, A&R was the only direction in which he could go.

Lieberson therefore had several options; he finally decided to combine A&R and Marketing at the Gallagher-Levy level, and then have each man report only to *him* on A&R. He thus sidestepped Adler, while satisfying Gallagher and Levy and, in turn, complying with the Harvard report.

Adler, naturally enough, was upset. He had persuasively advocated adoption of the new concept, for he assumed that this would lead to his control over A&R. Actually, it left him with *less* power. Both Gallagher and Levy, who formerly reported solely to him, now reported to both him and Lieberson. On paper he still was Lieberson's second-in-command. In reality, he had lost some of his influence.

I was largely innocent of these dealings. You rarely feel office politics in the making; the machinations are subtle, restrained and usually conducted without visible drama. Yet Lieberson was orchestrating a thorough restructuring of the company.

I was called to his office in June of 1965 and out of the blue offered the top job for Columbia's Musical Instruments Division (Fender Guitars, Leslie Speakers, etc.). I was making about twenty-five thousand dollars then, and the new position paid forty thousand—a nice raise. Yet I was not ecstatic. I enjoyed the entertainment business, and I felt that I had built up a feel for it. And besides, I had no expertise whatsoever in musical instruments.

Another problem was that many of the musical instrument operations were located in California; the job involved considerable traveling, possibly moving to California, and this was impossible. My marriage, which had taken place in 1956 soon after my graduation from law school, had ended in divorce, and my two children, Fred and Lauren, who were now five and three, were living with me. The separation agreement gave my ex-wife custody of them if I moved outside the state. Lieberson said that

I wouldn't have to move, but I wasn't happy with the idea of the job; at the same time it hardly seemed prudent to turn down such a large raise in both salary and responsibility.

Trying not to hem and haw, I told Lieberson that I'd *lean* toward taking the job if he felt it appropriate . . . but I wanted to think it over. I didn't know Lieberson was still playing his organizational chart game. Five minutes after I'd agreed—more or less—to take the job and had returned to my office, he called Adler into his office and said he planned to give Gallagher and Levy control over their respective A&R departments—yet not give Adler that cumulative power.

Adler said straightway he couldn't continue under those conditions. Did Lieberson have anything else in mind?

I'd been back in my office half an hour when the telephone rang. Lieberson had to "retract" the earlier offer. He was sorry but Norman Adler did not go along with his plans and a change was necessary; Adler would get the Musical Instruments operation. Creative Playthings and some other subsidiaries would also report to him. Adler, it became apparent, was quite happy with the change. He felt that Creative Playthings was the beginning of a major CBS entry into education and he would be at the helm of an exciting new venture in a field that fascinated him. So Lieberson and Adler had avoided a major confrontation without embarrassment to either side.

Lieberson meanwhile promised me he had "something" in mind. Which was fine. I'd had terribly mixed feelings about the Instruments job. And so, about a week later, he called me into his office again. The meeting was short and to the point. Lieberson had accomplished his restructuring, and I was to be offered a job titled Administrative Vice-President. My responsibilities would be equal to Adler's; yet my title was to be more restrained, for Adler still would be called Executive Vice-President and, though his responsibilities were totally altered, we both felt it would be a slap in the face to appoint a "Co-Executive Vice-President." I owed a lot to Adler and, what's more, I personally felt he had contributed enormously to Columbia. I certainly was not going to make an issue of titles.

Meanwhile I was going to have both Marketing *and* A&R report to me. I was stunned.

I suddenly had the job everyone coveted. My salary had nearly doubled. I was in charge of the entire Domestic Records Division.

I had responsibility for Marketing, A&R, Manufacturing, Engineering, indeed everything. And I had the opportunity, though I planned for now to explore it most cautiously, to test my creative instincts.

The bulk of the record industry was equally taken aback. I was virtually unknown except through my legal contacts. I had no experience in the business itself except as a lawyer. It was clearly a long shot on Lieberson's part. He knew it, I knew it . . . everyone in the industry knew it.

But Lieberson's chart games, brilliant as they might have been, caused me immediate trouble. For Gallagher and Levy had no plans to share their authority. Worse yet, Lieberson seemed to be defining my position rather vaguely. Gallagher and Levy got the impression from Lieberson that I was merely a "buffer" between him and the label operations; Lieberson, meanwhile, said to me that I was responsible for all domestic operations. So my authority was not fully defined, and perhaps was not intended to be.

My immediate problem was Gallagher. When Adler changed jobs, Gallagher assumed that he'd become Columbia's operations boss. Then I came out of nowhere. And he was extremely upset. He had several angry meetings with Lieberson, who defined my "administrative" title in ways that calmed Gallagher down. But Gallagher was not so easily dissuaded. I began to hear corridor gossip that I was only a figurehead for Lieberson. I also heard that Gallagher and I were feuding.

I felt pressure from Gallagher immediately. It seemed wise to avoid fueling this potential fire, so I did nothing to counter the pressure. He had a substantial reputation and considerable experience in the record business. I was a former counsel stepping on eggshells. I was in no position yet to take him on.

Yet the nature of the confrontation was clear. Lieberson had structured company operations so that he could lie back and take a rest while his underlings struggled for position and power. He had a way, then and throughout his career, of molding business life to *his* needs rather than the other way around. He was not a creature of the corporation; he traveled regularly and socialized at glamorous levels, and he kept up contacts with Broadway and the performing arts. He'd brought Columbia Records to considerable prominence in the classical and Broadway areas, and he had built up a tremendous personal reputation as a result. Obviously, I was extremely grateful to him for my appointment—and still am

—yet I hardly realized that he was handing me so many problems along with my new title.

The Gallagher conflict dragged on . . . and on, and the rumors of hostility caused a great deal of talk within the company, not to mention a growing tension in me. At one point I called Gallagher into my office. Until then, we'd gotten along well . . . on the surface. I told him that I'd heard these stories, and I thought they were quite unfair, and I certainly could surmise where they were coming from, since *I* wasn't feeding the rumor mills.

I said that I had no plans to challenge his reputation publicly. I would not—not *now*, at least—interfere with his prerogatives as Columbia's chief label executive. *But I hadn't appointed myself Administrative Vice-President; Lieberson had.* So I had no plans to let him run over me—and if he didn't operate his department well, I'd do whatever was required of me.

This led to the next immediate crisis. The A&R department had reacted with considerable uneasiness to Gallagher's newest title—and the department was no minor force to be reckoned with. Many of its individual members had industry-wide reputations and, as it happened, Gallagher was hard-pressed to have *any* of them report—much less listen—to him. I sat in on Gallagher's first A&R meeting. He walked into the room in an open-necked shirt and sweater. The pattern was set, for he'd always worn suits to work. This obvious attempt to change his image was transparent, and the A&R men around the table snickered privately at him. Gallagher simply didn't look the part, and it was a sad beginning for his campaign to secure their loyalty.

I should add that I was no more at home with the A&R department than he; but I solved *my* problem by watching and listening and keeping my mouth shut. And I continued to wear a tie.

Gallagher simply refused to recognize his limits. As overall label head, he was supposed to appoint independent heads for Marketing and A&R to handle day-to-day problems. He resisted this, preferring to hoard as much power as possible, and this soon blew up into a company crisis. The A&R men refused to recognize his leadership in other than the most minimal terms.

The department members had strong reputations to back up their feelings. John Hammond had signed and worked with Billie Holliday, Aretha Franklin and Bob Dylan in his career. Bob

Mersey was having enormous success producing Barbra Streisand and Andy Williams. Ernie Altschuler was well known as the producer of Tony Bennett, Jerry Vale and Ray Conniff. Teo Macero was an excellent musician in his own right and produced André Kostelanetz, Dave Brubeck, Miles Davis and Thelonious Monk. And Mike Berniker was a young A&R man building a reputation with Steve Lawrence and Eydie Gorme. Others in the department included Bob Johnston, who later produced Dylan; Ed Kleban, who worked in the Broadway show area; and John McClure, Tom Frost and Tom Shepard, who worked in the Classical area.

None of them felt he needed a marketing man's assistance in signing artists and producing records.

My problems with Len Levy were less urgent. We had been friends in the past and my new appointment hadn't raised any overt signs of hostility. I therefore tried to supervise him in as low-key a manner as possible; he returned the favor by speaking well of me among corridor gossips.

I saw early in the game, however, that neither Gallagher nor Levy could sign the right artists; as talented as they were, they simply didn't have the feel for this fragile and complex process. Yet there was nothing I could do about it. Lieberson had to please the Board and follow the Harvard recommendations somewhat; so he'd given them the power to test themselves creatively. I could only wait for the results.

Fortunately, they were soon evident and about three months after the new appointments were made, I asked Gallagher to begin searching for a good A&R man, the best.

My request shouldn't have been controversial; Gallagher was *supposed* to do this.

Instead, he tried to convince me that it was absolutely necessary for him to win over the men in the A&R department; and as soon as he won their confidence the department would be running smoothly. Clearly, he had no immediate plans to find a competent head of A&R.

One should understand the *tension* involved here. I was new; I had an uncertain mandate. I was confronted with evasiveness and resistance from a man of considerable stature who, understandably enough, felt poorly used because he had to report to a younger, less experienced executive. And, if I slipped and fell, he clearly planned to dance on my grave—he made no secret of it.

Now, in the early stages of this rather protracted problem, which lasted nearly two years, Gallagher must have thought me slow-witted. Or at least he *seemed* to, for his reasoning at each confrontation was excessively transparent. I had told him that I wanted the *best* A&R man in the business. After delaying nine months on the appointment, his first suggestion was a man who had previously reported to him in a sales capacity, one of his loyal followers.

I rejected the appointment, and I made my irritation clear. Encounters in corporate offices are tense, sometimes brittle, but rarely loud or passionate. They are more like diplomatic negotiations couched in polite language whose inflections carry an enormous amount of weight. Finally, Gallagher came to my office and I told him that I had a mandate to get Columbia's domestic operations in order and I intended to carry it out. For nine months, I had treated him with deference, as befitted his experience and accomplishments. But now it was time to do business. I gave him three months to appoint an appropriate head of A&R. Yet even then, rather than agreeing, he countered with the suggestion that he first appoint a head of Marketing and divest himself of his immediate responsibilities there. He even admitted that things had backed up in that area; he'd been spending 80 to 90 percent of his time supervising A&R.

Gallagher recommended a fellow named Bill Farr as the new head of Marketing. Farr was a solid citizen, a gentleman and a competent administrator. He did not have Gallagher's force or leadership abilities; he was not likely to make the Marketing people forget that Bill Gallagher once ran the department. Nonetheless, he was not one of Gallagher's unquestioning loyalists.

I accepted the appointment.

Gallagher had used the appointment, however, to stall on the A&R question. And now he was trying to stall further. I was extremely annoyed. I told him that one decision had nothing to do with the other. But it was clear that the problem was going to drag on.

By the time I was finally putting really strong pressure on Gallagher, my position on the corporate roster was better defined. In the summer of 1966, Lieberson had given me a new title: Vice-President and General Manager. Earlier, it was possible to quibble that I could only "administrate." But while the new title brought no new responsibilities, it brought reality home to Gallagher: I was his boss. I was operating head of the division. During the first year of the "administrative" job, my salary (forty thousand dollars) was five thousand dollars lower than Gallagher's; it was possible for him to tell people that my authority was limited. Now, exactly one year later, it became clear that I was fully empowered to run the domestic division.

When my change of title occurred, Gallagher went to Lieberson and complained bitterly. Lieberson simply told him that the decision was final, whereupon Gallagher backed off, saying, "Okay, that's up to you," thus avoiding a major confrontation. Further bitterness might have forced his resignation.

The pressure was building even more in A&R. Ernie Altschuler came to me one day and said that he could no longer report to Gallagher; *he* would like to be head of A&R. Our discussion was rather pointed; if Altschuler didn't get the job, he would take an offer from RCA to head their A&R department.

It was painful to say—but I had to tell him that I would stick by Gallagher.

Ernie had had several big hits with Tony Bennett and Ray Conniff, and he was a talented MOR producer. Yet, to me, he didn't have the credentials to become head of the department, particularly since I'd already begun to feel that most MOR albums were fading from the best-seller charts. So he left.

Bob Mersey and Allan Stanton came next. Mersey complained that he couldn't get along with Gallagher and, more important, that Gallagher wasn't the right man to run the department. Stanton, who was running Columbia's West Coast A&R operations at the time, agreed and said—rather emotionally, in fact —that *he* wanted to be considered as the new head of A&R, not *under* Gallagher, but substituted for him. Again, I felt that Stanton, like Altschuler, was talented . . . but not ideally suited to spearhead the direction in rock music Columbia would be taking. Stanton left to go to A&M Records.

I really felt pushed to the limit, and I finally told Gallagher that he had two months to find an A&R man—or be fired. I would do this very reluctantly, since his contributions to Columbia in the past had been considerable. But there could be no delay; I told him that I was facing mass resignations in the A&R department; the lapse had been intolerable.

In the fall of 1967, Gallagher resigned. He had received an

attractive offer from MCA to become operating chief of its Decca and Kapp labels.

I let out a long, silent sigh of relief and went back to work.

The problems with Len Levy had been much less severe. I told him that I planned to bring in Dave Kapralik, a former head of Columbia A&R who had gone independent, as head of Epic's A&R department, and that I was going to limit his own responsibility to marketing, his basic strength. Levy was not happy, but he did not contest the explanation that the move was not personal, but simply structural. Eventually, Levy was offered the Presidency of Metromedia Records, and he took it.

Neither Gallagher's nor Levy's careers stabilized after that. Gallagher didn't stay long at MCA. From there, he went to Gulf & Western's Paramount Records subsidiary—but that didn't work out, either. Nor did Levy stay long at Metromedia, or his next company, GRT Records. This is really very sad. The fact is that each is a tremendously able and energetic leader of men—but of salesmen, not A&R men. A&R can be an addiction. It derailed both Gallagher and Levy, at least temporarily, and their stories serve well as a warning to others in the industry.

# Three

**1** ══════════════════════════════

Donovan, in 1966, was my first signing. I'd been very cautious up to this point, sticking largely to the business side of things, learning about the unfamiliar parts of the Columbia operation and generally undergoing a quasi apprenticeship, while I watched the A&R Department—from a distance. After all, I was the lawyer, the Johnny-come-lately, and I was being watched carefully by many, both inside and outside the company. I felt that I understood music and creativity, but so does everyone else in the music business. I had to be extremely careful.

Donovan was a perfect beginning. He was under contract at the time to Pye Records in London and distributed in America through an affiliate label named Hickory; and, while he wasn't well known in America, he'd had several hits in England, where he was sometimes called a "British Dylan." I listened to several of his tapes and I was quite taken by the ethereal, lilting compositions. I felt that he had a good chance to emerge importantly in this country. Equally significant, his contract was about to expire.

I asked John Hammond, who also liked his work, to make an approach at the Newport Folk Festival. Donovan had already recorded "Catch the Wind," "Universal Soldier" and "Colours" and, while Hickory had gotten some chart action, Donovan was still considered an English artist very much in the shadow of Dylan—and a pale imitation of Dylan at that. I was deeply taken with Dylan at the time, and I think it was Donovan's lyrics which caught me. Like Dylan, he was one of the first contemporary singer-songwriters to convey really sensitive ideas in his lyrics.

Nonetheless, I thought that the comparison to Dylan was unfair. Donovan's music was entirely different—softer, melodic, even mystical . . . I strongly felt he could be a unique artist on his own. Moreover, I never objected to signing artists of similar talents who had genuine ability. I always resisted the impulse to close doors. The result was that Chicago comfortably joined Columbia after we already had Blood, Sweat & Tears; and Liza Minnelli signed a contract even though we had Barbra Streisand.

Negotiations with Donovan were never models of efficiency. Donovan's manager, Ashley Kozak, had told John Hammond that he was interested. But several months went by and we heard nothing. Finally I called Kozak in England. He reaffirmed his interest, but said that he couldn't begin discussions until they had taken legal readings on the Pye contract. It seemed like a stall, and I was anxious. I really wanted Donovan to be my first signing and everything was still up in the air.

A few months later, Kozak called and said that he and Donovan were in New York. I naturally agreed to meet with them and we had a long, long talk. Donovan seemed very much like his songs—gentle, warm and witty. He had an almost spiritual air about him. He was also an artist with very definite ideas. Yet, even when he asked for commitments, like our using his own art and design concepts for album jackets—an area very important to him—his manner was friendly and winning. His musical plans were far-reaching. He planned to make commercial records, but he also wanted to try a Broadway musical—and several different projects for children, the idea of which fascinated him. Fine. I told him of Columbia's strong Broadway tradition, and that we had just added a line of children's books and records to Columbia's catalog. He was impressed. I asked him whom he'd like to record with, and he mentioned Mickey Most, the top British producer who had made his mark with Herman's Hermits and The Animals. Epic, in turn, had just signed an exclusive producing contract with Most; a nice coincidence. Most also had a good feel for single hits, and it was clear that Donovan had a potential for getting very, very ethereal; marrying his artistic talent to Most's commercial instincts seemed perfect.

In fact it was—for several years at least.

Our risk exposure to Donovan was relatively small, signing him for one hundred thousand dollars and giving him a guaranty of roughly twenty thousand dollars a year for five years. I suffered no anxiety regarding this, my first artist-signing, since right from the start Donovan had a seemingly endless string of high-quality hits, "Sunshine Superman," "Mellow Yellow," "Wear Your Love Like Heaven," "Jennifer Juniper," to name a few. His concerts were major musical events, and he always succeeded in weaving a near-magical spell, appearing often in a flowing white gown surrounded by flowers, his songs and chatter never failing to lift his audience into an entranced state. He became an important spokesman for cultural change in both England and America. But the story doesn't end here.

With Donovan at least momentarily fixed in place, I turned my attention to the company's financial problems. Yearly pretax profits of $5,000,000 weren't much, particularly *after* you paid the taxes, which left less than $2,500,000. A few mismanaged contract negotiations could eat that up quickly. And so I began looking around for other ways to make money. It occurred to me immediately that record albums had become an outstanding bargain, selling even without discounts as low as $3.79 retail. Everything else had gone up—the price of movie and theater tickets, hardcover books, symphony seats. Producing costs and artists' royalties were rising as well. I began to compare the value of a record album with that of other entertainment. In New York, it cost as much as $3.00 to see a first-run movie—two hours of entertainment. By the same token, you could buy a record album for $2.50 . . . and get hundreds of hours of entertainment out of it. A Broadway show made an even better comparison: $15.00 for the evening or $30.00 for two. The cast album would cost you less than one-tenth of that amount.

Something had to change. I knew that rack jobbers and retail dealers would protest a price rise. They wanted to keep their present margins, and they were vocal in their stubborn belief that the public would not pay more for records. And, by instinct, a salesman doesn't like prices to go up; he wants them to *drop* . . . he assumes he'll get more customers and a greater volume of sales.

After lengthy rounds of discussions, I decided the rack jobbers were living in the Middle Ages and, at their own NARM (National Association of Record Merchandisers) convention in March, 1967, I introduced the concept of variable pricing. Three months later I put this into practice with the albums *Dylan's Greatest Hits* and *Paul Revere & The Raiders' Greatest Hits*. I raised the price one dollar and put a poster inside each to justify doing so. It worked. Each album sold extremely well. The controversy was never to arise again.

Next, I started looking around the manufacturing plants, and I was amazed at the number of records stacked up in warehouses. I was told that the duplication of stereo and monaural records caused most of these storage problems.

A thought kept recurring—why not price monaural and stereo identically? It would eliminate the problems of double bookkeeping and give us another raise in album prices. The stereo record was no longer any more expensive to produce, though the *myth* of its greater expense persisted. It seemed a golden opportunity to move toward better profit margins. At the time, the monaural list price for pop albums was $3.79, and the stereo was $4.79. I raised the list price of the monaural pop record to $4.79, assuming that this would eventually lead to a phase-out of monaural records, but gradually.

It eliminated monaural records practically overnight.

Bill Bachman, Columbia's chief engineer, had told me that stereo albums could be played on monaural phonographs, so it made sense for customers to buy stereo records now. But it was the rack jobbers and dealers who really sounded monaural's death knell. They simply stopped stocking them; they didn't like keeping double inventories either.

I expected some criticism when this happened, but I wasn't prepared for instant chaos. People came up to me at conventions and public events looking anxious and saying, "I hope you know what you are doing!" As with variable pricing, the rest of the record industry immediately followed my lead. Suddenly everyone was *swamped* with monaural returns. For a while, this caused a lot of economic confusion. I was blamed everywhere as the man taking the industry over a cliff.

Yet, a year later, this was considered a bold marketing move. Monaural albums were almost extinct, and the list price of albums had been raised another dollar. A lot of marginal record companies suddenly felt quite secure, and many messy inventory problems had been solved.

I frankly enjoyed these marketing moves. It was frustrating both waiting out Gallagher and restraining myself until I felt comfortable to move in the creative areas. I wanted to exercise some authority, and this was a good place to start. I based these pricing changes on the underlying belief that records are a very valuable cultural medium. It was time they became recognized as *equal* to movies and Broadway and best-selling books. It made sense to get the marketing and inventory problems out of the way. Music and musical tastes would soon be changing very fast.

# 2

*Mame* and then *Cabaret* showed just *how* fast. Since Broadway original cast albums had accounted for as much as 20 percent of Columbia's sales, these were important releases to us, and we promoted them as vigorously as we had any previous cast album. But when sales leveled off at three hundred thousand and two hundred and fifty thousand respectively, there was no way to explain the sales drop—except in terms of changing consumer tastes. Nor was it a simple problem, for Broadway people were putting a lot of pressure on me. Hal Prince, Broadway's most successful musical producer, called again and again to ask why the *Cabaret* album wasn't selling. He and Tommy Valando, who in his own right was fast becoming Broadway's leading music publisher, had worked together on the giant hit *Fiddler on the Roof*. Why wasn't *Cabaret* in *Fiddler*'s class?

There was nothing I could do about the sales trends. The pop music world and its Top Forty hits were simply changing. So I decided to make a move to give some direction in the creative area. It was a totally non-productive effort.

I began talking to the A&R men. I'd been listening a lot to the radio, in the morning, at night, whenever it didn't interfere with my work—mostly New York stations, WMCA and WABC. It seemed obvious that this was terribly important: you've got to *keep* listening to music that people are listening to and buying, however it changes. So I called a meeting of all A&R men and talked about this. A big speech it was. All these sullen A&R men around the table listening to an ex-lawyer tell *them* to listen to the radio to learn to understand and feel the new rock sounds. Outrageous! It was quickly clear that I was shouting in the wind.

For Columbia's A&R staff was trained in—and had made their reputations in—MOR and jazz. Mitch Miller's antirock rhetoric rang in their ears and they still believed it. No lawyer was going to tell them otherwise.

They felt quite threatened by my speech, as it turned out. History may have proven Miller tremendously wrong, but in 1966 and 1967 the case for rock was hardly clear. And A&R men as a group were much less flexible than I imagined. They simply tuned me out and went back to producing Ray Conniff, Percy Faith and Andy Williams, who, as they pointed out, were selling plenty of records. I had to begin thinking of going to independent producers to get contemporary records. I had been reluctant to do this, since the larger companies had always tried to do everything with their own in-house producers, but this was becoming more and more difficult. By the time the musical revolution of the late sixties had passed, the best record producers no longer worked in companies. The power of in-house A&R was considerably reduced.

Next, I approached the Broadway writers. It seemed obvious —again, by listening to the radio—that Broadway composers were unaware of the changes taking place. I arranged a lunch in early 1967 with Jerry Bock and Sheldon Harnick. They were right on top, having composed the score of *Fiddler on the Roof*. Additionally, they were working on two or three future projects. Could I influence them? I would try.

There was an additional problem. I could hardly have brought it up at the time, but I was also worried about quality. Broadway was simply not producing musicals that matched those of the forties, the fifties and the first half of the sixties. Shows like *My Fair Lady* and *South Pacific* led to fine, excellent albums filled with memorable and occasionally profound lyrics and melodies. But the theater of the late sixties, continuing until today—with exceptions, of course—is simply not producing this kind of musical experience. Broadway's current hit, *A Little Night Music,* has won Tony Awards and a score of citations. But nobody is *dying* to record its songs. Stephen Sondheim, in turn, is Broadway's fair-haired boy, and he is a brilliant lyricist; yet his melodies—with the exception of "Send in the Clowns"—are less than memorable. The result is that the cast album of *A Little Night Music* will probably sell around a hundred thousand copies. It is just not a compelling musical experience as an album.

The lunch with Harnick (Bock was sick) and his publisher, Tommy Valando, didn't help much. They were coming off a giant hit, and didn't quite understand my cause for alarm. I tried to tell them that Broadway music was losing the pulse of contemporary society; its *impact* might soon be lost. It was already being reflected in record sales. I offered to give Harnick carloads of albums by contemporary artists making it, or beginning to make it. He was polite, respectful; he listened. But it was clear that there would be no plans to write rock songs into new productions.

# 3

Broadway's hardening of the arteries included, I regret to report, the incomparable Richard Rodgers.

I ran into him outside Goddard Lieberson's office early in 1968. The tapes of Janis Joplin's first album had arrived, and I was extremely excited. Rodgers was waiting to go to lunch with Lieberson, and I stopped to talk with him.

I said that I'd discovered an artist in California who in many ways personified the enormous changes coming in popular music. I couldn't be as pointed about my Broadway theories with the venerable Rodgers as I had been with Harnick, but I wanted him to *hear* this new music, to react to it. Perhaps he could make some of its magic known to Broadway. I really believed in Janis's talent, and so I asked him to come into my office and listen to the tapes.

He walked inside and eased himself into a chair near my desk. I put on a tape of "Summertime," figuring that "Ball and Chain" first might be too dramatic a departure for him.

Rodgers listened very intently. He looked a little puzzled, however, and kept gazing up at the ceiling. When the tape ended, he didn't say anything. That made me nervous; I figured I'd play one more cut, a rock piece. Perhaps "Summertime" was a little too familiar. It was a considerably different version from the original. So I put on "Piece Of My Heart." After a minute and a half, he motioned me to stop.

He said that he just didn't "understand" it. He'd take my word that the record would be meaningful to young people—but he didn't understand what the music's appeal was, what the *basis* for the appeal was, why anybody would think this particular piece of music was good, or for that matter why anyone would consider *Janis* a good singer.

He became upset. He shrugged his shoulders and his left arm flailed as he talked. "If this means I have to change my writing," he said, "or that the only way to write a Broadway musical is to write rock songs, *then my career is over*. In no way could I possibly do this!"

I was really disturbed by his reaction. I wasn't asking *him*, the dean of Broadway composers, to write rock songs. I was simply hoping for more understanding of rock on Broadway. By now, I was used to pressure and complaints that suggested I was leaning too far away from traditional and middle-of-the-road music, the music that had supported Columbia for so long. I kept hearing that I lacked the proper appreciation for the Broadway art form, which was absurd. I had grown up with Broadway and loved its tradition and the great scores that came from it. But Broadway needed revitalization—it needed infusions of new blood. I had simply hoped that Rodgers and his colleagues could appreciate talent the likes of Janis's and welcome her kind of music into their creative family. I was tremendously concerned that music seemed to be pulling so widely apart, and I had hoped that its factions could be reconciled before they split off from each other completely. But there was no use; Rodgers's reaction was totally negative.

I learned an important lesson from that experience, as well as from the Harnick lunch and the abortive Columbia A&R meeting: don't try to *change* people. What comes to them naturally is fine, but you can't impose a new musical awareness on people simply through logic. I was wrong in trying, but then I suppose I had to find this out the hard way. It made more sense in the long run to accept Rodgers's great legacy—or that of Bock and Harnick—for what it was. If a revolution came, it would require new faces and new minds, not a cosmetic job done by past masters.

# 4

Following the same principle, rather than make over our own A&R staff, I turned to an outside independent producer and made a label deal with the master of them all, Lou Adler.

Lou had already made his fortune by forming Dunhill Records with Bobby Roberts, Hal Landers and Jay Lasker, and then selling it to ABC for several million dollars. He was one of the best producers in America, having had brilliant success with The Mamas and The Papas, Johnny Rivers and Jan and Dean. But he was having serious disagreements with Jay Lasker, who ran the company for ABC; the problems were so bad that Lou wanted out and, amazingly, Jay was willing to give him his release.

Lou had enormous style. He drank the finest wines, wore expensive clothes, drove expensive cars and always seemed to have a beautiful woman in tow. During the time I knew him best, he was most often with Peggy Lipton of "Mod Squad." In the studio, moreover, he was a consummate perfectionist, one reason why his relations with Jay Lasker deteriorated. His productions were excellent and frequently inspired; but he often took a lot of time, so expenses mounted up—an easy way to make a record executive nervous. Later, it turned out that his productions often were *too* good. He'd often find a good—but not great—artist, and then produce an album so excellent that the artist in concert could only be a disappointment.

Lou's very first record for us was a giant hit, Scott McKenzie's "San Francisco (Wear Some Flowers In Your Hair)," and it became a theme of sorts for the flower child era. It was also a big commercial hit all over the world. It seemed obvious to me that we should follow the single immediately with an album. I pushed my belief that albums and singles should go out at the same time, but Lou held with the old singles-oriented philosophy, which meant that he would allow the single to run its course before releasing the album; he wanted to wait. He was also afraid that Scott would become identified too powerfully with one song; he wanted him to have another hit *before* the album came out. Earlier, Lou had released Barry McGuire's album containing "Eve of Destruction" on top of the single, only to find that Barry faded as soon as his big hit faded. Lou took this badly and didn't want to make the mistake again.

Fine. Except that he wasn't able to find another hit for Scott McKenzie. The album was released late and did just *fairly* well, but it could have had a sale of three or four hundred thousand *more* units if the album had been released when the single was hot.

Lou's own label, then and now, was called Ode. As was customary in such label deals, he was given a budget to produce a certain number of single sides, and money beyond that for overhead. He also committed himself to produce a substantial number of albums for the company. As time wore on, he began falling short of this quota, but I figured that you don't push a guy like Lou Adler. You assume that he's a professional and that when he sees an artist he likes, he'll produce a record.

Beyond that, I was profiting from our relationship. Lou was a shrewd businessman and a great judge of talent. Talking to him and watching him deal with artists was very enlightening. Almost innately, he seemed to combine business acumen and creativity as though they were *intended* to be mixed. He was the one who taught me how to coordinate record campaigns . . . being sure, for example, that your record is reviewed at the same time you take out your trade ads. His close attention to album covers—and to the people he worked with—made a lasting impression on me.

Still, I was bothered by the *kind* of artists he seemed to be producing. All too often they seemed to be artists with no real potential. The only group he produced that I felt had a feeling for the future direction of music was Spirit, a strong aggregate. His other artists *sounded* as if they could have hits—but this was mostly the result of Lou's superb studio techniques. Music was coming into a time when word-of-mouth comment and public appearances mattered more and more. Except for Spirit, not one of his groups had the goods to go on tour.

I kept asking Lou about this. But it was hard to criticize him, for his records were great. At one point, for example, he put together a group of Los Angeles studio singers for a gospel album of Bob Dylan's songs. It was brilliant—but they were not a performing group, and there was no hit single. It didn't sell. He also recorded an album with Peggy Lipton, partially for personal reasons, I suppose, and it was superbly produced. Unfortunately,

Peggy was not an earthshaking singer; despite her public identification with the successful "Mod Squad" series, the record sold poorly. At one point, he produced an album with a group called The City. Carole King was involved in the group and, as everyone knows, she went on to become one of the best-selling album artists in the history of music. But on the only album for Columbia she was submerged in The City, and it didn't work.

We more or less broke even on the Adler contract, but the ending of it was personally sad to me. Lou simply hadn't accomplished what we'd hoped and, when his contract ran out, we decided not to pick up the option, which seemed too expensive. Actually, he had produced nowhere near the number of albums agreed to. It would have been possible—if we had chosen to do so—to suspend his contract and force him to complete them. But I was reluctant to do this, for Lou and Abe Somer, his lawyer—the most prominent Los Angeles music industry attorney and one of my closest personal friends as well—were now talking about going into business together. Abe suggested at one point that neither he nor I had had much experience in the music business when we originally negotiated Lou's contract and that the amount of product required was really excessive.

I didn't want to be hard-nosed about this, so I agreed to waive his contractual obligations and terminate the agreement. It was a favor, pure and simple, for Abe and Lou. Although Lou had not been successful at Columbia, he remained one of the best producers in the business and it certainly would have made business sense to keep him around.

Then a disturbing issue arose. I'd visited Lou a few months earlier in Los Angeles when he was recording the Dylan gospel album. Listening to the tapes, I kept hearing one voice. It just popped out at me. It turned out to be Merry Clayton, a well-known Los Angeles background singer, and I suggested that Lou sign her individually. He agreed to, and did.

When Lou was ready to leave the company, I decided I wanted to keep Merry for Columbia. We had the contractual right to retain any artist who recorded on Ode. The discussions became *more* complicated when Abe Somer decided in the interim to stay with his law firm. Now he was simply Lou's attorney rather than his business partner. This was sticky. I had agreed to let Lou out of his contract partly because of my warm regard for Abe and the business favors he had done for me. It was impossible now for me to say I wouldn't do that for Lou alone. Finally, however, a meeting was set up to designate which artists Columbia would retain. It was scheduled for a Friday around Christmastime and happened to be the same day I was giving a party for Janis Joplin, so I asked Abe and Lou to meet with Walter Dean, who was then head of Business Affairs at Columbia.

I had never informed Walter about my interest in Merry Clayton.

The weekend passed and on Monday morning Walter came to brief me. I asked him what artists we were retaining, and he mentioned Scott McKenzie and Spirit. I said, "Fine, but we also want Merry Clayton. You don't know about her, but I had asked Lou to sign her a while ago, and I would like to keep her as well. He can continue to produce her, if he likes. Just tell Abe. I'm sure there won't be a problem."

Walter immediately called Abe and conveyed this, saying he hadn't known about Merry earlier. Abe promised to talk to Lou. A few days later, he called to say, "Look, Lou feels he acted upon Walter's verbal comments. He's made a deal with Jerry Moss of A&M now, and one of the artists he's promised him is Merry. Lou thinks it was fair to act on Walter's word; he is Columbia's Vice-President. He feels he can't go back and tell Jerry he's not going to get her."

"But she's an unknown singer," we protested. "How could Jerry Moss be affected one way or another? Furthermore, we are gratuitously letting Lou out of a contract. We have an absolute legal *right* to retain Merry Clayton! Walter knew nothing of her when he talked with you on Friday night. And we called you right back on Monday morning. It would be wrong to call that a totally inclusive discussion."

Abe again said that he would call back. The next day he told Walter that Lou felt "very strongly" that he had the right to act on the oral agreement.

I was *most* upset by this. I called Abe—who was very uneasy to be caught between Lou and me—and got very emotional. I said that I wanted Merry Clayton, and it was not just a question of legal rights. *I was letting Lou out of an agreement.* He was free to go elsewhere and make a new label deal for a lot of money. But I had the *right* to keep Merry Clayton, and I wanted to do so.

"I'll tell Lou this," Abe said, and that seemed to be the end of it.

Several months went by. Lou was given his release. Then Merry Clayton began to get some publicity over the song "Gimme Shelter." The Rolling Stones were publicly enthusiastic about her performance of it, which was a tremendously important endorsement. I called Walter Dean and asked about this, and he said he assumed that Lou would be recording her for us. That had been his final understanding on the matter.

The following Monday I picked up *Billboard*—and there was the Merry Clayton single . . . *on Ode Records*. I couldn't believe it! I was *really* angry. We'd been good friends. I'd let him out of his contract. I'd suggested that he sign Merry Clayton. I felt that I had no choice except to sue to retain her.

Naturally, this created a rift between Lou and myself for some time, even though the lawsuit was not pursued actively by either side. It was eventually settled that Merry could stay on Ode, but only as long as Lou personally produced her. If he did not, she would automatically revert to Columbia. I had an ulterior motive here. Merry is a very talented artist, but I didn't think that black artists were really Lou's cup of tea. If Merry wanted hits, she'd eventually have to find a black producer. To do this, she would have to come back to Columbia. In fact, it nearly happened. I got a call from Alan Bernard, now Merry's manager, in 1972 saying that he'd spoken to Lou about having someone else produce Merry. He was told that she would revert to Columbia if this happened. Would I release her?

"No," I said, as calmly as possible.

As of this writing, Merry still has not broken out. Altogether, it was a sad break in my relationship with Lou. We see each other only occasionally now.

It bothers me—sometimes a lot—that human relations and business problems seem to conflict so often. Lou Adler has done brilliantly over the years; his name stands for taste and quality in the music business. I admire him enormously and I miss my relationship with him. Much too often in this business and, I assume, others as well, you are left with the ashes of friendships after the contracts are signed. I very much wish it weren't this way.

# 5

Let's go back to Donovan, over whom another kind of storm was developing. It was 1969 now, and I'd been getting unhappy calls, both from him *and* Mickey Most. It was, as I expected, a conflict between Most's commercial instincts and Donovan's experimental impulses. I tried to stay neutral in the fight, but it was easy to be sympathetic to Most. He and Donovan had been extremely successful; I didn't want to see them break up. The result in such cases almost always was a decline in sales.

On the other hand, you cannot sit on an artist. Like gifted children, artists have to be given room to grow. If you try to limit them to a particular area of creativity, however successful, the result is rarely good. By contrast, if an artist feels free to experiment, and fails, he or she will most likely rebound. Few artists have an unbroken string of successes anyway. There has to be a stubbing of toes. So I kept urging Mickey to give Donovan the room he needed. But now Most saw *his* reputation as being on the line. He was an exacting producer—and a successful one. If Donovan wanted to do things he didn't approve of, he felt that Donovan should do them with someone else.

A lot of phone calls went back and forth. And then Donovan disappeared. I heard that he'd gone to live in Greece; for quite some time he was completely out of touch. His father had become his manager and, though his father was a very pleasant man, he was not at all experienced in music. The lack of communication was disquieting to me.

More than six months later, I got word that Donovan was finally working on an album by himself. This raised immediate problems with Mickey Most, who was contracted to work with Donovan, but obviously wasn't. First, an agreement protecting Most's royalty rate had to be negotiated, which was done. Then Donovan's father, Donald Leitch, arrived in New York to begin negotiations for a new contract—the previous one was set to expire at the end of 1970. The talks bogged down quickly. Mr. Leitch assured me constantly that Donovan was happy at Columbia and would never leave. Unfortunately, we were very far apart on the question of money.

Then a promoter named Jerry Perenchio got into the act. He was later to become prominent for his work on the first Ali-Frazier fight, and then the Billie Jean King-Bobby Riggs tennis match. His arrival seemed a bad sign to me. He'd negotiated a few deals with Columbia before, and they never closed. He always asked too much money for my taste—but in his defense I should add that he always managed to come up with it from someone optimistic enough to pay it.

Well, we began talking to Perenchio, knowing only that Donovan was somewhere in Europe working on an "experimental" album. Beyond that, although Donovan had already earned the original guaranty many times over, we felt he still owed us three or four albums under the contract. But with someone like Donovan, you don't start writing lawyer's letters—or so I thought. Gentle methods are advisable, for personal relationships can be terribly important.

The negotiations proceeded by fits and starts. Donovan's father kept assuring us that Donovan was very happy at the company; Perenchio, on the other hand, wanted far more money than I was willing to pay. He also asked that Donovan be moved from Epic to the Columbia label, which I turned down flatly. Epic, as it happened, was created as a sister label to avoid overstuffing Columbia; also to resolve potential artist rivalries. Donovan, as I've noted, was sometimes called the British Dylan; it therefore made sense to keep him on a separate label from Dylan. And Epic, though smaller than Columbia, was not considered a country cousin. It had been attracting good names—Sly and The Family Stone, The Hollies, Poco, Edgar Winter and, in other areas of music, Bobby Vinton, Tammy Wynette, Charlie Rich—and it would have been disastrous to Epic's image if artists, as a mark of success, began moving over to Columbia.

Walter Dean, now Columbia's invaluable Executive Vice-President, and I had a number of meetings with Perenchio. We finally offered a two-million-dollar guaranty for a five-year contract requiring ten albums. I still believed that Donovan could be a big artist, despite his disappearance, and this seemed a very fair contract to me. Perenchio said it was definitely in the "ball park." He said he would recommend that Donovan make the deal, and then get back to us.

A deafening silence ensued.

Telephone calls to Perenchio were not answered; subordinates said that the Ali-Frazier fight was keeping the promoter extremely busy. I'd heard that Warner Bros. and RCA had made bids, but I didn't bother to check them; it didn't seem to make any difference. Our offer was solid; and we'd treated Donovan well in the past.

In the meantime Donovan was scheduled to appear in July, 1970, at our convention in Freeport, the Bahamas. He also planned to release the album he'd been working on, *Open Road,* and I was told that he planned to tour behind it, reintroducing himself to his fans. I wanted to talk with him. I wanted to have him in Freeport so badly, in fact, that I not only agreed to fly him and his group over, but also his fiancée. He'd been out of circulation for more than a year, and I felt that his new group would be an exciting way to close the convention's Saturday night banquet show.

He came, we talked, and it all sounded very promising. Donovan outlined his album plans, thoughts about working on a movie, ideas for children's projects and even his old interest in Broadway. And his show was brilliant; his magic remained hypnotic.

Then everything fell apart. Donovan suddenly canceled his tour, allegedly because of tax problems, and he disappeared again. Besides further confusing the negotiations with Perenchio, this meant his album would suffer as well. He'd been gone long enough to *need* a tour; he also needed a hit single. We got neither; the album sold about three hundred and fifty thousand copies, a good sale but not great.

And then I learned that he had signed with Warner Bros.

I was stunned. Beyond the usual business ties, I had an emotional attachment to Donovan. He was the first artist I'd signed; the company had treated him extremely well, and we were supposed to be on the best of terms. It seemed *astounding* that he could have talked about his future face to face with me at Freeport—without so much as a wink or a nod toward signing with another company.

I was hardly ignorant of big business dealings. You win some, you lose some. But this seemed particularly underhanded. Of course Warner Bros. maintained their innocence throughout. They said that they had no idea of Donovan's commitments to Columbia, including his undelivered albums. They simply were looking to sign a top artist who, in turn, was willing to negotiate with them.

I believed them and thought their goal fair; yet it seemed *unfair* that Donovan could get close to signing the Warners deal without Perenchio notifying us.

I decided to play rough: we suspended Donovan's contract. A "suspension" means activating a clause that requires an artist to fulfill his contractual guarantees, but extends indefinitely the time in which he must do it. Donovan would then be required to stay under contract to us to fulfill his album obligations—no matter how long it would take. He would not be able to go to Warner Bros. until afterward.

The odd thing was that Donovan didn't seem to understand what had happened. He knew he'd signed with Warner Bros.; but he had been advised that he'd satisfied his legal obligation to us. It turned out that Warners had offered him two hundred and fifty thousand dollars an album for ten albums, plus financing for a motion picture. He didn't know, of course, that it was the usual movie step-deal: the company puts up a certain amount of money, then looks at the first draft of the screenplay. Then it has an *option* to continue the commitment. By the time we were ready for court action, in fact, Donovan was in Los Angeles writing his screenplay and working on another album. The court would decide who got the album.

We began taking depositions. Donovan happened to be in New York, so we made a Columbia conference room available for the examination. I ran into him in the corridors as he walked toward the room. It was hard to be *personally* angry with Donovan. He greeted me very warmly; I greeted him the same way. We'd always gotten on well. I felt awkward . . . his lawyers were with him, and I was on my way to a meeting. So we talked only briefly. Donovan's magic as a performer was such that you almost had to believe him: he seemed no businessman at all. A lot of artists want their public to feel that they don't care about business problems and money; Donovan gave this impression better than most.

Then the strangest thing happened.

Donovan was sitting in the conference room, answering lawyers' questions and reading letters he and I had exchanged over the years, which were brought in as evidence to trace the history of his Columbia contract—and he suddenly realized that Columbia *had* been betrayed by the negotiations. The letters showed that we had gone to a great deal of trouble on his behalf, that we'd been told by Perenchio we were the number one contender for renewal and that we had thought his managers were recommending he re-sign with us—that we had had no idea he was closing a deal with Warner Bros.

He suddenly stopped the proceedings. He said he couldn't continue. And, without saying another word, he walked out of the room.

Three hours later, I got a telephone call from Allan Klein, the former manager of The Rolling Stones and the various Beatles, excepting Paul McCartney. Klein had been called in to help negotiate the original Donovan contract with Ashley Kozak. He also represented Mickey Most and thus remained indirectly interested in Donovan as well.

Donovan had walked across Sixth Avenue into Klein's offices. He said that his managers had screwed up badly, that he hadn't gotten the right information from them, that he now realized why I was angry. He wanted to stop the litigation, fire his lawyers and managers and negotiate a new contract.

Needless to say, I was pleased. Klein asked that I match the Warners guaranty. I did. I couldn't do anything about the motion picture commitment—and in fact a nasty legal battle still loomed with Warners. But the fight ended just as abruptly as it began. After a few months, Warners voluntarily bowed out, realizing that they wouldn't do well with a recalcitrant artist. And as it happened, Donovan's movie never appeared. Warners retained their motion picture rights, but they apparently didn't like the first draft of the screenplay.

Unfortunately, Donovan hasn't been very active since that time. He's released only two albums in the interim, but again he didn't tour behind either one—a serious mistake. His reviews are uniformly excellent, but without a tour and a really big single hit, the effect is muted. Yet Donovan's unique position in rock is secure and he remains an important artist. If he's willing to make a few commercial concessions, any album of his could be a major reentry; for Donovan's appeal is lasting.

# Four

## 1

My first meeting with Bob Dylan was disastrous; also, fortunately, forgotten. It was 1963, and I was Columbia's General Attorney. He was already an important voice of social protest. But I had to tell him that he couldn't record a song about the John Birch Society; it was libelous.

The problem began with Ed Sullivan. Dylan had been invited to appear on the show—quite a break for any contemporary artist at that time—and he planned to sing a new song titled "Talking John Birch Society Blues." It was a biting satire in which a member finds Communists under his bed, his stove, even inside his television set. Unfortunately, the song had a line suggesting that John Birch members subscribed to "Hitler's views," even though he'd killed "six million Jews."

It was a very potent line, musically—but clearly libelous. Nobody would argue that the Society wasn't ultraconservative, but it couldn't reasonably be said that they subscribed to *Hitler's* views, so the show's attorneys banned the song. Bob, in turn, canceled his appearance. He assumed, however, that he could still record the song on his next album, that Columbia wouldn't object.

We did. In strict legal terms, any member of the Birch Society who cared to could sue us when the album was released. I had to rule against it. It was a difficult decision—an awkward position for me. After all, I was a liberal. I'd worked for Adlai Stevenson during the fifties. I also admired Dylan, who I thought was contributing a great deal to progressive thought in this country.

But I was Columbia's lawyer, and I had to take a *legal* position. Bob was twenty-two at the time—I was thirty-one—and he asked to see me. When he came into the office, John Hammond was with him; but he couldn't say much, for Dylan was deeply angry, saying, "What *is* this? What do you *mean* I can't come out with this song? You can't edit or censor me!"

I was squirming terribly. I said, "God, I hate to do this. I feel awful. It has nothing to do with my being conservative, or the company being conservative." I kept apologizing and defending myself, saying I was a liberal Democrat, and so on. He obviously felt this was an establishment-oriented, conservative ruling, so I tried again and again to say that it had nothing to do with politics or liberalism; it was simply a legal issue. And I had no choice but to rule that, yes, this was libelous; and because the company had much more money than he did, we'd end up having to defend the lawsuits.

"It's all bullshit," Dylan said.

And then he stalked out of the room. He didn't want to hear any more—either we came out with the record or we didn't. He didn't want to hear any apologies or reasons or anything else. He was very angry; I felt bad. It was purely a legal issue, but it couldn't be sidestepped. Years later, when I was Columbia's President, I don't think he remembered I was *that* lawyer, which was fortunate. Or, if he did, he didn't let on. The anguish of that particular decision sticks with me even now. And the irony of it is considerable, in the light of my later fights on behalf of freedom of expression.

Another unpleasant moment—though not involving us face to face—preceded that one. Early in his career, Dylan was not happy at Columbia. His first album didn't sell well and, outside of Hammond and a few others, most people at Columbia thought he was a freak, at best a "different" performer. The upshot was that John Hammond called me one day in a state of anxiety, saying that he'd received a letter from Dylan disaffirming his record contract on grounds that he was a minor when he'd signed it. Could he do this, Hammond asked? Again, a legal opinion: yes, probably. In those days one didn't go to court to get a minor's contract approved; this meant, in effect, that Dylan could disavow it before he got to be twenty-one—which would happen in a few days.

John was most upset, saying that he was "totally amazed." He had had no idea that this was coming. He and Dylan were on excellent terms, and he assumed that this was a ploy by Dylan's lawyers to get a better contract deal somewhere else. Dylan had signed nothing but a standard form contract with us.

I asked John how good his relationship with Dylan really was. He said, "Very good." I suggested that he call Dylan—right away—and bring him into his office; then convince him that the company *would* get behind him in the future, find out if he was really *that* angry and, if he wasn't, get him to disavow the letter in writing.

It was a long shot, but it worked. Dylan signed a statement disavowing the disavowal, saying the contract was equally valid after he reached twenty-one. His attorneys were horrified!

It wasn't the last time I'd have to reach a considerable distance to keep Bob Dylan on the label.

# 2

In 1966, soon after becoming the operating head of Columbia as Vice-President and General Manager, I had a major, major problem. The contracts of Columbia's three top artists—Dylan, Barbra Streisand and Andy Williams—were set to expire *at once*. Each of the three contracts was to take nearly a year to negotiate— a difficult, taxing, frightening, grinding time for me.

Worse yet, each expired *while* I was negotiating them. Dylan, Streisand and Williams suddenly became free agents, quite able to shop around the industry and leave Columbia high and dry if other offers looked better.

Normally you try to sew up contract renewals well in advance of their expiration dates, but there was no way to push these particular artists any faster than their managers wanted to go. Williams was the star of a weekly television show and had become the best-selling solo artist in the country; Streisand was selling at least eight to nine hundred thousand copies of each new release. And Dylan by now was at the peak of his influence.

Three of the toughest managers in the business—Albert Grossman, Marty Erlichman and Alan Bernard—were representing Dylan, Streisand and Andy Williams, respectively. It was clear immediately that competing record companies *and* the managers themselves were watching me closely. The managers, in fact, became competitive among themselves, vowing that no one of them would get a bigger deal. At one point they thought of joining forces; apparently they were dissuaded by the legal problems involved.

Each negotiation was very rough, filled with tense confrontations. In a way, the one with Williams was the knottiest. The big problem, again, was precedent: Columbia in 1965 had never paid a guaranty larger than five hundred thousand dollars for a five-year, ten-album contract. Andy Williams, however, was a giant in the entertainment world. He'd recently sold more than a million and a half copies of his *Moon River* album, the same for *Days of Wine and Roses.* "Call Me Irresponsible" and "Dear Heart" had sold a million units. He was also a household figure because of his television show, which is always an enormous boost to record sales.

Streisand was a tremendously important star as well. Her album sales were consistently high. Her potential was unlimited. She was already making motion pictures—*Funny Girl,* for example—which would provide very valuable sound track albums.

Columbia's pretax profits, as I've noted, were about five million dollars a year at that time, and both Williams and Streisand were talking about guaranties of more than a million dollars. The wrong move in these negotiations could have been perilous to the company.

I knew that Williams was talking to other companies. Warner Bros., which at the time was a solid middle-of-the-road company with such artists as Frank Sinatra and Dean Martin, was the main competition. During a Florida A&R meeting I heard that Williams was talking actively to them. I got very worried. Bill Gallagher and Walter Dean were handling the negotiations, but I thought it might make a difference if Williams dealt with the head of the company, so I called him directly. He said that he'd been happy with Columbia—but this was a business matter, and Warners had made a very big offer.

I eventually offered him a guaranty of one and a half million dollars to re-sign for five years. It seemed like a gigantic deal, a precedent-shattering move; yet, looking back, it seems amusing that I was so worried. The price of popular music since then has shot up dramatically. That amount of money is often given to artists with nowhere near Williams's track record. And with all the things Williams had going for him, it wasn't that big a risk. As it turned out, Andy made the guaranty back with plenty to spare.

Yet these were hard-fought negotiations, and I periodically got terribly anxious about them. It is difficult enough to have one major artist out of contract in the middle of negotiations; it is unprecedented to have *three*: worse still to have this happening to someone recently promoted to head of operations. I felt that Columbia's future was very much at stake—not to mention my own—and I did find myself muttering about it now and then at home. It would cut into my thoughts during social and family conversations, kind of like living with a difficult pregnancy. We simply couldn't afford to lose the baby.

One way I hedged my bet against such a large guaranty was to stipulate that Williams had to record fifteen albums—three a year. It was a lot to ask, except that Williams, like Streisand, doesn't write his own songs: material is submitted to him and he records it. And so he was willing to promise this in return for the high guaranty. I eventually made the same arrangement with Streisand, asking again for fifteen albums for the five-year period. It wouldn't have been fair to give Barbra the same guaranty as Williams, since she didn't sell as well at the time. I therefore offered her a sliding-scale royalty, higher if she would accept a lower guaranty of one million dollars, which she accepted.

The Streisand negotiations were volatile. Erlichman would pound the desk and storm out of the office periodically, and then not call for three or four weeks. My general technique was to avoid returning emotion for emotion; you can't take these things personally. It's business. You want to sign the artist, and you want to do it for a reasonable amount of money. If a personal conflict develops between you and the manager, it can seriously damage negotiations. Besides, some of the temper tantrums were calculated; Erlichman or some other manager would be testing to see if I could be bulldozed. Other times, of course, they contained genuine emotion, for Erlichman and Bernard strongly cared about their clients *and* did not want to be outnegotiated by the other.

When Marty Erlichman stormed out, I usually called Walter Dean in and told him what had happened; then we'd wait a week for things to cool off and call Marty. It was sometimes quite upsetting; I'd sit in my chair and grind my teeth, thinking: *I can't close this goddamn deal!*

Finally, after having my back against the wall for what seemed an eternity, we came to terms, and the contract proved a tremendous bonanza for Columbia. Streisand not only brought the company tremendously successful sound track albums—*Funny Girl* sold more than one and a quarter million copies, for example—but very successful studio albums as well, especially those on which she performed songs by contemporary writers, such as *Stoney End* and *Time and Love*. At this writing she still hasn't filled the quota of fifteen albums, mostly because of her motion picture commitments, so the contract continues to bring in a great deal of money, long after the guaranty has been earned.

# 3

The Dylan negotiations were another question entirely. I felt that we simply couldn't afford to let him go; if nothing else, he was an unparalleled symbol of avant-garde musical thinking—a name that would help us sign other good acts in the future. Equally important, I felt that he would *continue* to be a major artist, despite the incapacity and silence that had lately plagued him. Yet there was a money problem.

Ironically, the best-kept secret in the business was Dylan's sales record. His influence as a performer, writer, poet and cultural innovator far exceeded the sales of his albums. He was easily as big an influence on pop tastes as The Beatles, yet his sales at the time stayed consistently below five hundred thousand copies, the amount needed for a gold record.

It was an easy secret to keep. His cult always besieged record stores when a new album arrived. The charts always reflect a concentrated buying spree, so any new Dylan album immediately zoomed to the top. Ray Conniff, by contrast, might have sold three times as many albums over a longer period of time, but nobody was rushing into the stores to buy him, so his chart action was relatively minimal.

This secret turned out to be an albatross. Since they didn't know his sales record, other companies assumed that Dylan's presence would vastly enhance their Bottom Line, and they were willing to offer a great deal of money for him. Columbia, meanwhile, was offering artists a 5 percent royalty rate, which was standard. The policy was not to go above it; and since we used mostly staff producers, paying them nothing extra except Christmas bonuses, we never gave independent producers more than 2 percent. Everything was pretty tight and uniform. The highest guaranty we'd offered an artist up to this time was five hundred thousand dollars; this was to Doris Day for a deal involving ten albums.

It made sense, therefore, to offer Dylan the usual 5 percent with five hundred thousand dollars up front, for a five-year deal; it seemed, in fact, generous. Unfortunately, other record companies weren't bound by such traditions. MGM, for example. When I made our offer to Grossman he came back and said that we were simply being outbid.

I asked what kind of money he was talking about. The answer was depressing: MGM was offering a 12 percent royalty and a million and a half dollars guaranteed for five years. They were taking an amazing chance—Dylan had suffered his motorcycle accident and at this point was totally incommunicado; Grossman would say nothing about his health or state of mind. Nobody even knew if he had his *voice*.

I tried to point out—as I always had to at Columbia—that royalties at MGM and many other companies don't take free records into account. Many companies make deals giving the wholesaler, say, two free albums for every ten he buys—and they don't pay artist royalties on the free ones. This lowers the percentage points considerably.

Here the argument cut very little ice. If we argued that MGM's royalties really amounted to 10 percent, they had still doubled our offer. There was little I could do. I had Streisand and Williams to consider as well. Streisand was selling eight to nine hundred thousand albums with each release; Williams was easily topping a million. Dylan, meanwhile, was not in that league. What could I say to Erlichman and Bernard?

Finally I decided that the company just couldn't afford to match the offer. I felt terrible.

But I couldn't get the Dylan matter out of my mind. Negotiations are sometimes like poker, and claims of competing money can be a matter of bluffing; yet I knew that MGM generally was throwing that kind of money around. They'd outbid us earlier for The Righteous Brothers, offering them eight hundred thousand dollars for a five-year deal. The Brothers were just coming down off their hit "You've Lost That Lovin' Feelin'" and they seemed very hot. Yet that kind of money is a serious gamble and, in that case, it was a disaster for MGM.

With Dylan, it just *seemed* that Columbia shouldn't lose him. Goddard Lieberson and Harvey Schein apparently didn't mind that much; they felt more strongly about not breaking policy lines. By contrast, I felt that Dylan was far more important than policy lines; *there had to be another way.* Again and again, I kept appraising the situation, and I finally called up Grossman and offered him a total royalty of 7 percent, including the 2 percent producer's fee. That meant that he could hire an independent producer and pay him, say, a flat fee of 1 percent and keep the rest of the royalty. Again he said it was out of the ball park—which meant that he was close to concluding the MGM deal.

Enter Allan Klein, the controversial but very successful music entrepreneur.

From managing Herman's Hermits, The Animals, Bobby Vinton, Donovan and The Rolling Stones, as well as distributing foreign movies, Klein had become a major stockholder in MGM. And the company was having a proxy fight. Most of MGM's board was motion picture-oriented, at best vaguely conversant with records. Now, the Records Division knew that it would be a major coup to sign Bob Dylan; but some of the board hadn't *heard* of him, and they were openly questioning the wisdom of signing an artist *they'd* never heard of for one and a half million dollars. Klein, meanwhile, was being courted by both factions in the proxy fight. He came to me at one point and asked what I thought of MGM's deal.

I admitted that I had mixed feelings about it.

I told him that I'd been personally negotiating for Dylan, as I assumed he knew. Then I told him that I had Dylan's *actual* sales figures; MGM didn't, and it was clear they were taking a major risk for their romantic notions.

Klein is no fool, of course. His instincts are among the best in the business—but this time he was wrong. After talking to me, he went to several MGM board meetings and brought up the Dylan matter, saying that their Records Division was in terrible shape and was about to make a very bad deal. The division was indeed in poor shape. For some odd reason, the company had earlier forgotten to renew options for a number of its important artists. Contracts are usually signed for one year with four renewable options, but MGM inexplicably had forgotten to pick up several options—that of The Lovin' Spoonful, for one example. As a result, the company had had to renegotiate that contract for much more money.

The proxy fight had led to incredible paralysis in MGM's executive offices. The Records Division had no authority to operate without the approval of corporate management; it couldn't sign contracts, including Dylan's, without word from the board. And the board was at war with itself. On the matter of Dylan, certain board members were afraid of alienating Klein, who obstreperously opposed the deal. Moreover, they *believed* Klein. The sales figures I had fed to him were genuine, and somehow they wanted to believe that the Records Division was screwed up.

I sweated this out for several months. I knew that MGM's deal with Dylan was fully closed; he'd *signed* the contract already. Now it was sitting in MGM's offices waiting for the corporate countersignature. But then MGM Records President, Mort Nasatir, got wind of Klein's and my discussions. Allan called me one day saying, "My God, they're going to sue us for conspiracy—they say I'm your tool to keep Columbia from losing Dylan!"

Nasatir at least knew Dylan's value. A lawsuit, however, was absurd. All MGM had to do was sign its own contract; I could hardly be accused of stopping this. And I couldn't be accused of fooling Klein. The sales figures were true; and Klein believed on his own that Dylan's future was in doubt.

One day soon after that, Albert Grossman called. He came to my office with Dylan's attorney, David Braun, and said, "Look, we've had an outstanding deal with MGM [I *knew*], but Bob is having second thoughts. He can't believe that MGM is taking so long to sign the contract; so I want to propose something unorthodox which is acceptable to Bob and myself, if you'll agree. Bob will require no guaranty if you'll ask for no minimum product. He'll make a five-year deal—no minimum number of albums—if you'll pay ten percent of retail royalties. There'll be no risk for you in front but, if we hit, we want to hit twice as big as before."

I thought it was a perfect solution, and I grabbed it. The royalties were twice anything we'd ever paid before, but it was worth it to keep Dylan.

I didn't foresee one bit of haggling, however, which threatened to derail the whole deal. Normally, at that time, when an artist was paid, say, 5 percent royalties in the United States, his foreign royalties would be half that. This was because his records were being sold locally by another company, and the licensing arrangements would eat up much of the profits.

Grossman, however, wanted 7 percent foreign royalties for Dylan. And this met with icy opposition from my old boss Harvey Schein, now head of Columbia's International Records Division. Schein and Lieberson were traveling in Europe at the time, and I called them. Schein said, "Forget it, it's out of the question. It would amount to triple the foreign royalties every other Columbia artist is getting, and set a horrendous precedent."

I argued that Dylan was a bulwark of Columbia Records. We had a once-in-a-lifetime, risk-free deal in the offing. *It wasn't an ordinary re-signing;* it was *terribly important* to the company. But Schein held firm, and Lieberson kept silent.

Now I had to call Grossman and try to get *him* to come down. He finally agreed to 5 percent for non-English-speaking countries, but he insisted on 6 percent for England—that was as far as he would go. Back to Schein. Still he wouldn't budge. Grossman was adamant too. Which left everything in my lap.

I finally threatened to sign Dylan for the United States alone, and free him of foreign obligations. This hadn't ever been done at Columbia, but I was convinced that we had to keep Dylan; when Lieberson saw this, he stepped in and began reasoning with Schein. After all, it was a very good deal for Columbia because of the no-risk factors—and Lieberson didn't want to tell me I *couldn't* sign Dylan. On the other hand, if I started signing artists strictly on a domestic basis, it would divide the company badly. After considerable soul-searching, Schein, one of the shrewdest businessmen in records, wisely gave in. After all, he technically had achieved his half-foreign-royalty goal—even if it was at 5 percent—and 6 percent for England, where we had our own company, wasn't so bad.

The Dylan negotiations had a comic-opera ending. MGM still had the unsigned contract in its files, and I was trying to make *our* deal as quietly as possible. For that reason, I asked David

Braun to meet me outside the CBS building to work out final details. We settled on the dining room of the Dorset Hotel, which was in the neighborhood but not a hangout for music people. Everything went fine until the dessert course—then the entire executive staff of MGM Records walked into the room.

I nearly died. I couldn't believe that they would choose *this day* to have lunch in *this place*. Fortunately, the dining room is fairly large, and they were seated on the other side of it. And since Braun, as it happened, represented other clients as well, they couldn't necessarily assume that we were discussing Dylan.

We finished dessert calmly—never looking in their direction—paid the bill and walked out.

That day, Braun sent a telegram rescinding Dylan's signature.

# 4

Dealing with Dylan, despite the mythology which surrounded him, was surprisingly easy—though it could be a fragile and murky business at times. A couple of years after signing the contract, he left Grossman. I never knew why. As it happened, I always got on well with Albert, who was somewhat controversial. Sometimes thought to be imperious—or even brutal—in his dealings, Grossman nonetheless was always professional, honest and to the point with me. I liked him.

At any rate, they stopped working together, and I began to worry that Dylan might become too isolated. He did not have another manager; I had the feeling that he needed someone to bring him ideas, goad him a bit, make suggestions, offer help if he needed it. This is not easy to do with Dylan, of course, and I had to tread *very* softly. I began calling him. I could never reach him directly, for he guards his privacy very carefully. The technique was to call his secretary, Naomi, who would call him; then, if he chose to, he would call back.

In these calls, I simply offered my services in whatever way he might need. I'd ask what he was doing, what his thoughts were about various things, if he was thinking of doing any performing, if I could arrange meetings with managers or producers or advisers he might need. On specific occasions, we talked of recording problems, or what single to choose off an album coming out. He was extremely polite in these conversations, saying he'd "consider" each suggestion and get back to me. Sometimes he did, sometimes not.

I never spoke to the press about Dylan. His need for privacy was obvious, and he had such a unique image that I felt I *couldn't* comment about him. An artist sometimes looks to a record executive for help in image-building; this can be a delicate problem, for a record executive has to be sure that *his* image doesn't interfere with the artist's. The executive must submerge himself in the promotion process; if possible, become nearly anonymous. In Dylan's case, of course, this was no problem. His career of writing and performing spoke for itself. My role was simply to advise and help him, if possible, and then to market his records.

Dylan's first public appearance after his August, 1966, motorcycle accident was at a special January, 1968, Woody Guthrie Memorial Concert at Carnegie Hall. Judy Collins, Pete Seeger, Arlo Guthrie and Richie Havens were there, but Dylan was clearly to be the main attraction, for he had been totally out of view since the accident. All the seats were sold out within an hour after they went on sale, and thousands of people weren't able to get tickets.

I had not seen Dylan since becoming head of the company. It was agreed that I should visit with him before the concert and perform the ceremonial act of presenting him with his gold albums. By this time, his *Greatest Hits* album had been released. Its sales gave Dylan his first million-unit seller and in turn motivated sales of some of his other albums to gold-record status.

I arranged a short meeting in his suite at the Park Sheraton Hotel. Grossman, Dylan's wife, Sarah, and a few others were present. It turned out that he *liked* receiving the gold record album plaques, however bourgeois the concept might seem. He was very mellow and friendly and seemed to be quite another person from the reputed Dylan of sharp words and piercing looks. He asked if I thought that *all* his albums might go gold, and I had to admit that three albums he recorded still had a way to go.

The concert itself, thanks to Dylan's long-awaited appearance, was a major event. Outside the hall, a crush of photographers and press along with a large crowd of onlookers created the excitement usually associated with a major movie premiere.

Inside, the crowd was unusually quiet, almost tense. What would he look like? Would his voice be the same? A great musical figure, Woody Guthrie, was being honored, but all attention was riveted to the return of the young, mysterious poet who had haunted so many minds.

Finally, the curtain rose. A number of performers came out of the wings at the same time. Judy Collins, Pete Seeger and Richie Havens were identifiable at once—and then a roar rose in accelerating volume as more and more of the audience identified the lightly bearded figure in the dark suit as Dylan. No fanfare. No separate big entrance. There he was, singing along with the rest, looking a little pale but moving with energy and assurance.

I felt a sharp tingle. He was back and it was wonderful seeing him on stage. For Dylan was not just a performer or a writer, he was a leader who had affected the thoughts and ideas of millions. Occasionally, during the concert, his individual turn would come and he'd casually step forward and sing some Guthrie songs: "Dear Mrs. Roosevelt," "The Grand Coulee Dam" and "I Ain't Got No Home." The crowd gave him a loving response, but, to him, this was a tribute to his idol, Woody Guthrie, and he never made any effort to take an individual bow.

The Park Sheraton meeting I had with Dylan was brief, but it established a working relationship between us. After that, he would send me tapes of each new album as it came out of the studio, and I'd work directly with him on such questions as the album jacket and choosing the single for AM radio play. The one time Dylan called regularly was during the period before a new album came out. He'd suddenly be very active, asking about release schedules, cover art and anything else that popped into his head.

Our area of greatest difficulty was singles. Bob always said that he would leave the choice up to me—yet he was invariably surprised by my choices, and sometimes balked at them. He didn't think about singles, he said, and he didn't think AM radio was *that* important. None of his friends listened to it.

I suggested that his friends . . . might . . . not constitute the average profile of record and radio consumers. But we never really resolved the issue.

Bob's first album after the accident, *John Wesley Harding*, was disappointing. It was great to hear him again; I enjoyed the album as any Dylan fan might. But it seemed quite below his capacity for classic writing and singing. I kept looking for something of "Like a Rolling Stone" or "Mr. Tambourine Man" caliber. But I found nothing similar. The album was a satisfying listening experience. I found myself interested in the material, but that was about all.

As a businessman, I was unhappy. I wanted a stronger album for his reemergence. I knew that the album would get FM play and occasional AM play, and would probably sell fairly well simply because of Dylan's reemergence. As it happened, the album sold about five hundred thousand copies. But with a good single hit in it, the album could have done twice that. Fortunately, Columbia was hitting well in other areas; my disappointment was nothing urgent.

By the time *Nashville Skyline* came along, however, I was worried that Dylan might be establishing a trend on the wrong end of the sales chart. It was a marvelous album—first-rate Dylan— and I loved it. Yet I was wary of the title. I tried to get him to change it; we talked several times. I felt that there was considerably greater universality on the album than a country-oriented title would suggest—the "Nashville" idea might be a turnoff to great numbers of city people.

He always listened to me—extremely politely—in these conversations. Then he'd inevitably say: "I'll get back to you." On this occasion he waited a month—calling on the day the album covers were to be shipped. He said yes, he'd been thinking a great deal about the album's title. Maybe it should be changed.

But it was too late. He asked if there was any way of holding up the shipment. I said no. Did I *really* think the title would hurt sales? I said I'd stand on my statement: it was a *limiting* title. But if the album got good reviews, and we were able to break out a single, sales would undoubtedly be good, though no one could tell what it *might* have sold. As it happened, "Lay Lady Lay" was a huge single hit; the reviews were good, and the album sold over a million copies. Bob was extremely pleased.

Considerable controversy followed with the release of *Self-Portrait*. I personally liked the album; it was a fascinating departure. On the other hand, I wasn't surprised by the stir it caused. An artist *has* to be unpredictable to have a long and varied career. Dylan had already shown his capacity to grow and change; so why be upset by *Self-Portrait?* It was simply another direction for him, and he'd shown with *Nashville Skyline* that new directions could be as profitable as old ones.

When artists evolve on their own, you can't be concerned about every change they make, or whether they will be accepted by the critics. Artists have to grow, and the record executive—and for that matter, the public—should simply ride with them. No one except the individual artist can dictate the dimensions of artistic change. Our criterion for judgment ought to be whether we like what an artist is doing. I *still* play the *Self-Portrait* album at home.

As it happened, Bob asked my opinion of the album's concept early on. My objections wouldn't necessarily have stopped the album, but I knew he'd been having some difficulty coming up with his own material, and I'd always felt that a good writer-performer can make a meaningful record using material from other writers as well, so I encouraged him. I discussed this idea in whole or in part with Paul Simon and Laura Nyro, and their attempts have been quite satisfactory—for an important artist brings a unique presence to *any* song. Simon & Garfunkel, for example, did very well with The Everly Brothers' "Bye, Bye Love," and, on Warners, James Taylor has done marvelously with Carole King's "You've Got a Friend."

In Dylan's case, the problem was more acute. He is known far more for what he has to say than for how he says it. Still, I encouraged him in the project. A substantial body of critical opinion later complained that Dylan owed his public more than rehashed versions of old songs. Yet it seemed important to look at Dylan's *whole* career; he'd probably be singing and writing for many more years. This was not a permanent departure from his traditional gifts, but rather a light album on the way to something else.

We continued to have our singles disagreements, restrained to be sure, but disagreements nonetheless. When he sent me the *Nashville Skyline* tapes, I decided immediately that "Lay Lady Lay" was the best release. It was vintage Dylan, and it had a bite to it—a strong melody and appealing sexuality. I also thought that it might cross over to middle-of-the-road listeners. It had warm lyrics and an infectious melodic hook. Fortunately, in this case, Dylan deferred to me, saying that he wasn't the best judge of singles appeal. We released the record and it became a big hit.

After *Self-Portrait*—which had no single release—we had a

similar problem with the *New Morning* album. Singles are enormously important. An artist of Dylan's stature can easily double an album's sales with a hit single. For this brings the album to the attention of consumers outside his hard-core, mostly FM-listening following. *John Wesley Harding* had sold 500,000 albums without a single; but *Nashville Skyline,* with "Lay Lady Lay" 's AM-radio help, sold 1.2 million. The singles principle can be almost mathematical. If Dylan had had yet another single hit on *Nashville Skyline,* for example, the album might easily have sold over 2 million copies. Simon & Garfunkel often sold this when their albums had two hit singles. And in those rare instances when an album has *three* hit singles, its sales can jump to over 3 million copies: *Bridge Over Troubled Water,* for example; Carole King's *Tapestry;* and Blood, Sweat & Tears' second album.

The singles principle does not work automatically. It has many refinements. It often depends a great deal on whether an artist has strong FM appeal; also on the quality of the single itself. For a single to push its album to the absolute top of the charts, it must basically appeal to everyone, at every level, who listens to music. It has to get extensive play on both Top Forty and middle-of-the-road radio, thus becoming a "standard"—which means that it will be recorded by other artists, sung in nightclubs and on television. And, because the performer in question is considered a "quality artist" by FM audiences, the hit will be exposed as well on that medium. In the parlance of the trade, the hit then becomes a "monster."

The effect of a hit single on album sales is subject to several considerations. If the artist would *not* otherwise sell albums—if he is unknown, or does not have an FM or MOR following—a number one hit single selling, say, 1 million copies, might create an album sale of two hundred thousand to five hundred thousand. Johnny Nash's big hit single "I Can See Clearly Now" led to album sales of about three hundred and fifty thousand; Billy Paul's hit "Me and Mrs. Jones" led to sales of seven hundred thousand. Paul's album sales were higher because his hit had broader appeal, reaching the large black rhythm and blues audience as well. By the same theory, a second big hit would have pushed sales of Johnny Nash's album to seven hundred thousand copies, but would have only added perhaps two hundred thousand to Paul's sales, since so much of Billy's potential audience had already bought his album.

Occasionally, a single hit by a new artist is so strong that it can take his album—which might have sold next to nothing without it—over the coveted Gold Album mark (five hundred thousand units), even to sales as high as a million. Don McLean did this with "American Pie"; America did it with "A Horse With No Name." In these cases, the hit not only gets Top Forty and MOR saturation, but also important FM play, establishing the artist's credibility to a basically *album-buying* audience.

One factor greatly affecting a record's ultimate sales is the timing of the album's release. Ten to fifteen years ago, most industry people had the odd notion that an album's release should be delayed until the hit single had run its course. They reasoned that the album's availability might interfere with the single's sales; the album's *other* cuts might be played on the radio, creating harmful competition. As a result, albums rarely had the stimulus of a single behind them in the marketplace; by the time they arrived at record stores, the hit was Top Forty history. In retrospect, it seems amazing that this idea could have taken such a firm hold on the industry. I strongly believed otherwise. My debates with the marketing people were *volatile*. Radio play is tantamount to free advertising, I argued; why not take advantage of it?

The argument was finally resolved by evolution: artists began recording albums first, rather than single cuts; you *had* to release the album as the public's introduction to the artist. After that, you hoped a single would break out of it. When it did, the catalytic effect of the hit single on album sales was obvious.

All this analysis aside, artists with hit singles are almost always disappointed by their album sales. It's endemic to the trade. They begin pointing fingers at the record company, sometimes threatening to take their contracts elsewhere. What they don't understand is that album sales—after a hit single has come out— simply adhere to the marketplace rhythms defined above. Sometimes a single can be nothing but a "turntable hit"—meaning that it gets tremendous air play, but little or no retail sales. Or perhaps a single hit can be a novelty thing, lacking the substance or depth that will bring the album-buying public into the stores. One example was the giant hit "Sugar, Sugar," by The Archies. It was the biggest single of its year, selling several million copies, but the group behind it was simply a collection of studio musicians given the name of a cartoon character. The group had no album credibility, so preteen buyers scooped up the single, but left the album stacked up in stores—no small disappointment to Don Kirshner, the well-known entrepreneur, who produced it.

Back to Dylan. When *John Wesley Harding* came out, he asked me at one point why it didn't sell more. I said that it was because he was only getting FM radio play; it needed a single. The point was made more emphatic by *Nashville Skyline's* success. Yet, when *New Morning* came out after *Self-Portrait,* he resisted putting a single out. I thought "If Not For You" was an obvious hit, but Bob said that he hadn't thought about singles when he recorded the album, and he didn't want to put one out. I tried several times to persuade him otherwise, stressing again AM radio's importance. I said that sales of more than five hundred thousand additional albums were at stake. As usual, he said he'd think about it.

Soon after that, Olivia Newton John "covered" the song in England and had a big hit. Just as it was breaking, Dylan called me. He'd been thinking about the singles idea . . . why not test-market it in England? But Ms. Newton John's record was too far ahead; I had to tell him that he would look silly trying to catch up. Result: *New Morning* sold six hundred thousand copies; it could have done twice that.

I liked Dylan enormously. But it wasn't always easy to do business with him, for sometimes—though not always—he was as mercurial and unpredictable as the legends said. He could be gentle, polite and cooperative—or indecisive, suspicious and quite impatient about things. In the recording studio, he was an efficiency expert's dream. I don't know how long it took him to write his material, but when he got into the studio, things happened fast. He does most songs in one take; he's never been caught up in the school of laying down instrumental tracks, then dubbing voice over them, and on and on. Simon & Garfunkel, by contrast, might take up to eighteen months to record an album. The result is beautiful artistry, technical perfection, endlessly fine detail—and gargantuan studio costs.

Dylan came into the studio, played his songs . . . and that was it. He took an extremely casual, almost lax attitude toward the recording process. To him, the song was the thing and everything else was secondary. Ironically, after he recorded an album, he *then* became impatient and occasionally demanding. He would call directly—no longer through his secretary. He couldn't wait for the album to come out. How long would the pressing take? He'd ask about the artwork, wanting to see it, and then frequently change his mind about the design or the title, holding things up for weeks at a time. When *Self-Portrait* was coming out, he called the day the artwork was supposed to be printed and said that he'd decided to do his own cover; I liked the idea—a painting of himself—and so we used it. The album was delayed a month, however. After an album came out, he again retreated to being incommunicado. I wouldn't hear from him again, unless *I* called to tell him about critical reaction or sales results.

Dylan was innately suspicious, checking and double-checking advice he got, asking further questions on a given subject among his friends, then sifting through the advice until he came to his own conclusion. I still felt that he needed more career guidance than he was getting. Isolation was hurting him. He functioned best when he was prowling around—dropping in at clubs and listening to new talent. I'd call sometimes and ask if he'd like to attend a Columbia sales convention, perhaps meet some other artists or managers there, just to get him in circulation. He'd say, "That might be fun. It might be nice. When is it?" But he never went. Occasionally, I'd ask him about performing, and he'd say he was "considering" it. But he had come to resist this. He didn't like motels. He didn't like the life he had led during the tours that had been necessary in his early career. I suggested hitting half a dozen major cities, skipping the smaller places. But The Band had gone its own way, leaving him without a group to work with.

I asked finally if I could aid in getting together a back-up group for him. He liked that idea and called one day to say that he'd written some material and was ready to go into the studio. Who would I suggest? I thought of The Byrds, and he liked that, and so I called Roger McGuinn, who seemed delighted at the opportunity. We set aside a date the day after The Byrds were scheduled to perform at the Academy of Music in New York. Bob would simply meet them at the studio and play his material, and they would back him up.

The recording date came, and Dylan called at 2 P.M. Where were The Byrds? I immediately called up Roger McGuinn, who rather sheepishly admitted that the rest of the group was on its way back to Los Angeles. I was angry. "From every point of view," I said, "this makes *no sense.*" The Byrds were clearly on the downward slide at that point; the session could have been a meaningful shot in the arm. They'd grown up with folk rock; one of their greatest hits was "Mr. Tambourine Man." They would have been perfect for Dylan. And from the simple point of courtesy, how could this happen?

Roger said that the group had been touring a lot lately; the boys were exhausted. He hadn't wanted to force them into the studio that day. They wanted to return to their families. I realized that Roger was basically a nice guy, but this seemed awfully strange. Suddenly, he began asking how he could make amends. He protested that he hadn't realized Dylan would really *count* on this session. Could he fly his band back from California? Could he talk to Dylan? I called Dylan at the studio on East Fifty-second Street. He was boiling; he no longer wanted to work with the group, and so we had to cancel the session.

Dylan finally called Al Kooper, who put together a group of local New York musicians, including David Bromberg (an old Dylan friend), Buzzy Feiten, Harvey Brooks and Russ Kunkel, among others. The *New Morning* album resulted.

One of Dylan's last studio recordings for Columbia was a single: "George Jackson." Bob hadn't put together enough material for an album, but he still wanted to release it. I told him that it would have limited sales; it would get mostly FM play, and the average FM listener rarely buys singles. But the subject matter changed that. It was Dylan commenting—a little late—but commenting, and it was good to hear. The single got enormous press coverage, for most people were delighted that Dylan was saying something again. The *Los Angeles Free Press,* for example, ran a huge picture of him on its front page, adding simply that he "was back."

The "Jackson" lyrics led to another problem—my chance finally to make up for the "Talking John Birch Society Blues" incident. For the record had the word "shit" in it . . . one lyric line said that Jackson wouldn't "take shit" from anyone. We got a substantial amount of negative mail. Yet I've always felt that a record company cannot edit artists merely for language. It was not a question of libel here; just public taste. Some radio stations complained, but most either didn't play the record, or bleeped out the word. To be fair, radio stations have an entirely different problem—government regulations. They can, of course, be cautioned ahead of time that a record contains potentially objectionable language and, armed with this, can decide whether to program it or not; in other words, they have the tools to fulfill *their* responsibility one way or another.

As for albums, I felt that a record company's responsibility is similar to a publishing house's. Artistic integrity has to be strongly defended.

From time to time, this issue of language arose. It became necessary, occasionally, to defend the use of the word "fuck"—so at one NARM convention, I said the word from the rostrum in order to defend its use. It surprised some people, but its effect was telling. I simply feel that nothing less than a blatant violation of the law could justify a record company's silencing or editing performing artists—particularly thought leaders—who might occasionally go too far. It is far healthier for society to deal with their excesses than to stifle their thoughts.

For now, I ignored the protests over Dylan's lyrics and went back to dealing with a "dry spell" in his writing. To fill the void, we came to the question of a Greatest Hits Volume II album. I knew that commercially it would be strong, but we both wanted to make sure that it would stand up, that it would be a meaningful listening experience. To stimulate his interest, I gave him a list of cuts I thought should be on the album. We agreed that to be complete it should be a two-record set. Then he called me and asked what I thought about putting some unreleased material on the album as well. I was concerned that this might make the term "greatest hits" a misnomer; on the other hand, Dylan was hardly an artist to be bound by tradition. We finally decided to put six new cuts on that album, many of which had never been released except through underground pirated tapes. He sent them to me, and I listened—and liked them, except that one or two had been recorded on monaural tapes with very poor sound quality.

I suggested that this might be a little . . . primitive. There were channels missing; the sound was extremely poor. Bob didn't care. He said that the particular cut, fuzzy or not, captured his voice and reading of a lyric line in a way he liked. He didn't want to go back into the studio; he might not be able to duplicate it. End of discussion. And another example of his choosing "feeling" over "technical perfection."

He *still* hadn't given me permission to release the album, and I was worried that the selections already made, plus the scratchy monaural cuts, might look as though we were stretching things to fill out a two-record set. I met with him at Folk City one night when David Bromberg was opening—George Harrison was also there—and we talked about my suggesting some additional cuts. He said he'd consider it when the whole album could be heard in sequence. I had to go directly from there to appraise a new artist appearing at the Village Gate. And then I went straight to the Village apartment of Don DeVito, a Columbia product manager, to get to work on the problem. Don and I, plus Mark Spector and Mike Klenfner, also with Columbia, stayed up half the night going through every Dylan song we could think of, and finally came up with three or four additional titles, plus a suggested sequencing for the album. The following morning, we put together a tape of the proposed album and I sent it to Dylan immediately. He liked it: we finally had permission to put it out.

# 5

I'm sure that Dylan will be a major force for a long time. His albums will be important, both musically and culturally. What is most significant is that he is out there now, widening his circle of contacts and experience. Interest in him is as high as ever. It was no surprise, moreover, when he went to New Mexico to work in film with Kris Kristofferson and the cast of *Pat Garrett and Billy The Kid*. Although the venture was not altogether successful, it was to Dylan's credit that he resisted pressure—including mine—to withhold his soundtrack album after the film was panned in *The New York Times*. I had advised that the album might be hurt by the film's failure, but he didn't care. He'd written the music; he felt good about it; he wanted it out. The album was released just after I left Columbia in June, 1973. A hit single came out of it, "Knockin' On Heaven's Door." The album sold well and it proved Dylan right.

When the time had come in 1972 to renew his five-year agreement with the company, I had negotiated a contract with David Braun, still Dylan's lawyer, and had it prepared for Dylan's signature. Everything seemed fine. But then Dylan decided not to sign it. He said he just wasn't able to make a commitment to *anyone* for that long a time. I don't think he objected to the contract itself, for it had been negotiated slowly and carefully over a six-month period, but he simply was emotionally unwilling to be tied down.

Ironically, there was another stumbling block: during the negotiations, Braun had asked whether I would insert a provision into the agreement allowing Dylan to break his contract if I left the company. This had happened before with other artists who felt that they were signing more for their relationship with me than with Columbia. And in Dylan's case, it was something of a personal matter, since he had dealt almost solely with me for the past five or six years. Nonetheless, I felt that I had to resist this; my motives might be misconstrued. It would put me in an awkward position with CBS if and when I were to leave.

Early in 1973 I finally did conclude negotiations for a new contract with Bob. Basically, it was limited to a commitment for two more albums, plus the *Billy the Kid* soundtrack album—there was no time period involved. The royalty was substantially higher, and the guaranty was about four hundred thousand dollars per album. Dylan had also asked to have some of his old catalog revert to him. This was unorthodox; a record company always tries to retain a valuable artist's catalog, both for the catalog's economic value and the company's own leverage, if the artist is negotiating contracts with competitors. However, here, the offers to Dylan from the competition were enormous. I had to come up with some plan which protected "the store" but pleased the artist as well. We finally settled on a deal giving Dylan the right, after five more years, to repossess first his oldest Columbia album (which would be seventeen years old in 1978) and on down the line—except for Greatest Hits albums—one for each new album recorded. Only if Dylan remained a major star would old catalog have real value. But if he retained his luster, as I believed he would, I wanted his new albums. It also was a powerful incentive for him to record more. Both parties were happy with the plan.

The strange thing is that Columbia backed out of the deal after I left. Since the *Billy the Kid* movie had just been released, Braun screamed that the soundtrack album commitment had to be honored; they couldn't go elsewhere in so short a time. So Columbia released it at the royalty rate agreed upon during my negotiations with Braun.

When the Dylan soundtrack album bulleted up the charts immediately after its release, Goddard Lieberson, who was again in charge of Columbia, realized that he may have been too hasty in saying the new Dylan deal was not a good one. When the single broke out of the album, and clearly showed Dylan's continued fertility, Lieberson tried to resume negotiations. Talks were started, but there was one major problem, similar to the situation of six years ago: Lieberson did not quite see the stature of Dylan, the artist, continuing in the same way as did the competition. This time, no one at Columbia was around to fight for Dylan—the new head of Columbia's Domestic Operations, Irwin Segelstein, came from television, and couldn't be expected to have a knowledgeable opinion so early—and by this time Dylan was talking elsewhere and meeting other people. Soon, David Geffen, the enterprising new head of Elektra/Asylum Records, moved in and locked a deal up pronto.

And then a fascinating behind-the-scenes battle developed. Normally, the Asylum contract would have tied Dylan up for a few years. But Dylan was still wary of long-term commitments; he had limited the contract to *one* album. No one knew this; the way the deal was trumpeted, everyone in the business thought Dylan was bound to Geffen for quite a while.

I was amazed, then, to get a call from David Braun in March, 1974, saying that Dylan was considering *not* giving his next album, the live one of his tour with The Band, to Asylum. He was very disappointed with the sales of the *Planet Waves* album and couldn't reconcile those numbers, around 700,000 at the time, with the five million requests for tickets that greeted the announcement of the tour itself. Bob now strongly wanted to do something unorthodox—sell the tour album himself through a saturation mail-order campaign on television. I was told that he missed my guidance in the handling of the *Planet Waves* album. Now he wanted to talk to me about this new idea. I was very negative. It seemed—at best—undignified to have Dylan huckstered on a crash television campaign. What's more, the campaign would bypass retailers, rack jobbers and distributors, a bad precedent for the industry.

At Dylan's request and expense, I flew out to Los Angeles and met with him and Robbie Robertson of The Band to discuss this idea. During the meeting, I made an alternative proposal—that we set up an entirely new distribution system and sell the album directly to rack jobbers and distributors. This would give Dylan and The Band a much higher participation in each album sold and yet not jeopardize their standing in the important retailing community. Both artists liked this approach so much that they immediately scotched the mail-order idea.

The only question was the extent of their obligation to David Geffen. David had been instrumental in putting the tour together, and he felt he was owed the album, morally if not legally. Dylan and Robertson acknowledged that a debt existed, but they felt that both the moral and legal obligations had been satisfied by Asylum having obtained *Planet Waves*, the first album after the tour. Otherwise, why was their contract limited to one album in the first place?

I moved aside to let them wrestle with the problem and deal with Geffen. Not having been at the original negotiations, I didn't know who was right. I knew only that each side might be blinded by emotion or dollars. Geffen had parlayed his signing of Dylan to tremendous heights; he had gotten wide personal coverage in the national media for the signing coup. But the press clearly had the impression that he had Dylan for a longer period of time. He would look extremely bad if he lost the very next album.

It was clear that Dylan and The Band would give the tour album to Asylum if the economics were roughly equal. But my marketing plan was very attractive to their business advisers—and to their own business instincts, which were considerable. They would earn about one dollar *more* in royalties for each album and would also have room for a much heavier national advertising commitment. If the album sold one million copies, the difference to Dylan and The Band would be one million dollars; if it sold two million copies . . .

The situation became more intense when Columbia got word that the album might be up for grabs. Despite all its press bravado that Columbia could get along without Dylan, and would not make a "no profit" deal, the media coverage had hurt. The press had printed Geffen's version—which was true—that Dylan hadn't gone to Asylum for a big guaranty. In fact there was hardly any guaranty at all. Geffen had wooed and won Dylan in fair competition.

Now Columbia wanted to get Dylan back—seemingly at any cost. They had come to understand their loss. They didn't know of my involvement, but they knew Dylan was considering marketing the album himself. They offered about sixty cents more in royalty than Asylum had bid. This was less than my own proposal, but it came very close to closing the differential.

By this time I was watching with amusement from the sidelines. After all, I had no company affiliation; I had suggested we set up a new marketing approach, but I realized that Dylan and David Braun were now using the specter of that approach to throw these two major companies into a spirited bidding contest from which only Dylan could benefit. And they succeeded. Geffen came up to match the Columbia bid. Now things were roughly equal, and Asylum got the album.

So when the smoke had cleared, it was apparent that Columbia *was* willing to make a very limited profit deal to get Dylan back. Geffen, in turn, was forced to pay much more than he wanted in order to make his original deal look good, and Dylan succeeded, with a little help from a friend, in making a lot more money. Bob had surely come a long way from the days of Folk City hootenannies.

# Five

**1**

In a sense, it all began for me at the 1967 Monterey Pop Festival.

I'd spent my time until then productively enough: negotiating the Dylan, Streisand and Williams contracts, signing Donovan, making the Ode label deal with Lou Adler, dueling with Gallagher, changing marketing pricing strategy, visiting record-pressing factories and checking out unfamiliar company operations. But it was all vamping in a sense. I knew in my heart that the job ultimately came down to whether I had the creative feel.

I often looked around the industry and saw company presidents postponing tests of their creative instincts. They traveled a lot, dedicated a manufacturing plant or a new tape facility, inspected operations in foreign countries and generally *looked* busy. But you can't do this forever. A company president must sooner or later test himself. And if he is to be anything beyond a paper shuffler, he must enter the creative wars with a vengeance. Donovan had been an important signing, but not a major test of my instincts; for he'd had some previous success.

Beyond that, the question of music's future direction remained. The top acts at the time—The Mamas and the Papas, for example—were softer and sweeter versions of the rock to come; it was still hard to know where music was going.

Lou Adler and Abe Somer approached me in 1967 to suggest that I visit the Monterey Pop Festival. Both men were on the festival's board and they said that it would be a chance to see new acts perform, watch several of my own (The Byrds and Simon & Garfunkel), and a perfect opportunity to be exposed to San Francisco's newly flowering musical culture.

It was a glimpse of a new world.

I remember the young people most of all: bright kids, open faces, flowers everywhere, a readiness and willingness to talk of the joy they felt. So much of this became seedy and desperate in the East Village later, but in 1967 they were trying to communicate their warmth and trust. The road into the festival was jammed with them, walking and in cars, but instead of the honking and fist-shaking that dominate a New York traffic jam, everyone seemed to be saying hello and sharing things. I was with my wife, Janet, whom I had married the previous year. We started giving rides to the kids and talking to them—and everything seemed so open; people seemed to be reaching out. So many of their words were later manipulated and twisted until they became clichés and gimmicks, but at the Monterey Festival you could honestly talk of "love" and enjoy communicating with people. The festival *exuded* love, brotherly love, the idea that love could cure ills and solve problems, the feeling that the world's problems would go away if people just loved one another more.

As Janet and I walked around the grounds, people came over and offered us flowers and beads, making a continual show of friendship and good will. It was exhilarating; it had a contagious effect. The music added to this feeling, and the audience in turn seemed completely in tune with the events on stage. I was stunned at the degree of respect and attention given to the great Indian sitarist Ravi Shankar, for example; his was, of course, a totally different music from that of The Mamas and the Papas and The Byrds, and yet you could have heard a pin drop during the performance. Even the local police, who had grumbled at first about the size of the crowds, were won over. At one point, several were introduced from the stage.

You caught yourself saying, in the middle of all this, "Hey, maybe this *can* happen." Maybe this spirit *can* affect human relations; maybe warmth *can* melt people down and we can trust each other more openly. I was truly taken by youth's disdain of materialism, appreciation of nature, and desire to be more open and candid and understanding of the frailties of others. Janet and I would meet these kids each day riding back and forth—I rarely told anyone that I worked for Columbia—and simply talk. I think of myself as a *very* realistic person, and I'd analyze what was happening sometimes, and find it difficult to believe that this wasn't a put-on . . . or a fad.

Yet I was a believer that week . . . far more than my usual caution would have allowed. At one point, I gave a party at my hotel just to meet more of the musicians and people involved. For the festival was a beautiful thing to watch. Looking back, it is clear that much of the festival's "love" was eventually forced to give way to the harsher demands of the larger society. But at the time, it was beautiful. And I honestly think society *was* affected by the ideas and emotions of Monterey and what followed. So many of us became more flexible in our lives, embracing new ideas and life-styles, even such simple things as long hair, or different music, and greater naturalness and informality in clothing. It *was* a revolution, a wonderful moment to be part of.

One jarring postscript:

Janet and I drove to Los Angeles immediately after the festival. We were still airborne from the good feelings left behind, flowers in the car, beads and necklaces strewn about—when the Los Angeles police pulled me over. I had been driving in the middle lane of a broad avenue, late for a meeting and looking for a particular cross street, and I must have been straying out of my lane, perhaps more than once.

The cops were incredibly harsh. I was wearing a necklace and smiling happily . . . and the next thing I knew, they were frisking me. Then they asked me to walk a straight line—I couldn't believe it! I said I was perfectly sober, and they said, "Come on, buddy, move over and *walk that line.*" Hostility. Abusiveness. It must have been the necklace, or the flowers—a rude return to reality.

**2**

Most of all, Monterey meant Janis Joplin.

I'd never heard of her. She had no records out, and she hadn't appeared outside of San Francisco. But she was to become a touchstone of much music to follow, a symbol of the electricity and power that music meant in the late sixties. She didn't sing a song; she ravaged it, tore it to shreds, made it explode. And she lived like the fire in her voice—the flame symbolic of both her momentous talent and her incredibly tortured life. No song meant more to me at the end of her life than "Me and Bobby McGee"—her reading of it, the emotion and pain she put into it. I cried when I heard it the first time. It was as simple as that . . . I wept.

It was a warm afternoon. The groups were doing thirty-minute sets and, about midway through, an unknown group from San Francisco called Big Brother & the Holding Company came onstage. Janis was not billed separately but, from the moment she took the microphone and unleashed the throaty, sensual wail that made her famous, she was in command.

She was electrifying. She strutted up and down the stage banging a tambourine, and as the audience got turned on, she got *more* turned on, almost childlike in her exhilaration. For me it was spine-tingling . . . awesome . . . hypnotic. My eyes riveted wherever she went. She was choked up at one point, laughing at another. She just couldn't contain herself, and you didn't know how to take it all. It was ebullience thrust at you in the most basic, primitive ways . . . trembling . . . shaking . . . almost a violent tremor when she got extremely *into* what she was doing. She seemed bursting with emotion; and it was so *pure*.

I knew immediately that I had to go after her. I didn't tote up any executive balance sheet. I didn't care who managed her, or if she was under contract to another label. I just wanted her!

As soon as a break came, I went backstage and found the group's manager, then Julius Karpen. I said that I was really knocked out. Karpen suggested that I get in touch with the group's attorney, Bob Gordon, which I did. At that point, matters became complicated. Gordon said that Big Brother was under contract to Mainstream Records, which is run by Bobby Shad, but he added that they were unhappy. Shad was about to release an album they'd recorded as a demonstration tape, and the group violently opposed this. There was a question about money: Mainstream wouldn't let them return to the studio to rerecord the tape. Gordon thought that this was probably grounds for breach of contract.

I made my interest clear immediately, inviting Karpen and Gordon to a Columbia convention in Miami. It was a showcase technique I used often: a chance for artists and their managers to see the company in action. They stayed for three days, and we started to discuss contract terms. I offered the group twenty-five thousand dollars to sign and fifty thousand for delivery of the first album, which was to include recording costs. At the time, it was a generous offer. We were signing most brand-new artists in those days for five or ten thousand dollars, and perhaps twenty-five thousand for delivering the first album. The extra money here was both to demonstrate my interest, and to provide money in case they had to buy their way out of Mainstream.

This was August, 1967, and Big Brother had indicated its interest in return, promising to begin talks with Shad immediately. Contract negotiations, however, are not for the impatient; the smallest twist or turn can take months to settle. In this case, Shad could not be talked out of releasing the demo tape. It was a poor album at best—but the bigger problem was that it would help spread the word about Janis. Word of her Monterey performance was already getting around; and the band was starting to tour outside of San Francisco. It would be only a matter of time before other companies began bidding.

One of the earliest bids, in fact, came from my old colleague Bill Gallagher. He'd gotten word of the deal and had made an offer for MCA.

Meanwhile, Big Brother's representatives were researching the Mainstream question. They concluded that Shad's demo album release might not be *quite* enough to get a breach of contract ruling—and the court costs would be prohibitive anyway. They then tried to *buy* the contract from Shad, beginning with a twenty-five- or thirty-thousand-dollar offer, which Shad refused. At some point, the group also had a falling-out with Karpen, who was fired and replaced by Albert Grossman. By this time, rumors were spreading through the industry that Big Brother's contract might be up for grabs. I tried to convince Grossman that Columbia should have exclusive negotiating rights, pointing out that Gordon had called *me* about Grossman, and that I'd recommended him—and that we'd come into the picture long before any other record company including, certainly, MCA.

My relationship with Grossman went back to Dylan and, as it happened, we had also talked right after Monterey about the new, exciting music. He had then proposed an all-inclusive deal to sign three artists at once, The Steve Miller Blues Band,

Quicksilver Messenger Service and The Electric Flag, for a hundred thousand dollars up front. I was ready to agree to it. But he couldn't get management rights for Quicksilver or Steve Miller; and I ended up paying fifty thousand dollars for The Electric Flag, a great band that featured Mike Bloomfield on guitar and Buddy Miles on drums.

The Big Brother deal, meanwhile, ballooned considerably. Grossman settled into serious negotiations with Shad, and returned with a two-hundred-thousand-dollar deal! As he explained it, Columbia had to pay Shad that sum outright. One hundred thousand dollars could be charged as an advance against Big Brother's future royalties—and we had to swallow the rest. Mainstream also was to get a 2 percent override on the next two albums. The mathematics came to this: Big Brother was a hundred and fifty thousand dollars in the hole—one hundred thousand dollars of its first album royalties, plus fifty thousand dollars recording costs, which are also normally charged against royalties. Columbia, meanwhile, was risking two hundred and fifty thousand dollars; one hundred thousand was a straight expense. The rest could be recouped if the group was successful.

That was a lot to put out there, but we signed the contract in the spring of 1968; it had taken nearly a year since Monterey to close the deal—a long, long time, it seemed—but worth the difficulty of every twist and turn along the way.

# 3 ══════════════════════════════════════════

I still hadn't met Janis. Grossman called one day as the contracts were being prepared and said that the group was in the building touring the art department—would I be willing to come down to the tenth floor to meet them? I guess he was asking about the propriety of it. Should they come *up* to the eleventh floor to meet me instead? This was the last group in the world I wanted to stand on ceremony with; I said I'd be down to the tenth floor shortly.

"You know what Janis would really prefer to do?" he added. I said I didn't. "She's talked about meeting you," he continued, "and she thinks it only fitting and proper that she go to bed with you to cement the deal. That would be her way of showing this is a more meaningful relationship—not in *lieu* of signing, but in addition, a way to make the signing different from what it normally would be in the business world."

I sort of . . . deferred . . . the offer. I said that I'd be down to the tenth floor anyway, and that I was very much looking forward to meeting her.

I got there about five o'clock. The group was in a conference room; I went in and shook hands, and we started some preliminary talk. It was a little awkward—it always was with groups the first time. Here I come, in my suit and tie, looking to the musicians like the president of a large establishment record company (which I in fact was, having been given the official title of President in the summer of 1967 right after Monterey); and they are usually in a typical under-thirty uniform, T-shirts and dungarees. Nor was Janis wearing a bra. I was trying very hard to make them feel comfortable, saying that the building might be formidable—the press always had called it "black rock"—but that I knew the difference between the two styles of life, and they shouldn't be put off by the austerity of their surroundings. Everyone in the company, I said, was accessible and informal.

Suddenly one member of the band looked at his watch and said, "Wow, we've got a press meeting at six . . . we'll be late!" We'd been talking for nearly an hour; everybody was pretty relaxed. One member of the group said that he had to get into his clothes, and another threw them across the table to him. He was sitting across from me, and he had no shirt on. But I assumed he was wearing underpants . . . or something.

Then he stood up to get the pants thrown to him. He was totally nude! My reaction was pure male protectiveness—I was embarrassed for *her*. At the very least, I wanted to close the conference room door. Imagine the rumors if people in the hallways saw this!

Janis, meanwhile, got a tremendous kick out of the whole thing. I'd just finished telling the group how informal Columbia was; she guffawed and said, "Well, this is how informal *we* are." Then she laughed again, and pretty soon I was laughing too.

Janis could be like a little girl, expansive and enthusiastic with bubbling innocence one moment, then blunt, sarcastic and coarse the next. When her career was beginning, she would delight in each new experience—public appearances, new recordings, advertisements, a hit single, a party I gave her one night at my home after a Madison Square Garden performance—and she would beam and grin from ear to ear, girlishly feminine, childlike and vulnerable, all at the same time.

And when her albums were recorded, she'd play cuts for me, squealing with delight at musical nuances that caught her. But, unfortunately, this was often masked in what came to be known as the Joplin "cult personality"—the tough, wisecracking, blunt-speaking girl turned broad turned star. At these times, she seemed to revel in her bawdiness, her talk constantly salted with direct references to sex and her desire for it. For she was clearly a sensual person, and yet she was also desperately trying to make sense out of the alien world of superstardom. She was vulnerable and often quite helpless among people alien to her and her music, leaning on anyone close who offered—or appeared to offer—help.

As her career wore on, she adjusted considerably to the business end of music, becoming intensely aware of money and the importance of wealth. She was also better at giving orders than taking them. She had always been a focal point of the sixties' anti-establishment mood, yet after a while she began worrying about accumulating as much money as possible for future security. Her life and her moods were a series of striking contrasts. She could be insecure yet strong, innocent yet worldly, exuberant and shy, bitingly sarcastic, and then smiling and cheerful. Wearing frilly clothes, she was coyly feminine—then suddenly she was a swaggering, drunken sailor with her bottle of Southern Comfort.

Yet despite her contrasts, one thing remained consistent—her vital, seething, raw talent. She honed and fed that talent with every last ounce of physical and emotional energy at her command. And the result was a force so compelling that it rode down fatigue, strain and the limits of endurance, to reach the very core of human capacity. Few artists have ever mattered so much to me as Janis.

# 4

After the signing, I was looking for a way to introduce her—and the music which she represented—to the company. Earlier, in February, 1968, I'd introduced The Electric Flag to the National Association of Record Merchandisers' convention by first cautioning the audience that they might want to put cotton in their ears, that it was a "big" sound, but I warned that it was *the* sound soon to be heard around the world. I'd felt very strongly that Columbia had to make an important and visible commitment to this kind of music. NARM happens to be a fairly conservative group, accustomed to entertainment like Tony Bennett and Frank Sinatra, but these people were responsible for 80 percent of the records sold in America. It was time to turn them on to something new.

The same was true for Columbia itself. Along with Janis, I'd now signed other artists capable of producing the searing, powerful sounds that I expected would soon dominate popular music. I therefore arranged a show at the 1968 Columbia convention in Puerto Rico, aimed at rattling the walls: Spirit, The Chambers Brothers, the newly formed Blood, Sweat & Tears and, lastly, Janis.

Even in the beginning, she adjusted to the company hustle very well. She mixed with the salesmen at the convention easily, smiling and making warm small talk, like: "Oh, you're going to be selling my album? I hope you like it." Or something slightly rougher: "I hope you can sell the shit out of this album, man!" She was enormously friendly, laughed often in her well-known, high-pitched, melodic cackle that was both startling and disarming at the same time.

The show opened that night with Spirit, a very exciting group from California, whose totally bald drummer, Ed Cassidy, caused a lot of comment. Then The Chambers Brothers came on. They were coming off a giant hit, "The Time Has Come Today," and they had a tremendously exciting rock-gospel act. The house was completely turned on. They were followed by Blood, Sweat & Tears, whose fusion of rock and jazz was pioneering a tremendously exciting musical trend.

The Blood, Sweat & Tears show, with their new vocalist, David Clayton-Thomas, was sensational, bringing the audience to its feet again and again; and as the ovations continued, Janis became more and more frightened, standing beside me backstage with her bottle of Southern Comfort, saying, "Jesus, how can I follow that?" It was a typical show of Janis's odd insecurity. When she went on, she gave a tremendous performance, a stunning one, yet the crowd had been taken to such highs with The Chambers Brothers and Blood, Sweat & Tears that they simply couldn't get any higher. They were too tired. And that made Janis unhappy: she wanted to have a *unique* effect. She had an incredibly strong competitive spirit and set the highest possible standards of excellence for herself.

Now I had the problem of introducing her album to the public. Music after 1967 was distinguished often by long album cuts, opportunities for musicians to get further into their compositions and improvise with individual instruments as jazz performers had done before. This was a welcome addition to the repertoire of pop music, but it also posed some commercial problems. They began, fittingly enough, with Janis's first album.

Pop album sales, particularly when FM radio wasn't as important as it is now, depended on Top Forty single hits. As in Dylan's case, a chart-climbing single could easily double the sales of a good album. And with a brand-new artist, a hit single was imperative. Janis already had a following—but hardly big enough to overcome the two-hundred-and-fifty-thousand-dollar deficit of her initial signing. We needed to sell half a million albums at least.

So when I listened to the first tapes of *Cheap Thrills*, I knew we *had* to pull a good single out of it. I settled immediately on "Piece Of My Heart," which posed another problem. The album cut wasn't quite right. It had a good hook—the phrase or the lyric line that sticks in your mind later—but this particular hook, the words "Take a little piece of my heart, baby," didn't come back often enough. It wasn't stressed enough to be *indelible*. A song like "Raindrops Keep Fallin' on My Head," for example, leaves you with an impulse to whistle or sing the title lyric line. It is a classic hook and it comes back often enough during the song to be a theme within the theme.

I decided that "Piece Of My Heart" had to be restructured. It was no small decision. For another characteristic of the new music was the professed independence of the new musicians; they didn't want to be—or at least *appear* to be—commercial. They were antiestablishment—or so they said—and what could be more "establishment" than having the President of Columbia Records alter an album cut for *commercial* reasons? Beyond that, I had my own pressures to contend with; my creative reputation was on the line. Joplin and artists such as Blood, Sweat & Tears *had* to be successful. I had put a lot of money down. If I was to continue to operate the company with a relatively free hand, I had to establish my artistic credentials *and* my good commercial sense. In a sense, a lot of this rested on "Piece Of My Heart."

It seemed safer to do the cutting and splicing and *then* show Janis the results. If she objected, I wouldn't put out the single. On the other hand, if I asked up front, there might not be a chance to try it at all.

I got a recording editor, and we listened to the tape in my office. I listened several times, then told him to keep the first forty-five seconds, then take out the next twenty seconds . . . and so on. I didn't know enough musical terms to give him technical instructions—just shorten this, leave that, cut this out. Basically, this meant cutting some long instrumental passages and then bringing the hook in one time more than the original recording had it. I later did this kind of single editing many times at Columbia, always using the same rough shorthand.

Next I called Janis at Albert Grossman's office and asked her to drop by the building. I said that I had something I wanted her to hear.

I was tense when she arrived. "I'm not going to come out with this if you don't like it," I said. "But it's extremely important for you to have a single hit. Strictly speaking, you don't owe me anything in the way of singles; yet this is where a record company comes in. We have to consider sales, and without a single hit your album might sell two to three hundred thousand copies. *With* a hit, you could sell six hundred thousand, eight hundred thousand, maybe even a million albums. Your album is out, and I obviously don't intend to change anything in it. But we have to get a single out right away and, rather than fool around and go back into the studio, I've edited one of its cuts in a way that I hope doesn't offend you."

I was being extremely solicitous, and I kept repeating that I wouldn't put the record out if she didn't like it. Finally, I put the tape on.

Janis listened very impassively. She obviously wasn't thrilled, but she shrugged her shoulders and said it was okay . . . if I felt this had to be done, do it. She obviously wasn't into the singles concept, and she knew that most of her existing fans listened to FM. But this was a business decision. She wanted to make it big. It wasn't such a large compromise. The idea didn't offend her as much as I had expected.

There is always a funny twist to the singles question. When a group has a single hit that is edited differently from their album cuts, they find concert audiences requesting *that* version. They even have to change their stage act. This happened to Big Brother when "Piece Of My Heart" reached the top of the charts. But I suspect they didn't mind terribly; for, thanks to the single, the album sold more than a million copies. Janis was very excited and called me constantly to ask how the single and the album were doing.

It was never easy to have *one* reaction to Janis. For her brashness was clearly a cover for pain and insecurity. I remember once going to the Fillmore East to see The Voices of East Harlem. While I decided against signing them, I felt that I should go backstage and at least say hello, making my feelings clear rather than prolonging the issue. Janis was backstage too. She'd been drinking heavily, and she looked at me for a moment, and it was awkward. She was the star of the company right then, and so I naturally should have stopped and spent some time with her. Yet she could see that I had business to do.

Suddenly she said: "I understand you're on a gig—so go upstairs and do your thing. I know you didn't know I was here." Her perception was acute. She might not have loved the idea of me moving on, yet she understood—this time.

But there was a time when Janis became quite jealous of Laura Nyro. During one of Janis's first New York gigs, I took Laura backstage to introduce her. By now, Janis was becoming a big star, while Laura was a shy, breathless sort of girl who wasn't well known. That night, Janis was very indifferent and cold. Laura wanted to tell her how much she'd loved the performance, but Janis barely nodded a greeting as she drank straight from a Southern Comfort bottle and talked to a new boy she was eyeing. It got worse after Laura's songs began to be sung widely by other groups, such as Three Dog Night and The Fifth Dimension. She was getting a tremendous amount of publicity, and Janis's visibility had lapsed slightly because she'd split with Big Brother and was in between albums, forming a new band. Record promotion tends to slacken during these periods; there's just so much you can say about an artist without it becoming hype, so you inevitably cool things off.

"I can see I'm not the Number One female in your eyes anymore," Janis said one day on the phone. "You're turned on to Laura now."

It was, again, awkward. I explained that Laura was getting publicity for purely business reasons; that it was silly to set up competition between them, and that I didn't feel publicity at this point would do Janis any good. She'd just left Big Brother, and I knew it was a lot of strain putting a new group together. I couldn't apologize for liking Laura; all I could do was tell Janis that I would do everything possible to see that her music got the largest possible audience, and that I cared about her.

The split with Big Brother was particularly difficult for her. I had called Grossman, when her first album was about to be released, to suggest changing the title to Janis Joplin *and* Big Brother & the Holding Company. I felt even then that she should have separate status; word of mouth was spreading about her, and she clearly stood out from the band. It soon got worse. The reviews were relentless, saying again and again that she was far superior to the musicians backing her. She called one day to ask my opinion about leaving the group. I could tell from the way she spoke that she'd already made up her mind.

These situations were always difficult. Musical groups form and break up as seasons change, and at some point in the process someone asks my opinion about it. It is extremely difficult to say the right thing. If the group is successful, I don't want them to break up. But by the time they've come to me, the decision is really made. It does no good to point out that separate members of a successful group rarely make it as big as the group did—*if* they make it at all. Group members on the verge of breaking up aren't interested in logic; they want support for the wrenching dislocation that is about to come. The result is that I usually end up holding various hands and doing little else.

In Janis's case, it was a different problem. Stepping away from Big Brother's shadow made sense, and it was clear that she was calling primarily to touch base. I asked her reasons; she said she felt that she could branch out more by dealing with stronger musicians. But it had taken a long time to make the decision: she had the strongest possible personal tie to the group . . . they'd started their careers together, lived together and been through a number of rough-and-tumble times together. She felt very bad about the whole thing.

I was pulled both ways by the problem. On the one hand, the group *had* achieved a strong national reputation, and there was always a possibility that a split could affect Janis's career in the wrong way. On the other, I'd been continually worried that Janis was too limited in her musical contacts. I was extremely pleased when she started working with Gabriel Mekler, a producer of considerable intelligence who is nobody's yes-man. Janis later worked with Paul Rothchild, also a talent of major proportions. She did not surround herself with yes-men; yet I had a nagging doubt that Big Brother really could grow any further. However, I did feel personal ties to the band itself, since I had signed the band and not just Janis after Monterey.

When the split eventually came, I agreed to continue with the group as well as with Janis. Big Brother did two more albums for Columbia, each getting decent reviews and selling about a hundred thousand copies, which meant that they had some audience of their own. Unfortunately, they toured very little after that and as a result didn't build up a separate identity.

Besides everything else, there was always the question of longevity . . . where Janis would go once everyone *was* exposed to her style, where her material would come from, whether or not she'd burn herself out musically. The verdict was still out. There were constant questions about her voice—would it last? I frankly didn't know the answer and, for that matter, couldn't have done much about it if she *did* lose it. For now, she was hot; she was a truly great performer and singer; heiress, if she lasted, to the tradition of Billie Holliday and Bessie Smith.

I tried to deal with one problem, however. She'd begun to get rather shoddy publicity, particularly after she was arrested in Florida for using what the police chose to call "obscene" language. I personally was sometimes repelled by her coarseness; she could be quite insensitive to the feelings of those around her. Every now and then, for example, we'd be together on some public occasion and she'd break off the conversation in midsentence after seeing some guy across the room, saying, "Wow, I'd like to ball *him!*" And then leave and make a beeline for this guy.

It occurred to me that some of the more scruffy stories might be offset if I gave Janis a tasteful party, one exposing her to other parts of the musical world. It was around Christmas, 1969, and she was scheduled to appear at Madison Square Garden, a very important concert for her. I called Myra Friedman, later the author of an excellent book on Janis but then a former Columbia publicity writer working for Albert Grossman, and said that I'd like to throw a party for Janis at my home, a sort of midnight supper, after her Garden appearance.

Word came back that Janis was delighted. I planned to mix musicians and industry people from all sectors of the music world, everyone from Miles Davis to Bob Dylan to Tony Bennett to Ahmet Ertegun (the head of Atlantic Records), and have the party catered and semiformal as well, a scene of candlelight and subdued conversations, champagne and caviar. For Janis was now clearly one of the most important singers of an era and, while the *rest* of the musical world took her seriously, I wasn't at all sure that she saw *herself* in that light. It was time she did.

The idea of a formal party brought out Janis's best instincts. I visited her dressing room before the Garden concert, and she was very warm. When we were alone, she grinned widely and bragged that she would be an absolute knockout at the party. She'd had an outfit made especially for it, and she couldn't wait to put it on. She seemed more feminine that night than at any other time we ever talked, no longer "one of the boys," as she was tagged for so many years. It fascinated me . . . here she was getting ready for one of the most important concerts of her life, a major appearance after leaving Big Brother, and she was thinking about what she'd wear at a party afterward.

Her performance itself turned out to be fairly routine. But at one point, Paul Butterfield and Johnny Winter joined her onstage, and the electricity between Joplin and Winter was awesome. Winter played a searing, booming guitar and Janis faced him nose to nose, holding the microphone and wailing right back at him, each raising the other to a higher energy level. By the end of the set, Janis was dripping wet, bushy hair flying in all directions. The crowd went wild.

After Winter left the stage, Janis did a few more numbers, then cut her encores short with a good-natured announcement that "a friend" was throwing a party and she had to change and get ready. Amazingly, the audience let her get away with it. Even the newspaper reviews the next day mentioned this in good humor.

The party went extremely well. Bob Dylan made a rare social appearance, arriving at midnight and staying until 3:30 A.M.— though he never took off his hat and jacket. Albert Grossman, Lou Adler, Jac Holzman (then President of Elektra Records),

Neil Bogart (then head of Buddah Records), Abe Somer, Larry Utall (then head of Bell Records) and Ahmet Ertegun represented the executive side of the business. Johnny Winter, his brother Edgar, Miles Davis, Paul Butterfield, Rick Derringer, Tony Bennett, Laura Nyro and Dylan were among the artists there. The rooms were also filled with key managers, music critics and other industry executives and, soon enough, columnists Earl Wilson and Leonard Lyons arrived.

Janis arrived at 1:00 A.M. She'd taken some time to fortify herself for the event, and was plainly high. Yet she made a spirited entrance, wearing long black satin pants and a low-cut, see-through black chiffon top. She literally *glowed* at the attention, talking with Dylan—whom she'd never met—and meeting other music luminaries. Linda Gravenites, her San Francisco roommate, approached me at about 2 A.M., saying that Janis was "flabbergasted." She couldn't *believe* the trouble I'd gone to; the party really glittered.

There were funny sidelights. Laura Nyro arrived shortly after Janis, wearing a white promlike formal gown. She made a beeline for a bedroom where the coats were being kept—and rarely left it all evening, saying that she was afraid to step in the way of Janis's spotlight. At one point, Dylan found out she'd arrived and asked to meet her. Laura literally went into shock upon seeing him. She giggled and could barely talk, and Dylan for once kept the conversation going practically by himself, saying that he was into her albums and that he admired her music, waiting patiently for her to collect herself . . . which never happened.

At the end of the evening, Janis had tears in her eyes, thanking Janet and me repeatedly. She was deeply touched by the evening.

# 5

The news that Janis had died came to me at home. My son, Fred, heard it on television early in the morning and rushed in to awaken me. I was stunned and remember thinking only of empty space, of a sudden, terrible void. It seems almost mawkish to say that Janis's death was a tremendous loss; obviously it was. How much more she meant to all of us can best be indicated, I suppose, by the silence left behind. She gave us the energy of an entire lifetime in her few short years, and, if nothing else, I am grateful simply as one of her fans. It would be wrong to pretend that I wasn't upset over the *commercial* loss as well; I was, for the music business is a business.

Yet I think of Janis in far more than business terms. For, in a strange way, our lives were intertwined; Janis's good fortunes were mine as well. Finding her meant finding a new musical world. And, given a gentler time than the sixties, she might have lived longer; but it also must be said that she might have burned less brightly. It is with awe that I finally remember her—awe that one human being could attempt to give so much.

When Paul Rothchild sent me the acetate of the *Pearl* album, I couldn't help crying. The album showed that her talent was truly flowering. I kept playing "Me and Bobby McGee" over and over again. It stood out instantly as a classic; her reading of it was brilliant, filling every word, every note, with feeling. I took the acetate along to a country music convention that week in Nashville, gathered all the promotion men and salesmen in my suite and just put it on. The effect was electric. This group of tough, often cynical men, who'd seen thousands of records come and go, became as choked up as I was. And when "Me and Bobby McGee" came on, many wept openly.

That was the effect Janis had. She captured and captivated you. Soon after her death, Columbia was flooded with tapes made at her live performances. I got together with Albert Grossman and Bob Gordon, and we carefully went over the kind of material we thought should come out after her death. I was worried that a lot of half-baked tapes of live concerts might emerge, none of which would reflect well upon her memory. Then I asked Elliot Mazer to assemble an album of her best live performances, which we simply called *Joplin in Concert*. For that was Janis's testament: her records and her concerts. She had always said: "Live for today and let tomorrow take care of itself." Moderation was not in her vocabulary; life had to be lived full tilt, until the crutches she needed to sustain that energy finally did her in. Now it is her records that remain, and as long as they are played, which will easily cover all of our lifetimes, she'll never be far away.

# Six

## 1

Few groups symbolized musical change as much as Blood, Sweat & Tears. Eddie Mathews, a Columbia A&R man at the time, called me one day in the fall of 1967, and insisted that I see the group, not just listen to their tapes. Eddie was a fast mover; he and I went right down to Cafe Au Go Go in Greenwich Village one afternoon to sit in during a rehearsal. I immediately sensed something very unusual. The group was highly professional, and they were excellent musicians. They were the first group to fuse rock and jazz in a very identifiable and compelling way—the end product seemed extremely sophisticated and yet accessible to the rock music follower.

I was excited. I returned to my office and made an offer right away. They wanted twenty-five thousand dollars up front, which was high. We were signing groups for ten or fifteen thousand dollars, and my business affairs people and I—even at this early date in the rock explosion—worried constantly about escalating the cost of doing business. We used to sign unknown artists for *nothing*. Then it went to five thousand, then ten . . . and eventually to twenty-five thousand in very special cases. Yet I didn't want to lose this group, and I knew that they could get the twenty-five thousand from smaller companies, since they don't have to worry much about precedents. Additionally, the group was not exactly unknown; at least three members had been with The Blues

Project, an earlier group that had received considerable critical acclaim.

So I signed them for twenty-five thousand dollars. Al Kooper was then both *ad hoc* spokesman and musical thinker for the group and we spent a lot of time together. Al had long black hair and dark eyes, a wiry build, and he was extremely conscious of the way society—as well as music—was pulling apart at the time. I once asked him why he spent so much time in the Village; he said that he felt *hostility* when he ventured into the midtown areas, as if all the businessmen resented his long hair and relaxed clothing. This was still 1967, and long hair was not yet "in" for the business community.

The first Blood, Sweat & Tears album got uniformly excellent reviews. *The New York Times* hailed the group as one of the most exciting to emerge in pop music history! Still, at the beginning, the album didn't sell phenomenally. No single emerged; FM radio was only beginning to be a force in pop music. Sales first went to forty thousand, then fifty-five thousand and then seventy-five thousand. This was okay, but it was just scratching the surface of the audience I felt the group could have.

Then they broke up.

Al Kooper appeared at my door one day. "I've got bad news for you," he said. "I'm going to be splitting from Blood, Sweat & Tears."

I was dumbfounded! "How in the world can you be splitting up *now?*" I asked unhappily. "You just formed! The company is behind you; a tour is about to begin; why so *soon?*"

"We have a difference of musical opinion," Al said. "We've more or less hidden it from you, but it looks like something permanent. We just can't agree about the type of music we should be getting into, or who should be playing what. There's just too much discord." Al described the conflicts only vaguely, but it seemed that other group members were challenging his right to do the vocals. They wanted a stronger voice, and differed with him on the type of music to be played. Throughout their career, Blood, Sweat & Tears *always* seemed to be having identity crises. They never really ceded direction to a manager, and participatory democracy among nine musicians works poorly at best.

"My God," I argued, "you're killing the album if you break up now! Without public appearances, it won't go any further." Al said that they planned to go through with the tour, saying nothing about the breakup until afterward. I said the usual cliché things: give it another shot and see what happens, have an open mind—all that. But it didn't work; words rarely do in these cases. Kooper left the band shortly after the tour.

Then the rest of the group came to me. My relationship had been almost solely with Kooper, but they planned to keep the name Blood, Sweat & Tears and bring in another vocalist. They asked me to help them keep going. I believed that the group's musical concept was still exciting, that their musicianship would remain and that momentum had been built up, so I approved a loan for them of ten thousand dollars to keep them eating, and waited. A few months went by, and band members Bobby Columby and Steve Katz came to say they'd found a new singer from Canada named David Clayton-Thomas. They were very excited, and they wanted me to return to the Cafe Au Go Go again.

He was staggering—a powerfully built singer who exuded enormous earthy confidence. He jumped right out at you. I went with a small group of people, and we were electrified. He seemed so genuine, so *in command* of the lyric lines, a perfect combination of fire and emotion to go with the band's somewhat cerebral appeal. He was almost . . . animalistic. I knew he would be a strong, strong figure.

Jimmy Guercio, who later worked so successfully with Chicago, produced the group's second album, and it was an absolute explosion. Three gold singles broke out of it, one right after another, making it one of the best-selling pop albums in music history: almost four million copies sold. They were in demand everywhere, appealing to the broadest demographics and age span of any rock group. It seemed that they could do nothing wrong. I was thrilled. I had trusted my musical instinct and it was working! Joplin had become the biggest female star in the business, and Blood, Sweat & Tears had emerged as the most important American rock group. But then the group ran into problems again.

For one thing, they didn't want to work with Jimmy Guercio anymore. They wanted to produce the next album themselves. They wanted to manage themselves. In effect, they wanted to run *everything*. And, worst of all, they had no sense of public relations; this turned out to be their biggest weakness.

When a group breaks through by appealing to an avant-garde or FM audience, it must maintain credibility with them. This will be the nucleus of its following. The problem can be delicate when the group starts getting single hits, for this can turn off the FM audience. I tried to warn Blood, Sweat & Tears about the danger of surrounding themselves with establishment show business people, the kind who like to get into the latest fad.

"Don't be surprised," I joked once, "if Sammy Davis, Jr., calls up to say he'd love to spend time with you. Maybe Richard Burton and Elizabeth Taylor will come backstage." The reigning Hollywood establishment is always into the latest fad, style of dress or political movement, and I knew that this would hurt the group. And sure enough, just a few weeks later, I heard that Sammy Davis, Jr., had agreed to introduce them for their Hollywood Bowl appearance. They began to have their pictures taken with movie stars—important talents all, but hardly consistent with the Blood, Sweat & Tears underground image and following.

The group finally hired a business manager named Larry Goldblatt. I hoped things would change now. I had the feeling that I was a lone voice in the wilderness trying to advise them. But things got worse. Goldblatt called me to say that the group had decided to play Caesar's Palace in Las Vegas. He touted this as a "breakthrough"—the first contemporary rock group to play Las Vegas. I was upset. This would damage their underground credibility even more.

When Goldblatt called to ask how much advertising support Columbia was giving to the gig, I said none. I thought the appearance would hurt them badly. He got very angry, arguing that it was Columbia's duty to support *all* their engagements. I said the company would *not* support a tour that would hurt record sales and their future. I had no power to cancel the booking, but I wasn't going to support it either. A record company's duty is to sell records; the Caesar's Palace appearance would ultimately have the opposite effect.

This was 1970. Hollywood and contemporary rock music mix more easily now. Singers such as Mick Jagger live in both worlds with no harm—possibly even with help—to their images. But at that time a good part of the contemporary music audience was extremely antiestablishment. It made no sense to fly disc jockeys into Las Vegas, run radio advertisements and create a lot of hoopla over this appearance which might erode their base of underground and FM support.

That year Blood, Sweat & Tears made still another mistake, albeit with good intentions. The group accepted the State Depart-

(1970)

ment's invitation to tour several Iron Curtain countries. The tour was extremely successful, and they came back highly impressed by the young people they met. However, they were turned *off* by the despotic governments they encountered. Government officials sometimes tried to make them cut their hair before performing; they tried to control the audience responses at the concerts and regularly attempted to keep the group from talking to local people.

So when Blood, Sweat & Tears returned to the United States, they gave some very anti-Communist interviews. Nothing is *wrong* with this—except that it compounded their establishment image. Suddenly Blood, Sweat & Tears was the superpatriotic group playing Caesar's Palace and hosting movie stars backstage. Granted, this had nothing to do with the group's music, which remained exceptional. Yet these public relations mistakes led to an almost total loss of underground support. The group suddenly had a middle-of-the-road audience and found itself increasingly dependent on single hits for large album sales. Their albums continued to sell well by objective standards, but the decline from the lofty top was quite precipitous. From their giant four-million seller, their next album sold a million copies and the one after that about seven hundred thousand. However, they were still in demand. Each album was being certified as a gold record and their confidence was very strong, mainly due to the warmth and natural ebullience of Bobby Columby, their drummer, who was emerging more and more as the leader of the group. But they needed help and didn't want to admit it.

Occasionally I had the group in for lunch. We'd sit down in my dining room and I would urge them—whether the problem was one of public relations or choice of new material—to get some assistance from a good producer. They needed an outsider to help them keep perspective—to help them satisfy both the need for hit songs and the necessity to be loyal to their jazz origins, a tough double requirement. I tried to get them to work with top producer Richard Perry at one point. He agreed to do it as a favor to me, but the relationship didn't last long when it became clear, as it did in several of their other arranged producer-marriages, that the group seemed determined to make it on its own.

Now it was 1972. David Clayton-Thomas met me in San Francisco to say that he was splitting. I was staying in the Mark Hopkins Hotel, and we talked for nearly three hours. He no longer felt "musical rapport" with the group. He didn't enjoy them as people any longer, and he even thought that they were making fun of him onstage, mimicking his movements and laughing behind his back. There simply was too much hostility; he couldn't be with them four or five days a week on the road anymore. Most important, he said, he wasn't singing the kind of songs he felt he could do best. It was the old conflict between jazz and vocals that had plagued the group from its inception.

I believed in David as a singer. He was distinctive; he had a style and a sound of his own. Occasionally he gave a superficial reading to a lyric line, almost a glossy coating to it, but when he was on, he could be unbelievably good. On the other hand, he was mercurial, given to violent bursts of temper followed by sudden calm—smiles and love—then violent temper again. He was extremely upset when his first solo album following the split sold only about fifty thousand copies. This was a hard pill to swallow after Blood, Sweat & Tears' giant sales, and he didn't take it well at all.

It was, again, the old problem of group versus individual identity. The record-buying public rarely crosses over when an individual leaves a group. They relate to the group, and to the group name, rather than to its individual performers. The critics liked David's first album, but no single broke from it. We shipped seventy-five thousand albums to the stores and a substantial percentage of them came back. We had done a good job of advertising and promoting it—but still the album didn't sell through.

David was not satisfied. At first he seemed to be contemplating a Tom Jones-style career, appearing in front of large orchestras. Then, when that didn't look promising, he tried to put a group together. He seemed to be floundering but he did have a big talent, so we put out a second album, shipping about forty thousand copies this time.

He was tremendously upset.

I tried to tell him that the last album's sales *merited* nothing more. Equally important, the record industry—unlike book publishing—can manufacture thousands of albums in a matter of days if the demand warrants it. We don't have to get them out on the first try. Recording artists, nonetheless, always wanted to know how many albums you shipped out. If the number was less than they thought appropriate, they were always upset. Yet the fact is that record companies constantly deal with fast-breaking market demand; we are equipped to add ten to twenty-five thousand albums to the market in three or four days. *If* the demand is there.

David wasn't interested in technicalities, however. He demanded his release from the Columbia contract. I agreed to this—except that I wanted to retain the opportunity to recoup our losses. We were substantially in the hole over the first two albums, and it seemed fair to me that we have a shot at getting our money back. There were plenty of precedents for this: buying Joplin's contract from Mainstream; purchasing Earth, Wind and Fire's contract from Warners. Unfortunately, he didn't agree. After I left CBS, he sued Columbia and me allegedly on grounds that we were interfering with his right to go on with his individual career. I never saw the complaint, as I was never served. He eventually recorded an album with RCA which didn't sell either. Musically, he probably deserves a better fate.

The group, meanwhile, replaced Clayton-Thomas with another vocalist. Unfortunately, between Caesar's Palace and the bloodletting with David, they had fallen considerably short of their earlier success. And then further personnel changes came about, making their progress a rough, uphill struggle. All of this is sad, because even with an almost totally restructured group, Blood, Sweat & Tears can create musical excitement onstage. The original concept that started it all still has validity. The high musical standards the group set for itself at the beginning have been retained. They finally have a manager, Fred Heller, who knows what to do with them, given the opportunity. Now, they can only hope that a "Spinning Wheel" or "You've Made Me So Very Happy" comes their way again, giving them one more chance to regain some of their past glory.

# 2

One of Blood, Sweat & Tears' best-known hits—"And When I Die"—was written by Laura Nyro, whom I signed in early 1968.

I was very taken with Laura. She was shy and vulnerable, with dark, deeply set eyes, and she had an odd inability to express herself, which made her even more endearing. In the studio, for example, she'd ask the sidemen for "blue" or "orange" sounds; she couldn't say precisely what she wanted. Yet I felt that she was one of the most talented artists to emerge in years, probably more for her writing than her performing talent, though she could be very striking onstage as well.

I had seen Laura perform at Monterey—badly. She was invited partly on the strength of the songs on her first album, released by Verve. Her stage appearance, however, was amateurish and overdramatic. She came out in a flashy costume, backed by two black gospel singers, and the act simply didn't work.

Still, I was very impressed with her writing, and I agreed to a meeting one day after her manager, David Geffen—whose career was just getting underway—called to ask for an appointment. Laura auditioned in a small room on the eleventh floor. Auditions are vitally important to an artist's career, yet they always seemed to happen in incongruous places. The room here contained only a piano, and a few pictures on the wall. A room I sometimes used in the Beverly Hills Hotel was better suited for weddings, with workmen frequently coming in to move tables and chairs to get ready for the next function there, while I would be trying to listen to an artist at the piano. Sometimes I used my office—members of Dr. Hook & the Medicine Show created instant chaos there and literally danced on my desk. And I'd hesitate to count the obscure lofts and matchbox-sized studios I've visited to seek out tomorrow's talent.

Laura complained immediately about the room's lighting—too much of it. We turned off the lights, and she played by the glow of a television set. I was knocked out! She played what eventually became her *Eli and The Thirteenth Confession* album and the strength of her writing was so obvious that I decided to sign her immediately.

By the style standards of the sixties, she was quite an unusual artist. She wore full-length skirts, and her black hair was long and stringy. When she first saw me, she said that she wanted to be a "star." "I've seen the kind of star Barbra Streisand is," she said that day, "and I know I've got the goods to make me one as well." She was the first young artist I'd ever signed who talked like that; and it was clear she meant it. Laura had both old-fashioned ambition and very clear ideas about her music.

She also had a full share of artistic eccentricities. She talked in a soft whispery voice, and her emotions were right on the surface . . . riding on very, very sensitive antennae. She lived fully for her music, and cared enormously about it. She once decided that one of her albums should be fragrant. I got estimates and found that we could put a fairly pleasant smell into the vinyl for a reasonable price.

One day I got an urgent call from Laura saying that she'd picked up a few copies of the album to send out to friends, and she couldn't smell a thing! I called the factory; they had indeed stopped putting in perfume. To keep Laura happy, I asked them to start again.

In regard to music itself, Laura was very demanding. You had to be very tolerant of her in the studio, for she spent a tremendous amount of money. She knew exactly the kind of feeling she wanted to get into an album, but she often couldn't explain this to her producers and engineers except in terms of colors. Eventually, people who worked with her caught on; in the meantime she had to be treated with kid gloves.

The biggest problem was that she had contradictory commercial instincts—which was unfortunate for someone who wanted to be a "star." Her talent was obvious: The Fifth Dimension, Three Dog Night, Blood, Sweat & Tears and Barbra Streisand were having gigantic hits with her songs. But her *own* albums sold between two hundred thousand and four hundred thousand copies, mostly to a cult audience. Profitable, yes; superstardom, no. When she finished an album, it was clear that one or two changes in a particular song could produce a big single hit. But she refused to let me make them. Felix Cavaliere, of The Rascals, produced one of her albums and tried to convince her to make changes. Again, she refused.

As a result, Laura's albums became—in effect—demonstration records for other artists, who subsequently sold millions of albums of her songs. Cavaliere might ask her to tone down a falsetto, or change pace or tempo on a particular number, and she'd turn him down. When she recorded a rhythm and blues album with famed producers Gamble and Huff in Philadelphia, one cut was a sensational version of the old Drifters' hit "Up On The Roof." But her record wasn't quite right for singles play, for she'd ended with a long, self-indulgent, repetitive passage which was really a trip of her own. I asked her to let me cut it to release as a single; she said no.

Nevertheless Laura got plenty of attention. Her fans were devoted and worshiped her at concerts. They threw flowers and left mementos and asked again and again for encores. She responded in a coy, playful way that endeared her to them even more. She had—and still has—the potential to become a major, major star, but success soon became more and more elusive.

Laura had a small apartment on New York's West Side when I first met her, and a passion for tuna fish, which she ate nearly every day. She eventually moved to a more fashionable place on Central Park West; the tuna fish came along too. Her publishing company, in fact, was named Tuna Fish Music. She eventually got into Yoga and meditation as well, and made several trips to the Orient pursuing these interests. But part of her remained the shy, impulsive girl who first auditioned by the light of the television set; the girl who became speechless when Bob Dylan asked to meet her at the Joplin party, and then left at my house the next day a present for Dylan, beautifully and personally wrapped with a bow, with a note asking me to deliver it. I never asked or found out what it was.

Laura never seemed to be interested in money, but it happened that Columbia's acquisition of her publishing company was to become very bitterly disputed, leading to a personal rift between me and David Geffen.

David by now had become the manager of Crosby, Stills, Nash & Young and was having much success. One of his major assets was a 50 percent interest in Laura's publishing company. We had begun negotiating Laura's contract renewal, but since we had decided to build up April-Blackwood, CBS's music publishing companies, it made sense to discuss both the record contract and music publishing together. The discussions lasted almost a year, and during that time CBS stock—which was involved—kept fluctuating. David and I had agreed that Columbia would pay Laura 75,000 shares of stock for the purchase of all of Laura's copyrights—all the songs she had written. Included in the deal was a long-term recording contract which would have *no* guaranty, a songwriter's long-term agreement with her and a substantial amount of money that had been retained in the music publishing company that was being acquired. At one point during our talks, the stock was at 40 points, making it a 3-million-dollar deal. Then it went down to 25, and the deal was suddenly worth only 1.7 million.

It sounded like a lot of money, and the trade press played this up enormously. But the fact was that we were not only getting a long-term recording artist agreement with no risk money advanced, but we were purchasing a publishing company that already had earned over half a million dollars and would automatically continue to earn substantial income as an annuity from past copyrights such as "Stoned Soul Picnic," "Eli's Comin'," "Wedding Bell Blues," "Stoney End," "Time and Love," "And When I Die" and many other great songs destined to be classics. At this same time Warners had made a deal with Dionne Warwicke for more money and only for her *recording* contract, since she was not a writer, and there was no fuss at all.

The real problem in the negotiations involved the price of CBS stock; when the stock went substantially below forty, which was the price of the stock at the time of the original discussions, David had wanted an adjustment made, and one was made. Several months later, after the deal had been closed on an adjusted basis, the stock went to forty-eight. This time the CBS corporate people wanted an adjustment to be made. The papers were still not signed.

David was outraged. He insisted that we had closed the deal at seventy-five thousand shares; he would not make any changes. I tried to calm him, saying that CBS was not backing out of the deal but just wanted the same kind of flexibility that it had granted *him*. But he would hear nothing of it, and he became convinced that *I* was pulling the strings, rather than the other way around—and that I could get William Paley and Frank Stanton to change their minds if I really wanted to. I couldn't.

The result was a great deal of bad feeling all around. David and I had been close; he'd touted me onto several good acts— Chicago and Mac Davis, for example—that he wasn't managing, and we had spent a great deal of time together, often on weekends. After the uproar over Laura, we didn't talk for nearly a year.

The problem was further complicated by Laura's future. David was forming Asylum Records, and he wanted Laura on the roster. I opposed this. A manager who decides to form his own label can't take all his artists with him. Were Janis Joplin alive, and had Albert Grossman tried to sign her when he formed Bearsville Records, I would have fought that too.

The publishing deal had included a long-term extension of Laura's contract. The papers were being drafted, but still nothing was signed. I began to hear that David planned to scrap the whole thing and sign her to Asylum; some of the trade papers said that it had already happened. Laura, meanwhile, was in Philadelphia recording her rhythm and blues album. David was taking the position that the album would go to the record company which signed her. I was very concerned about this. And then, out of the blue, I received a letter from Laura.

She said that she couldn't believe I hadn't gotten in touch with her. She'd always wanted to be on Columbia, and she felt that she'd been cared for and treated well. But if the company was too large—not willing to fight for her—she was heartbroken. I called her immediately, and we spent several hours on the telephone talking it out; soon after, she agreed to stay with the company and signed the contract.

David was mortally wounded. He had a hypnotic attachment to Laura and identified with her completely. He complained bitterly that I had called Laura directly instead of dealing through him. He felt it was unethical to go around her manager—which I thought was silly. After all, he was also competing *against* me. I felt that I had to fight as hard as possible, and there was no other way to do it except by talking to Laura directly. This caused more bitterness. It became a very painful period. David is tough to have as an adversary. He's emotional and loyal, and when he's your friend, he's great. But when he's aggrieved, watch out.

I never had a taste for the "feud" and underneath it all felt a warmth and fondness for David that current events couldn't erase. It must have been the same for him because, after about a year, he called me at home on a weekend and said, "Look, my emotion is spent. I haven't been happy since we fought. We were such good friends before, let's be that way again." I agreed; I didn't want to carry this any further.

In the meantime Laura had become very upset by all the publicity about the deal. She wasn't materialistically inclined, and she felt that the stories about stocks and dollars and numbers were obscene. Whenever David was quoted in a magazine or newspaper article—often inaccurately, he claimed—she would cringe in horror and call me to ask if there was any way to stop these stories. She even had her lawyers explore the possibility of tearing up the whole agreement.

The publicity may have led, in part, to her long silence. She got more heavily into meditation and Eastern religions and this also may have taken some of the edge off her creativity. I don't really know. She was a prodigious talent during her early years, boiling over with ideas; recording one album, she would be two or three albums beyond it in ideas. But then she got married, moved out of the city and lived for a long while on Cape Ann, in Massachusetts. I think that this isolation may have affected her as well. Laura grew up in New York City, and her musical roots are there. She was very strongly into rhythm and blues, very much a product of the rooftops and tenements of New York's West Side.

The biggest problem, obviously, was her split with Geffen. David is tremendously able. He works extremely well with artists at both business and creative levels. If Laura and he had stayed together, I'm sure that he could have put her career back on track sooner. He is clearly one of the most talented music men in the business. Without him, Laura isn't productive—at least not just now.

I've spoken with her several times. One night at dinner with her and her husband, she told me that the time simply wasn't right. She had to feel the mood to write again, and the mood hadn't struck. I hope it does. Her silence is a terrible waste.

# 3

In 1968 Columbia launched a new era in contemporary music. I had signed Joplin and Big Brother & the Holding Company, The Electric Flag and Blood, Sweat & Tears. I wanted to introduce these groups, plus The Chambers Brothers and Lou Adler's group, Spirit, to the public in a particularly special way. For it seemed wrong to market them simply by releasing individual albums. I felt a *revolution* in the making, and a special approach had to be devised to herald this new sound in music. But it was also important not to blur the artists' distinctive talents. A performer's individual artistry is far more important than any concept, revolutionary or not.

It seemed important, nonetheless, to release Joplin and the others at the same time—thus bringing Columbia recognition in the industry and among the general public as a major force in this area of change. Unfortunately, at one point I let the marketing people go too far in the "concept" direction.

It seemed to me first that we needed a way to introduce this new music to the rack jobbers and retailers of records. Performances at the NARM convention in Miami in March, 1968, and at the 1968 Columbia Records convention in Puerto Rico, where several of the acts appeared—and collectively brought down the house—helped. But we also needed a marketing campaign to get these acts solidly into the retail stores. Eventually the marketing people suggested something called "The Rock Machine" and argued very strongly for it.

I never understood what the hell it meant.

It was sort of a robot. And the robot, which looked somewhat human, might sit in a store window with a lot of record albums in his claws, or have them coming out of his electrical innards. It was a visual concept—and sometimes these have little or no *literal* meaning. The idea was that Columbia was a repository of electronic music; it was a "rock machine." I disliked it intensely. It was a "big business" approach to creativity, not really sensitive to the meaning or nuances of the "new music."

As it happened, the concept proved a very strong sales technique. It excited those whom we had to excite—the retailers—and although the groups were unknown, their records were stocked everywhere. It also firmly planted Columbia's new image—and music—in the minds of retailers. Still, the image seemed entirely wrong to me, and worse, it was out of sympathy with the individualistic, creative, pioneering ways of the musicians it represented. It was a last vestige of an old way of doing business. Salesmen and promoters until that time always looked for "umbrella" concepts to merchandise records. This had to, and would soon, change.

Fortunately, the "machine" was short-lived. It worked for three months; after that, I succeeded in quashing it. Columbia, meanwhile, wasn't the only company to make this mistake. RCA introduced a group of rock albums as "Groupquake" and MGM tried to merchandise something called "The Boston Sound." In each case, it proved to be a terrible error. No good performer will tolerate having his artistry lumped into a merchandising package for very long. No one wants to open *Rolling Stone* and see his act advertised as part of the "East Flatbush" sound, or whatever.

Equally important, consumers tend to shy away from musical

"concepts." They want artists or groups they relate to; they need a reason to buy an album, and they are unlikely to get it from an umbrella concept. "The Rock Machine" and other industry campaigns which imitated it in one form or another were simply unfortunate attempts to make the new music fit into old-fashioned molds.

New ways of doing things, however, can cause problems. The Marketing department was changing. I'd tried to hire younger, more contemporary people, who would understand the new music and know how to deal with it. Predictably enough, this brought some radical thinkers into the company. For a while some departments nearly lost a sense of what Columbia was all about. The problem was that Columbia's roster was not—and could not be—strictly rock. It was important to stimulate the kind of thinking in the company that could capitalize on the talents of Joplin and others; yet I had to be very careful not to disenfranchise our substantial roster of middle-of-the-road, country, jazz and other artists.

It was an extremely delicate problem, an important and sensitive responsibility. Unlike Warners and Elektra, two of our chief competitors, I couldn't allow Columbia to acquire a solely contemporary image. This would severely damage relations with artists such as Barbra Streisand, Andy Williams, Ray Conniff, Miles Davis, Johnny Cash, Tammy Wynette, Vladimir Horowitz, Leonard Bernstein and many others. Already the company was becoming too rock-oriented for some of them.

On the other hand, the new music would soon represent at least 50 percent of the market. Warner Bros., for example, had jumped almost totally into the contemporary scene. During the early sixties their artists were mostly middle-of-the-road: Frank Sinatra, Petula Clark, Bill Cosby, Nancy Sinatra and Dean Martin. Then the careers of Petula Clark and Nancy Sinatra lost steam; Bill Cosby's comedy albums stopped selling, Frank Sinatra went into retirement and Dean Martin's sales dropped. They had to replace a lot of volume in a hurry, and they weren't deeply into country or black music.

What they hit upon was a very successful technique of poking fun at themselves in print, maintaining a sort of clubby rock-consciousness image. Meanwhile, they acquired a powerful roster of contemporary talent. Their advertising ideas came mostly from

Stan Cornyn, their very imaginative Vice-President of "Creative Services." He managed to establish a low-key, self-deprecating image for Warners which aided them enormously.

For all of Warner Bros.' success, however, a totally contemporary image can be limiting. They often find themselves crossed off the shopping lists of talented nonrock artists who have something to offer a company. When Liza Minnelli was looking for a contract, for example, she was inclined to talk only to Columbia. Our roster was diverse enough to make her feel comfortable. As much as I admired what Warners was doing, I concluded that it didn't make sense for Columbia to imitate it. I basically believed that our label's image had to be almost faceless. Let the artists create the image through their own quality. Don't establish a particular style that would disenfranchise anybody.

Eventually, Warners was forced to broaden its approach; even its artists started complaining. Then, too, music began to change and become far more diverse. However, while it lasted and served a purpose, their advertising campaign was the most effective one to come out of the industry in years.

Rock consciousness at Columbia, meanwhile, very nearly got out of hand. The problem surfaced when Morris Baumstein, who had worked imaginatively on the company's advertising in one capacity or another for several years, brought in an ad written for several underground publications and titled "The Man Can't Bust Our Music." I thought that it was an effective ad, and an original approach, but I was disturbed by it. Again, what did it mean? It was identifying the company much *too* closely with the counterculture. After all, Columbia Records in the public's mind was a large company, *the* large music company. We might have created a climate hospitable to many irreverent thinkers, but we also were involved in all of music, and must have seemed to some like General Motors.

I asked Morris to have the ad elaborate on the meaning of the phrase. He did, and I rejected the copy. About a week later, he came back. He said, "Look, I've never done this before, but the entire Advertising Department believes in this ad and we think you are dead wrong." He had gladly asked the copy chief to rewrite ads on previous occasions, but this time he felt strongly enough about the ad to reject my rejection. The ad was *not* going to *The New York Times,* he argued, but to the rock press and various underground papers. He persisted.

I was sitting on my departments quite strongly at the time. In fact, two or three of my executives had warned me recently that excessively strong leadership could result in problems. There were complaints that I was scrutinizing too many ads. "Give them more rope," I was advised. "Let them make their own mistakes." I was uncomfortable with this approach. I had always felt I should provide examples of what I wanted, standards for others to follow. Only then could my department heads know what was expected of them. Also, I felt a responsibility to guard the image of the artists I was personally signing. I believed that I owed this to them.

But the thought kept gnawing at me: was I being overprotective? Was I too cautious? I considered all this in weighing my response to Morris and I concluded that I should give in.

I was wrong. This was not the occasion to delegate judgment. For the ad had really missed the mark. *Rolling Stone* had a marvelous time ridiculing the company with it, talking about Columbia's "identity crisis," how we were trying to be hip, etc. They were right. I may have resented them singling us out for ridicule (I often did that when people made fun of Columbia), but they *were* right.

# Seven

## 1

It was a time almost of frenzy. As 1968 ended, Columbia was clearly established as the leader of the record industry. Its share of market in the industry was rising dramatically; it had been 11 percent when I became Administrative Vice-President in 1965; now it was 17 percent. Joplin and Blood, Sweat & Tears were filling concert halls across the country, and selling millions of records. Simon & Garfunkel were doing extremely well, though they hadn't yet reached their high point of the *Bridge Over Troubled Water* album, and Sly Stone, a former Memphis disc jockey, was beginning to take his audiences Higher everywhere he went. The appetite for contemporary artists seemed to be insatiable.

The year 1969 was to begin with a bang. I had just signed an exciting Latin rock group out of San Francisco called Santana, and was contemplating their launching, when a friend who'd been at the Fillmore East the previous night called me at home on a Saturday morning. Al Kooper had invited a guitarist from the audience onstage, and my friend said it was an eye-popping spectacle! A slender albino figure, tall and catlike in his movements, had mounted the stage. He brought the house down. The display of virtuosity was electrifying.

Sunday, a review in *The New York Times* hailed Johnny Winter as a major new discovery.

And then things happened fast. On Monday, Steve Paul, manager of a New York club called The Scene, called. The Scene was one of the "in" spots in town. Musicians often dropped in after their gigs at two or three in the morning to talk or jam. The club never made money, because Steve found it somehow inappropriate to charge for their drinks either the artists who jammed or the music executives who dropped by and could be persuaded to bring in their artists. Nonetheless, he ran the club with considerable style and flair.

Steve wanted to talk to me about Johnny. He was candid: he'd read about Johnny in *Rolling Stone,* and had flown immediately to Texas to persuade him to come to New York. The unscheduled Fillmore East appearance had created instant interest in Johnny everywhere and Steve wanted to talk right away. Steve was about twenty-six at the time, but he'd been around a while, and he had some definite ideas about managing Winter's career.

He planned to meet *only* with the presidents of companies. And he planned to consider only Columbia, Atlantic and Elektra, whose images he liked. I agreed to the procedure, and Steve, Johnny and I met. We spent about two hours together; from the beginning it was hard to keep my eyes off this striking fellow with flowing white hair and an oddly mellow look in his pink eyes. Johnny was very articulate, and he knew the business fairly well, having made some earlier albums for smaller companies. As with many artists, he wanted to know about creative freedom, art and design, advertising and promotion.

The only problem was Columbia's studio situation. The company owned its own studios, and our engineers belonged to a union. Atlantic and Elektra, by contrast, had no union problem. At Columbia, the current collective-bargaining agreement required that union engineers be present and work the "boards" (the engineering console) at sessions involving Columbia artists which took place in the studios, or within several hundred miles of any one of them. This was thought to show considerable flexibility on the union's part; the contract used to be much more restrictive, requiring that only Columbia studios could be used for Columbia recordings, period.

The studio problem had long been a thorn in my side. I felt strongly about artistic freedom—and in the rock world this means that artists may want to handle the boards themselves, or choose a close friend or associate to do it. In 1972, after a major confrontation with the union, the rule was finally relaxed. But for now, I could only tell Winter to look at the Columbia studios; I was sure that they would meet his standards. And if he didn't like them, I promised him that he could record in Texas or Florida or any one of about thirty states where it was permissible to record freely.

Still selling hard, but low-key, I took the two of them on a tour of the art department; it was quite a sight. Steve Paul dressed *always* in blue; today he was wearing a huge floppy blue hat. Winter walked beside him, his heavy Texas accent rolling through the corridor.

When people turned to find the source of the voice, they saw—and stared at—this striking white-haired figure. Curiosity abounded.

So far, we hadn't talked about money; the conversation that day involved music and art.

Three days later, Steve called to say that RCA had offered Winter a six-hundred-thousand-dollar guaranty. They hadn't even been asked to *bid*. I was shocked; I figured Winter was gone. I just couldn't go that far. But then Steve took a position that surprised me. He *still* wanted to go with the companies he'd originally selected. Money—within reason—didn't matter. The musical home was crucial too. I breathed a sigh of relief and asked what the price was. Atlantic had offered between three hundred and fifty and four hundred thousand, and he said he would expect to get that from Columbia, or very close to it, if we wanted Winter. And he volunteered that Winter would choose Columbia without hesitation if we came up with the money. We had the best "vibes."

I still had the problem of precedent. There was no doubt that I wanted Winter. Yet this would be Columbia's most expensive signing thus far—for a new artist. The Joplin deal had involved *buying* her contract from someone else; that was different from this. Those negotiations, complicated or not, hadn't escalated the price of other contracts. Our royalty rate, which had risen slightly to 8 percent of retail sales or 16 percent of wholesale, including the producer's share, was still the lowest in the industry. We were signing the most important new artists for twenty or twenty-five thousand dollars. The Winter signing might upset all this.

Our Business Affairs negotiators, Dick Asher and Elliot Goldman, who were first-rate, worked sixteen hours a day to keep up with the new frenzied activity, trying to hold the advances within manageable limits. I stayed within these limits *almost* always. But

I did have a weakness when I sensed that an artist was a truly unique talent. And Winter seemed just that. He was an instrumental virtuoso, often a major index of durability. And he was clearly a showman as well. I just *had* to make the deal and trust my instincts. I offered Steve Paul fifty thousand dollars an album for six albums over a three-year period, with an additional two-year option for four more albums.

Steve called almost immediately to say that he and Johnny would be coming to Columbia. I was delighted.

Publicity problems followed. Steve wanted a dramatic signing; he wanted Johnny's friends present, the press in attendance, and an auspicious setting. Steve, Johnny and Johnny's friends were all living on a rambling, heavily wooded estate in Westchester county, and they asked if I would attend a luncheon they would arrange for the signing. I did, and the signing took place there. It was all proceeding smoothly, but I began to get apprehensive when the publicity started to break. The stories said that I'd signed Winter for almost a million dollars, or seven hundred thousand, or five hundred thousand, none of which was true.

Publicity—if excessive or unwarranted—can hurt an artist's career. Steve Paul is one of the most professional men in the business now, and one of the nicest to deal with. But in 1969 things were getting a little out of hand. Johnny hadn't cut an album, or toured, yet Steve had scheduled a press conference the following week at the Plaza Hotel. He'd taken a corner suite, a very elegant setting.

I asked him to cancel it. Johnny's Texas background and first appearance at the Fillmore simply did not jive with the Plaza. His image might be badly distorted. Continuing stories of a high-priced signing appeared everywhere. One of Johnny's old albums had surfaced and was getting on the charts as a result of the widespread publicity. Johnny wasn't even ready to record his first Columbia album. I was very worried that all the press and money talk would make it difficult for the album to get a fair hearing.

Fortunately, Johnny delivered everything he promised. He was a charismatic performer and guitarist, and although enormous skepticism was voiced throughout the industry as to whether Columbia would recoup its guaranty, we did, handsomely. Johnny's sales averaged about four hundred thousand units for each release, more than triple the number needed to break even. And my relationship with Johnny and Steve led to another unexpected plus: the signing of Edgar Winter, who was to become a giant star in his own right.

An additional note on Johnny Winter is sad. He kept up a hectic touring pace, and he eventually encountered serious health problems which involved drugs. Steve came to see me at one point and said that he was very worried about Johnny. He felt that he was almost losing control as a manager; for the act, with Johnny's albino hair, stylized clothes and dramatic stage presence, had a momentum that was difficult to control. Finally—and luckily—Johnny committed himself to a hospital. He was out of commission for nearly a year. He had been close, literally, to killing himself. But the deaths of Janis Joplin and Jimi Hendrix, both kindred spirits, affected him deeply, and the strong urging of Steve and other close friends convinced him that if he didn't get help he'd die.

I was thrilled to see, a year later, that Johnny had recovered and was returning to the rock world. On his first day out of the hospital, he flew to New York and, with the ever faithful Steve Paul, came to see me. All he wanted to do was assure me that he was well, and was ready to "make music." He looked fine, and talked freely and directly about his problem and his life-and-death struggle to conquer it. Two months later he was back at work.

# 2

Santana came out of nowhere and suddenly exploded all over the charts. I received a call one day from rock impresario Bill Graham suggesting that I watch them perform at Graham's Fillmore West in San Francisco. Santana was a local group, and no one had yet heard of them. Bill soon became involved with the group; but at the time he was thoughtful enough to call me simply as a friend, and so I flew up directly from Los Angeles.

I was knocked out! Latin music combined with rock was absolutely infectious. More important, the group was solid musically. I agreed to sign them. The ensuing negotiations introduced me to Brian Rohan, who was soon to become one of the most prominent and colorful figures on the San Francisco music scene. He was the attorney for both Santana and the group called It's a Beautiful Day, whom I also saw at Bill Graham's urging at Fillmore West. Both deals were negotiated at roughly the same time.

Santana's debut was staggering. We considered them mostly a local group, since they'd appeared primarily in the Bay Area up to that time. But I had *no idea* of the strength of their word-of-mouth following. When their first album was released, it sold out of San Francisco's record stores the same day. Our local promotion people got very excited. We sent a second allocation of albums—and it sold out as soon as it reached town. The phenomenon spread; this was a time of great excitement in FM radio, and we found ourselves struggling tremendously just to keep up with Santana's FM listeners. The album sold out of stores in San Francisco, then Los Angeles, then all over the country. San Francisco fans alone bought fifty thousand copies.

Then "Black Magic Woman" emerged as a single; the album began selling a hundred thousand copies a week! Bill Graham would call me every Wednesday to get the latest sales figures—two, three, four, five hundred thousand, one million units, finally two million. The group was on fire. Their second album, *Abraxas,* went to 3 and a half million; their fame spread and Santana became the rage of Latin America and several countries in Europe. They were absolutely on top.

And then, as happens so *often,* the group's success began to level off in 1972. Santana had had a falling out with Graham. Then they let their manager go. Next, the group members had trouble among themselves and there was substantial personnel reshuffling. Finally, Carlos Santana himself underwent a complete metamorphosis. He cut his hair, began watching his food intake, got into meditation and changed his musical direction completely.

Carlos and I never had a real relationship. He was very quiet, and whenever we met, there never seemed time to talk. At a Santana performance, I might go backstage, and we would shake hands. But dressing rooms are always crowded and noisy; it was difficult to have meaningful conversations. However, at one point he did tell me with great emotion and feeling how his new religion had changed his life, how liberated he felt and what a tremendous experience it was. He had become friends with John McLaughlin of Mahavishnu Orchestra fame—they shared the same guru—and he began to get further and further into progressive music. The Latin influence could still be felt, but the street-Latin beat—that infectious, melodic rhythm for which Santana became so famous—was gone.

Thus far, the critics are saying that Santana's new music is the best of their career. There is more depth, more feeling, greater musical insight and cohesiveness. The group has matured a lot and they're more stable. They have won many new admirers. But, unfortunately, they also have temporarily lost a lot of their mass appeal. And that, as they say, is the music business.

# 3

With Santana, Johnny Winter and It's a Beautiful Day joining Joplin, Blood, Sweat & Tears, Laura Nyro, Sly & The Family Stone and The Chambers Brothers in selling out the contemporary music section of record stores all over the country, Columbia often seemed to be a rocket ship running on explosive fuel. *Chicago* came next; from the first day I heard of them, our relationship was as stormy as it was rewarding.

David Geffen called me about the group, which was working with Jimmy Guercio, and said that he was hearing good things about them. Guercio had signed a contract with Columbia earlier, giving us first look at all his artists until we selected three. All I had to do was wait for Jimmy to bring them around, or so I thought.

At this point in the contract, Columbia had picked two groups, The Firesign Theater, a successful choice, and Illinois Speed Press, an unsuccessful one.

I didn't bother to ask Guercio about Chicago; I assumed that he would introduce them when he was ready. And, sure enough, he did call, saying that he wanted to talk about the newest group he was bringing me.

I then heard from Mike Curb, who later, as President of MGM Records, became a minor hero of the Nixon administration for his crusade against musicians who were alleged to be drug users. For now, Curb was a West Coast producer and independent businessman who dealt in sound tracks and surfing music. He was "doing some business" with Jimmy Guercio. Would I mind if he came to the meeting? I knew that Curb was involved with Transcontinental Investing Corporation, a company rapidly expanding its interests in the music business, primarily rack jobbing, and that he was going to organize some creative activity for them. He was talking to Jimmy about doing some producing for him in return for stock in Transcon, as it was called.

Jimmy is a short, bespectacled fellow with dirty blond hair—soft-spoken, low-keyed, but chock full of big ideas and ambition. He always was fascinated with the world of big business and wanted to be a part of it. Curb, on the other hand, looks like a Hollywood movie actor, modishly dressed, slim, blue-eyed, nicely tanned . . . and he did all the talking. Neither one knew, of course, that I had already heard about Chicago; I waited for them to tell me about the group.

Curb said that he and Jimmy had a new group to submit to us. They were very exciting, and he thought I would be pleased. Then the surprise: I'd had this group under contract *before,* but I really hadn't seen their potential. Jimmy, on the other hand, was tremendously excited about them. He thought that they had big potential. I began to shift in my seat. I'd never had anyone from Chicago under contract.

"What group?" I asked uneasily.

"We're suggesting The Arbors," Curb said.

I was amazed. The Arbors were a clean-cut, Lettermen-like act who'd had several modest hits a few years earlier on one of our subsidiary labels, Date Records. They had a smooth college style—but we had dropped them eight months ago. They weren't making the chart-busting music of the future. Not even close to it. And here I was being offered . . . the Arbors! Curb was sitting in *my* office talking to me in a low-key, *trusting* way, batting innocent big blue eyes at me . . . trying to sell me a group I'd already dropped so that Jimmy could get out of his contract with Columbia!

It all came to me in a flash, and I tried to suppress my anger as I turned to Jimmy. "I want to hear this from your own mouth," I said. "Is this the group you're so *excited* about? You know our agreement: if you're not *wildly* enthusiastic about a group, don't even bother submitting them. Is *this* the third group under the contract?"

Jimmy was suddenly squeamish. He looked at the floor, squirmed in his seat and said, "Well, I don't know if I'd go quite as far as Mike is going, but I *do* believe in this group; and I believe that I can bring them hits." He was deeply embarrassed by the whole approach, and so I stopped talking. I said that I wouldn't be taking the group but told them to keep in touch.

After they left I called Dick Asher, Vice-President of Business Affairs at the time, and told him the story. I asked him to call Guercio and Curb and tell them that I'd known about Chicago all along; and then tell them that I planned to turn down *every* group submitted until they were offered to us. Word came back to me that Guercio and Curb were very embarrassed when they got the news. More important, I got Chicago.

# 4

Chicago's career began very much in the shadow of Blood, Sweat & Tears. The comparisons were obvious: the brass and jazz sound; the earthy, metallic vocals; the large size of each group. Moreover, Chicago's first album had no immediate single hit, keeping the group clearly behind Blood, Sweat & Tears for the first year.

Then things turned around. Blood, Sweat & Tears couldn't follow its giant second album with a big hit; and it began having all its public relations problems. Chicago, meanwhile, began criss-crossing the country, playing to increasingly large audiences, and started building up a great repertoire of single hits. By 1970, they had clearly passed Blood, Sweat & Tears and emerged on their own as the premier American group, known for such great records as "Questions 67 and 68," "Does Anybody Really Know What Time It Is," "Beginnings," "Colour My World," "Make Me Smile," "25 or 6 to 4," etc.

My relationship with Chicago had some special moments. After their celebrated week-long series of Carnegie Hall concerts in April, 1971, I threw a large party in their honor at Tavern-On-the-Green in New York and especially invited Miles Davis and Stevie Wonder to meet them. They were star-struck at meeting Miles and Stevie and were knocked out by the entire evening. The following Monday, they gave Janet and me a beautiful antique music box from Germany, six feet tall, that booms out the sound of metal oom-pah-pah records, an eye-catching piece of furniture. I was deeply touched at their generosity and thoughtfulness. Not every group acts that way.

Unfortunately, we had other exchanges that were not as warm. One problem was that they didn't like to be edited. They approached music in admirably pure terms, and they liked long album cuts with extended brass and guitar solos. I never had any quarrel with this except in one area: singles. Lengthy cuts almost invariably turn off AM radio audiences, and that's where big success clearly lies. Fortunately, Jimmy Guercio is a pro and he understood this; so did their industrious business manager, Larry Fitzgerald. Both men were able to convince the group that some compromises were necessary.

However, editing of their material *always* offended Chicago. Their singles often had to have a minute—sometimes as much as two minutes, or more—of instrumental passages taken off. Occasionally the single would have to be entirely reconstructed. The group felt, understandably enough, that this badly compromised their artistic integrity, but I didn't know how to have the hits without the editing. If I took out a particular guitar solo, or a brass passage, I'd hear through Guercio that they were extremely unhappy.

The editing problem plagued each new album. I'd bring up the question of editing, and the first answer was always no. They wanted the same version of a song to play on both AM and FM radio. I established the practice of doing rough edits first in my office with a company engineer, and then sending the tape to Jimmy, who would go into the studio and produce a polished version. It didn't score any points. Even though Guercio was eventually able to persuade them to accept the edits, and the records became smash hits, the group remained annoyed.

Then we ran into other problems. For example, Chicago never settled for a normal package. It was always a two-record set, or three records, or *four* records. And, they objected to our retail pricing. They wanted us to release three- or four-record sets and charge the public as if we were releasing a one-record album. This was impossible. They were not suggesting a cut in royalty for themselves, only a cut in our profits. We did bend over backwards to accommodate them by keeping the list price as low as possible, beginning with their first album. At the time, the list was $4.98 an album. Two-record sets were listing for $9.98. We charged $5.98. For the second two-record album we charged $6.98.

One of the problems complicating the economics was the group's approach to packaging. Frequently they wanted the kitchen sink—and then some. For their Carnegie Hall album, Chicago wanted half a dozen posters, gilt-edged foil wrapping and a ready reference list outlining voting registration procedures for newly enfranchised eighteen-year-olds. We naturally got into heated arguments over this and finally settled for the registration booklet, a very large poster, a medium-sized poster and four records. Despite the inclusion of all this, they were extremely upset that they didn't get the whole thing. Talk about the age of creative freedom!

One telephone conversation is particularly etched in my memory. I was arguing with two group members about the gilt-edged foil wrapping and other things, and I said that I thought the package was utterly gluttonous. "Not only would it cost enormous amounts of money," I said, "but it could hurt your career. Too elaborate packaging is a turn-off to critics, also to FM audiences. If you insist on including everything, it will distract from your music. Which is, after all, the reason for the album in the first place."

It was 1971. Janis Joplin was dead. Blood, Sweat & Tears was no longer selling major numbers of albums, and Andy Williams and Johnny Cash were off television. Chicago was clearly our number one group. The band members had always been verbally polite when we talked directly, but this conversation was almost bloody. They said, "*Look,* we're making you millions of dollars. We're your number one group. You're hot because *we're* hot. We *know* who you've got. Blood, Sweat & Tears has broken up; Joplin is dead, and Simon & Garfunkel have broken up. You have to rely on us—so *don't alienate us!*"

I hung up the phone. It was too crass, simply too raw. I was angry; so were they. I was willing to compromise, but there were limits. The problem had gotten out of hand. And it took quite some time before things eventually settled down.

I was always upset that my relationship with Chicago wasn't better. Here was a supergroup continually selling millions of albums—almost unprecedented success. They were making a fortune and so was the company. It seemed ridiculous to be fighting over the packaging and pricing of albums. But *this* was a case where I had to fulfill my business responsibilities before indulging the creative artists. If I gave in to their demands everyone would suffer: our profits would be cut to ribbons and they would receive more critical abuse than they did—and they did receive quite a bit—over their packaging ideas.

The lines were drawn; realistically, I was the only one who could give the final No. Bruce Lundvall, whom I had appointed as Vice-President of Marketing to replace Bill Farr, tried valiantly on many occasions to resolve the issues, but the group felt so strong that eventually the problem always came to my desk. And this was no time for me to win a popularity contest.

It bothered me greatly because I was genuinely fond of Guercio and Fitzgerald, who were both doing a superb job guiding the group's career. The constant haggling had created a strain in our relationship. There never seemed to be time to pause and celebrate our success.

I was also frankly worried that these arguments might damage Columbia's image among other artists. Our reputation for genuine sensitivity to an artist's creative needs was very high; I was concerned that our problems with Chicago might surface and change this, since artists on a label frequently compare notes.

Actually, it never happened. Guercio and Fitzgerald wisely kept the lid on and, of course, so did we. And Chicago kept right on making hits and selling millions of albums. What's more, their packaging now is much simpler and to the point, a sign that they are finally allowing their music to speak for itself.

# Eight

## 1

CBS's corporate atmosphere always bothered me. It sometimes seemed that the company went out of its way to be impersonal, as though this was good for business. The "Black Rock" building had a cool, glass-and-steel feeling about it, and corporate relationships inside reflected this. You rarely had a sense of camaraderie or, God forbid, friendship, in high-level dealings. A dramatic increase in your operating division's profits might bring a polite smile, but little else.

The building seemed a perfect CBS symbol. Its "facilities" regulations were designed for corporate robots. A corporation has to have standards, but to CBS austerity was almost a religion. When we moved into the building in 1965, nothing was left to chance. Employees were allocated precise amounts of office space according to their corporate grade, and then were told what they could or could not *do* with it. This caused some annoying—and occasionally funny—problems.

Vice-Presidents, for example, rated fifteen-by-fifteen-foot rooms. No one else could occupy equal space. The problem was that management actively discouraged division presidents from having large numbers of vice-presidents. So that if a vice-president resigned, or was promoted or fired, you were discouraged from immediately appointing another one. But you couldn't put anyone of lower rank into his room! Office space was scarce . . . but management preferred to leave the room empty rather than let you stretch the rules. You had to find *someone* to fill the departed vice-president's job; and you were likely to give him the appropriate responsibility, perhaps a raise. But you couldn't give him a bigger room or a new title.

Other problems involved office decorations. Record companies are not the same as banks. People who inhabit the music world tend to be loose, noncomformist types. They like informal clothing, and they hang album covers and pop posters on their walls. They also play loud music (for good reason) and tend to put their feet on their desks. This inevitably led to corporate problems. It made no sense to force Columbia Records employees to look or act like IBM executives—both for humane *and* business reasons. Creative people work best when they are happy; and happy creative people boost a record company's profit margins—that, at least, the CBS board members understood.

Still, the facilities staff people were tough enforcers of the rules. When CBS first moved into the new building, people tried to hang pictures or favorite posters or paintings on their walls . . . only to find them missing in the morning. Maintenance men would come by at night and *take* them. I had to run interference constantly for my employees. When I hired Kip Cohen, former manager of the Fillmore East, as head of East Coast A&R, he complained that he couldn't get permission to turn down the lights in his office. He was also informed that certain kinds of pictures couldn't be hung on the walls.

I told him that I would personally take care of the complaints. I felt that I had to protect Columbia Records from corporate stultification; I had to foster an atmosphere *both* creative *and* businesslike; a relaxed, happy one where artists felt welcome and young people were motivated to get into their work. A music company with a button-down mind will find it hard to prosper. I felt it was extremely important that we create an infectious enthusiasm toward work. This would distinguish us from other large companies which were choking with bureaucracy. Talented people in long hair and blue jeans *had* to feel comfortable here.

To that end, I led a sort of double life. My clothing had to be appropriate to the day's demands. For a board meeting, I wore relatively subdued color combinations; if I was meeting with artists and managers, I was much more casual. I always wore a tie, but there are ways of combining colors that suggest a livelier mentality than the cool authority of the CBS building, and I always tried to do this.

The biggest problem was that CBS, even in the late sixties, perceived itself almost entirely in terms of television and broadcasting. Even while pop music exploded all over the country, clearly replacing movies as the glamour and moneymaking industry, CBS still looked at us as finger-popping nonconformists operating somewhere on the fringes of the corporate ledgers. This simply was no longer true. Columbia Records was leading a giant cultural explosion. It now had a top position among CBS divisions; its profits had jumped astonishingly.

Yet few members of the CBS hierarchy seemed to recognize this. There were polite nods and I saw a few smiles when Columbia's sales charts—whose lines looked like inverted lightning bolts—were shown to board meetings. But there seemed little recognition of the significance of this. Elsewhere, record executives' salaries were rising fast; not at CBS. I began sending memos to corporate people. Columbia's success was the result of the talent and foresight of a number of key executives under me. I felt that their salaries should go up commensurately.

Unfortunately, CBS was not structured flexibly enough to permit this—without a fight. Salaries of executives were rated on corporatewide grade levels, determined largely by a man's assigned responsibilities and the amount of money he controlled. Each grade level had a range of maximum and minimum salary levels. A man might make 20 or 50 percent of his grade maximum; when he reached maximum, he would be rated to see if he should move up another level. The problem was that the corporate Personnel Department wasn't rating jobs the way *we* felt they should be rated. The department served all of CBS; many of its members were well on in years. They'd reached their positions when records were not a major factor in CBS's earnings.

The problem soon became critical. Columbia's Director of Promotion, Tom Noonan, made twenty-five thousand dollars a year; Motown wooed him away for forty. Sales and Distribution Vice-President Don England went to a tape company for a substantial increase. Then Bob Cato, Vice-President for Art and Design, went over to *McCall's* magazine for more money. These were strong, valuable men and their departures hurt me badly. Middle-level executives—who also were leaving—could be replaced, but you have a serious problem when men of vice-presidential caliber move on. (All those empty fifteen-by-fifteen-foot offices!) I began sending memos to John ("Jack") Schneider, the corporate Executive Vice-President. I was getting pretty hot under the collar, and when I got no immediate response, I asked Personnel for competitive salary evaluations.

Fortunately, Personnel found that raises would be justified. I then requested a meeting with Schneider and asked why my memos and the evaluations by Personnel seemed to have been ignored. I raised the point of bonuses as well. These were given out at the year's end, and the procedure being used allowed little room for discretionary judgment. I felt that it was the wrong approach. The record industry was changing enormously; I wanted more flexibility on awarding bonuses than the computer-allowed 10 percent.

Schneider's first reaction was muted negativism. He argued that television had carried records for *many* years; now it was the Records Division's turn. I argued that the old breed of records people was no longer around the building. I had new people working for me, younger and more dynamic. We'd had tremendous growth—as had the entire industry—and I was close to losing more good executives if something didn't change, and fast.

It was hard to blame Schneider for his ambivalence. He was then thought to be Dr. Stanton's likely successor as President of the corporation. He was supposed to have authority for the entire CBS organization, but in reality he was being watched closely by Paley and Stanton, and while he was on trial for a bigger job, he was quite handcuffed in making decisions. I was asking him to break *tradition*. Even if he were sympathetic to my position, he knew that Paley and Stanton were looking over his shoulder.

An additional problem was that Columbia's growth hadn't made much difference in CBS's stock. Television earnings had declined mainly because of the loss of cigarette advertising; diversification and acquisition programs outside of records (CBS bought into books, toys, baseball and movies, for example) had also done badly. The result was that Columbia Records had saved CBS a lot of face on Wall Street, but overall corporate profits weren't higher.

Finally, after repeated meetings, memos, arguments and counterarguments, I was given approval for several key salary increases. The computerized bonus plan was also amended so that a Division President could have a 30 percent range of discretion. I should have felt good—but I was exhausted. It was a long, hard fight and it should never have taken place.


# 2

My own raises came even harder.

By 1970 I had been President of the Columbia Records Division for three years. Harvey Schein was President of the CBS International Division, which was a separate operation. We both reported to Goddard Lieberson, whose responsibility as a group president included Schein's and my domains as well as the Musical Instruments Division, which encompassed Fender Guitars, Rogers Drums and Leslie Speakers; a mail-order division housing the Columbia Record Club; and the new motion picture division, Cinema Center Films.

My division was the domestic records operation. This meant, in essence, that I signed artists and was responsible for distributing their records in the continental United States. I had other responsibilities, as well, including the supervision of factories in New Jersey, Indiana and California which pressed records; tapemaking or duplicating plants in Connecticut and Indiana; a research and engineering lab in New Milford, Connecticut; sales and promotion offices located throughout the country; and music publishing activities.

The music publishing operations, April-Blackwood Music, housed not only the copyrights of artists signed to Columbia, but also those for songs written by composer-singers such as Harry Nilsson of RCA and James Taylor of Warners. Our pressing operation also serviced other companies, including Warner Bros., Elektra, A&M, Vanguard and Buddah. It was a custom manufacturing service which had no artistic or contractual connection to the artists involved. And finally, we had something called Special Products, which assembled material for records that companies, say, Goodyear Tires, might sell as premium offers for Christmas and Thanksgiving.

In 1969, we had decided to diversify even further, and we bought Discount Records. This operation grew from eighteen to sixty retail record stores by the time I left the company. The stores were full-catalog ones, since we were concerned that rack jobbers in department and drugstores were giving exposure only to best sellers rather than to a complete line of product. We wanted to set an example in order to encourage the full-catalog Sam Goodys of the world to expand, so we showed that we were willing to put up our own money for this purpose. We also used our stores as a market research device to watch the movements of the retail world. For the most part, stores were located around college campuses; our "market research" was done among the prime record-buying populations.

Finally, we purchased a small, growing chain of high-fidelity component stores in California called Pacific Stereo. I did this despite the doubts of several top members of the CBS hierarchy. This has proved to be one of the few really successful nonrecord-company acquisitions of CBS.

Supervising all this involved fifteen- and eighteen-hour days. I delegated as much authority as I could, for I still felt that my main efforts should be in signing and promoting artists, and I had to be free principally to compete in the signing wars against Mo Ostin and Joe Smith of Warners and Ahmet Ertegun of Atlantic. Still, a perfectionist streak made it impossible to stay *really* far away. I got so heavily into the business that I began to worry that my life was focusing far too much on my job. My days began with breakfast at my desk and ran until eight or nine o'clock at night. After going home, I'd spend an hour at dinner with my family and begin my night's reading . . . the record charts, sales memos, trade papers and *Rolling Stone*. Several nights a week, I had rock concerts to see or nighttime auditions to attend.

It got to a point where I had time for little else. I kept up with current events by reading *The New York Times* daily, and *Time* magazine each week, but I had the feeling that my range of contacts was becoming more and more localized. I had no time to read books; my wife and I struggled to keep up with our season tickets to the symphony. It was hard even to devote Sundays to my family. At least part of them had to be devoted to reading the early editions of *Billboard, Cashbox* and *Record World,* and the specially delivered reports of Bill Gavin and Kal Rudman, the two most widely read radio advisory services.

Yet I was enjoying myself enormously. The job was exhilarating, dynamic, glamorous and challenging. Time-consuming, frustrating and burdensome—all these, too; yet I felt stimulated, fulfilled and well rewarded.

Except in one area—salary.

For CBS was hardly bullish about raises. After my promotions to Administrative Vice-President and then to Vice-President and General Manager, all raises came by confrontation. CBS showed neither imagination nor initiative in this area. They were glad to see the division's profits go up thirty million dollars, and the group's profits go up more than fifty million, but I got no notes from Paley and Stanton about this, no congratulatory lunches, and nothing came down that gave the Records Division any special recognition. When the Records Division's gargantuan profits were announced, I got a smile or two. That was all.

My salary as President of the Records Division was then a hundred thousand dollars a year, plus a bonus of about forty thousand. It had gone from forty thousand a year as Administrative Vice-President to seventy-five thousand and then to a hundred thousand. Clearly, I wasn't starving. Yet it seemed ridiculous to be making Columbia tens of millions of dollars of new profits and getting much less compensation than the President of Capitol Records—which was losing money. My salary and bonuses were simply not competitive. Moreover, I had no chance to build up equity in CBS stock. I was offered the customary stock options but CBS stock was falling, since the decline in television revenues and the unsuccessful new diversification ventures offset the increased profits from records. The options were worthless.

In April, 1970, Mo Ostin of Warners called. He offered me two hundred thousand dollars a year plus substantial stock options if I'd switch companies. It was an extremely attractive offer. Warners by then was "Warner Communications"—a complex owned by the Kinney Corporation which included the Warners and Reprise labels, Atlantic Records and Elektra Records. Warner Communications seemed a much less impersonal company than CBS. The Kinney people had been wise enough to retain the various company heads—Ahmet and Nesuhi Ertegun and Jerry Wexler of Atlantic; Mo Ostin and Joe Smith of Warners-Reprise; and Jac Holzman of Elektra. Each was a major, colorful figure in his own right, with his own particular style and abilities. They were all free to run their own operations and, as far as I could determine, everyone was getting along quite well.

I was envious.

The Warners stock offer was also excellent. Mo promised me at least twenty thousand shares—at one dollar each. Kinney stock was selling at more than twenty-five dollars a share, and they expected this to go up to forty at year's end. In short, the offer could go as high as a million dollars. I had received, and would continue to receive, other offers—Jac Holzman had offered me a significant partnership in Elektra before he sold out to Kinney, and David Geffen would offer me a full partnership in what was to become Asylum Records—but this was the closest to what I wanted. I was sorely tempted.

The problem was that Mo couldn't *define* the job. It sounded as though I'd be working for all of Warner Communications in some sort of large-scale managerial capacity; Mo promised that he and Joe and Jac and Jerry Wexler would report to me. But that left Ahmet uncommitted, and he was in Europe and planned to stay there for several weeks. Meanwhile, I had to take or leave the offer; the dollar stock option plan would run out in ten days.

As attractive as the job seemed, I was vaguely put off by it. The new position might take me out of the day-to-day creative wars, for the men who *said* they would be reporting to me might easily resent my interference in their operations. After all, we had been competitors. It also occurred to me that Warners had good reason just to get me *out* of Columbia Records. Industry competition was localizing between Warners and Columbia. A million dollars spent to get me off their back was cheap compared to the artists they might lose in our bargaining wars.

I took the offer to Jack Schneider: another confrontation. Previously, I had tried to work through Goddard Lieberson. He was always sympathetic, saying "Get it if you can," but *he* couldn't help. He just couldn't get anywhere with the corporate people. This time he was in Japan, and so I talked to Schneider directly. I told him that I'd had several offers before this and hadn't mentioned them. But this time Columbia should make a competitive move. "I don't expect you to match Warners' offer," I said, "but I *do* expect you to make a substantial change in my compensation. And I need your answer within ten days."

They had several powwows and finally offered me an additional twenty-five thousand dollars. To sweeten the deal, they added an option of another ten thousand shares of stock. This was nowhere near Warners' offer, but it was an improvement. More important, I was happy at Columbia. I was proud of my accomplishments there, and the company was now built to some extent in my image, staffed by people I had hired and promoting artists

I had signed. It was also possible to keep CBS's corporate austerity at a distance by immersing myself in Columbia's looser, happier life-style. We were, after all, the "fringe" group, and I liked it there. I really didn't want to leave.

Yet, even after talking with Schneider, there was trouble. The stock option was promised—but it didn't materialize. Paley and Stanton had made the offer at a time when they expected a general stock option to become available shortly. Then they changed their thinking and they decided not to grant any stock options to executives. Still, they had promised one specifically to me, and I kept reminding them of it. I'd turned down a giant offer from a major competitor. Finally they admitted that they had a moral obligation to follow through.

It took them two years to find a way.

At the time we'd begun talking, CBS stock was selling at about twenty-five dollars a share. Not long after that it went up to forty-five and later above fifty. Stanton kept saying that he recognized the company's moral obligation—but he couldn't find a way to settle it that would make it a capital gains transaction. I finally said, "Look, give me two hundred and fifty thousand dollars in cash"—the difference between the option price when they first proposed it and the then current price—"and I'll take it as ordinary income and pay taxes." By this time it was 1972; I was afraid I'd never see the money at all.

One more twist. Since a "gift" of two hundred and fifty thousand dollars would be difficult to explain to the stockholders —I'd become a Director of CBS by this time and the money would have to be reflected in the proxy statement—they wanted me to sign an employment contract. I didn't like this; it seemed almost insulting to do this after I'd turned down literally millions of dollars in competitive offers. But I was told that CBS needed a quid pro quo to show the board why they were spending the money. I had no intention of leaving the company so I signed it, reluctantly.

By now, the whole money question had become terribly irritating—it was like pulling teeth. It always irked me that my work was appreciated so much more *outside* of CBS. I knew that CBS's other divisions were not prospering. Except for television, the other operations were either making minimal contributions— or losing money. The purchase of Holt, Rinehart & Winston had occurred when book publishing was very profitable. CBS paid a tremendously high multiple of the earnings of the company to get it. Then the Government cut back Federal grants to education—and hurt the textbook business considerably. CBS's attempt to get into the audio-visual recording business had gone awry and they were about to get out. Their venture into Cinema Center Films had gone badly and they were about to dump that as well. Nor had the New York Yankees or Creative Playthings become profitable.

And so it was largely Columbia Records' performance that had kept CBS stock healthy. I couldn't even get a note of thanks from Paley and Stanton. Relationships within the corporation were far too cold; nothing seemed to warm them up. CBS had enormous pride in its television operation, and talked often of its news operation. Yet the record operation's unprecedented profits were taken in stride. But *inside* Columbia Records, there was a tremendous camaraderie and warmth—the kind of dedication that made almost everyone stay until eight or nine o'clock at night and some people willing even to sleep over to get a job done. It was sometimes called the "Camelot" era. The door was wide open for any bright, young, ambitious record man who loved music and wanted to make it his life's work.

Fortunately, when it came to operating business decisions, the corporation was thoroughly decentralized. I was very grateful for this. Once I had demonstrated my abilities in the creative field, there were no questions when I wanted a million dollars to sign Streisand or four million to sign Neil Diamond. You would get the capital you needed to compete—as long as you made money. And we made money.

After much anguish, an overhaul of personnel and economic benefits was finally made. McKinsey & Company, a management consultant firm, made a thorough study of company operations and managed to bring the increasingly severe problems to the attention of the corporate people. Thereafter, CBS did attempt—now that so many voices had been raised—to become responsive to our needs. An attractive incentive program was established and salary maximums were improved. I was able to pay my heads of A&R and Marketing at least fifty thousand dollars a year. Below that, I could now pay thirty to forty-five thousand to department heads in promotion, artist relations and advertising. Still, the fight to reach these levels during 1969, 1970 and 1971 was so painful, involving so much effort, that the "new awareness" could not erase the scars for a long time—if ever.

It's readily apparent now that American corporations have to become more progressive if they are to survive. Tomorrow's executives are emerging from the ranks of today's long-haired youth, and corporations are going to have to be more flexible to deal with them. Corporations *must* loosen up their bureaucracies, and they must allow for greater individuality within the ranks in order to retain the young people's loyalties. It's beginning to occur; it has to.

# 3

I had occasion at the end of 1970 to raise my own flag for corporate nonconformity. Goddard Lieberson called to say that he might be leaving the company shortly—CBS wanted me to move up the ladder now, and later take his job. This meant becoming Executive Vice-President of the CBS-Columbia group. Reporting to me would be the Domestic and International records divisions, the mail-order operation, the Musical Instruments Division and Cinema Center Films.

I didn't like it. It meant that I would have to appoint a new head of Columbia Records. None of the men under me was ready for the job; and, more to the point, I didn't *want* to give it up yet. I liked my work enormously, and I was making Columbia a lot of money. From both a personal and a business point of view, it made no sense to move me. And I flatly had no interest in taking another corporate job just to move up the ladder.

This raised a few eyebrows. Business executives rarely—if ever—turn *down* promotions, at CBS or anywhere else in the business world. Lieberson asked me to visit with Dr. Stanton, CBS's statesmanlike President, and explain my heresy.

Stanton's office was not an easy place in which to relax. It was extremely large and reeked with efficiency and cold beauty. Stanton has a tremendous eye for high-quality art—but the art is all abstract sculpture and paintings in cool colors: imposing but, in some ways, sterile.

Naturally, Stanton wanted to know why I was turning down the promotion. I thought the move would be a terrible mistake for the company, I said. I was signing artists worth millions of dollars. It would deprive the company of a major asset—and I was not at all interested in musical instruments or mail-order problems.

I added, however, that I wasn't anxious to have CBS appoint *another* Executive Vice-President under Lieberson. I suggested that they give him an administrative assistant of some kind if he needed help. Stanton listened to all this politely enough, no doubt concluding that I was no longer a candidate for the CBS Presidency. I was something of a maverick now.

But the fact was that I loved music. I didn't want to leave the creative wars, and I really had no aspirations to become President of CBS. Stanton was in his sixties and it was known that he would be retiring in a few years. But I was not interested in playing those corporate chart games.

The pressure to do something about the Lieberson group continued, however. There were just too many businesses in it. Finally, a few months later, the decision was made to split it up; Harvey Schein and I were asked to become Group Presidents. Harvey was given responsibility for Musical Instruments, Creative Playthings and the mail-order division. I became Group President of the Domestic and International records divisions. Lieberson was given the somewhat vague title of Corporation Senior Vice-President, and the unenviable task of presiding over the dissolution of Cinema Center Films.

Even after the reorganization, I was a thorny problem for the corporate chart people; I didn't think that I should replace myself as President of the Columbia Records Division. I did make Walter Yetnikoff, whom I'd originally brought in as Assistant General Attorney from the Rosenman firm and who was now a very able General Attorney, President of the International Division, and then refused to suggest a President for the Domestic Division.

The domestic job was the basic heart and blood of my use to the company; I had the increasingly burdensome responsibility of keeping up the dramatic growth pace and I wasn't going to take myself off the firing line for structural tidiness. For a Domestic President must have the power to sign artists; logically I should retain that. On the other hand, *if* I retained that *and* appointed a President, he'd have no balls. He'd have no power. The corporation finally agreed to let things stand, allowing me to be simultaneously a Group and a Division President. True to form, of course, they tried to avoid giving me a raise. I had a major promotion, a new title, additional millions of dollars of responsibility, a seat on the Board of Directors—but they didn't see any reason to pay me more money. Eventually, I got a ten-thousand-dollar increase, but only after I pressed the matter several more times.

With Janis Joplin at the party after she signed her contract, 1968.
*Photograph by Elliott Moss Landy*

With Lou Adler, at the time of the launching of Ode Records, 1967.

With Johnny Winter at Anti-Defamation League Luncheon, 1970.
*Clive Davis personal collection*

With Paul Simon and Miles Davis at Anti-Defamation League Luncheon, 1970. *Clive Davis personal collection*

Presenting Santana with their first gold album, 1970.

With Jann Wenner, 1971. *Photograph by Bruce Steinberg*

With Bill Graham at premiere of the movie on the Fillmore, 1972.
*Metropolitan Photo Service Inc.*

With Sly in California, 1972. *Photograph by Stephen Paley*

Being greeted by Tammy Wynette and George Jones for the
Nashville CMA Convention, 1972.
Nashville Banner *staff photo by Charles Warren*

With Judy Collins and Mrs. Woody Guthrie, 1972.
*Photograph © by David Gahr*

With Loudon Wainwright at his first performance
after signing with Columbia, 1972.
*Photograph by Bob Gruen*

With Ornette Coleman and Donovan at Ed Wynn Humanitarian
Award Dinner for me, 1972.
*Clive Davis personal collection*

Backstage with Liza Minnelli, Mac Davis and Andy Williams, after introducing Liza at NARM Convention, March 1973. *Emerson-Loew*

With Elton John and Bernie Taupin after Elton's Carnegie Hall appearance, November 1973. *Photograph by Bob Gruen*

With George Harrison and Richard Perry during Ahmanson Theatre Week, May 1973. *Emerson-Loew*

With John McLaughlin, 1973.
*Emerson-Loew*

With Bruce Springsteen at
The Bottom Line, 1974. *Photograph by Peter Cunningham*

Lauren, Douglas, Janet, Fred, and Mitchell.
*Photograph by Trudy Schlachter*

Al Hirschfeld drawing from
*The Margo Feiden Galleries, New York*

# Nine

## 1

It was the end of 1970 and suddenly—after three years of stunning success—a serious crisis loomed.

We'd hit everywhere. Profits more than doubled in 1968, doubled again the following year and rose dramatically again in 1970. Columbia's growth patterns were meteoric, almost topsy-turvy. Records had jumped from a tiny percentage of CBS's overall profits to about one-third of its Bottom Line. We were making hit records as fast as the charts could absorb them. I'd begun to feel finally that I could relax. We had breathing room, an unprecedented depth of artists to call upon who represented a broad diversity of musical tastes. I felt that I had time at last to rekindle my energy—perhaps even coast a little. Was I wrong!

Suddenly, in less than one year's time, all this threatened to become ashes. Janis Joplin died. Simon & Garfunkel announced that they were splitting up. Andy Williams, Johnny Cash and Jim Nabors *all* came off television at the same time in a bloodletting of variety shows. Blood, Sweat & Tears were threatening a breakup. Dylan was not prolific. Sly had a highly publicized drug problem.

For the time being, thanks to the continuing momentum of current releases and catalog sales, we were safe. But the crisis soon began to gather speed. I had an additional personal problem: my anxiety obviously could not be public, for Columbia's success, like any record company's, was based in part on aura and reputation—

the belief, true or not, that Columbia was the best. Not just the biggest, or richest, but also the company with the best pipeline to creativity, and the best ability to nurture it, promote it, merchandise it and publicize it; in all cases, to apply the highest standards of excellence. We were *the* company, an objective for artists, a standard of industry success. This reputation gave Columbia an enormous edge in negotiations that neither money nor persuasion could buy.

And now it was ominously threatened. Could I possibly replace the kind of volume produced during the previous three skyrocket years? To compound the problem, I knew that CBS had learned to count on major profits from Records. At corporate levels, no one really understood the mercurial nature of the record business; they understood only profit. Budget 10 to 15 percent growth for next year, they said—we are counting on you. CBS stock will be badly affected if you fail.

They simply didn't comprehend the fragile, boom-and-bust nature of the industry. The Cash, Williams and Nabors weekly television shows, for example, had been all-important. Williams was selling more than a million copies per release. Johnny Cash had sold a staggering six and a half million albums in 1969, more albums than any individual artist had ever sold in one year. Nabors had sold as high as eight hundred thousand copies per release and was a consistent best seller. But without the attention a weekly show focused on the host, I knew that Williams, without a hit single, would soon drop to sales of four to five hundred thousand albums per release; Cash would fall to three or four hundred thousand an album and Nabors might drop as low as seventy-five thousand copies per release. Quite a comedown! A different—but equally disastrous—principle could affect Simon & Garfunkel. *Bridge Over Troubled Water* had sold more than nine million copies worldwide. As individuals, Paul and Artie could not attract this kind of audience. In the United States they might sell one million copies of each release, a truly excellent sale but not the historic volume of their former days. And Sly was simply not producing albums at all. I heard stories that he was laying down hundreds of instrumental tracks in Southern California studios—without vocals. There was strong speculation that he would never sing again.

I estimated that serious P&L (Profit & Loss) trouble was a year away. The company's momentum could keep things afloat during that time. Yet I had to view the problem in a very cold light. In four years, Columbia profits had grown about 600 percent. Our share of market had been about 11 percent when I took over; now it was over 20 percent. We could continue signing and recording only new artists and carrying on as before . . . but I knew that this would *not* do the job.

For new artist breakthroughs were no longer generating the sales they once did. For example, we would soon be developing The Mahavishnu Orchestra, Loggins & Messina, and Dr. Hook & the Medicine Show. The sales of two new Mahavishnu albums might total 700,000 albums. Two Loggins & Messina albums might total 1 million, and Dr. Hook's first album might sell 250,000 copies. Fine. Except that the total sales of these three new acts, with five albums among them, was about 2 million. *Blood, Sweat & Tears' second album alone had sold 3.8 million copies.* This would just not replace the volume we'd been having. Our past success had become a tremendous albatross and now standard good fortune would fall considerably short.

Columbia's position and image were very much at stake. There is always backbiting in the business, there are always skeptics who are ready to ask what you've done *lately,* and I knew that Columbia's sales problems, should they arise, would be watched with great interest—if not drooling jaws—all over the industry. I felt the competition keenly. I knew that I had to roll up my sleeves and work harder than ever before, harder than I'd ever worked in my life. The problems seemed insurmountable. I became very intense, marshaled my closest aides—Walter Dean, Elliot Goldman and Kip Cohen—and embarked on the heaviest talent-raiding campaign ever conducted in the history of the music business.

# 2

Ultimately, the campaign brought a great deal of new energy and strength to Columbia—and screams of anguish from the rest of the industry. The list of "raided" artists became substantial. It hardly endeared me to my counterparts at other record companies. Beginning with Ten Years After in 1971, it included Neil

Diamond, Liza Minnelli, Mott the Hoople, Dave Mason, Earth, Wind & Fire, West, Bruce & Laing, Mark Almond, The Isley Brothers, Herbie Hancock and—one of the biggest catches of all— Pink Floyd. New artists—or artists yet to break—signed by us during this period included Loggins & Messina, The Mahavishnu Orchestra, Dr. Hook & the Medicine Show, New Riders of the Purple Sage, Aerosmith, Loudon Wainwright III, Bruce Springsteen, David Bromberg and Billy Joel. Through Gamble and Huff's brilliant productions on the Philadelphia International label, we also had success with Billy Paul, the O'Jays, MFSB, Harold Melvin & the Blue Notes, and The Intruders; we acquired Kris Kristofferson through a label deal with Monument Records, and Isaac Hayes and The Staple Singers under our national distribution arrangement with Stax Records. It all added up to a staggering array of talent for the company.

Several of the artists were English, a clear benefit of the corporate shuffling in 1971 which gave me responsibility for all foreign operations. Ten Years After, for example, was English. Alvin Lee, lead guitarist, had become a major star overnight following his appearance at Woodstock (and in the subsequent documentary film). As a performer, he had the ability to excite an audience quite apart from the quality of his music. I personally liked his musicianship though the critics gave him mixed reviews; even so, it didn't matter. He had a stage presence that suggested raw sexual energy, and he could whip an audience almost to a frenzy—as evidenced by the Woodstock crowd's reaction to him. The group came to my attention when Normand Kurtz, a New York attorney, called to say that success was not making Ten Years After happy at London Records. Chris Wright and Terry Ellis, the group's very astute managers—who also managed Jethro Tull and Procol Harum—wanted to know if I was interested in the group. I obviously *knew* of the group but, since I expected that a sizable advance would be asked, I said that I first wanted to check them out at an upcoming Madison Square Garden performance. The ticket arrangements were made quietly. A talent raid is considerably different from an audition. You go directly to your seat and you don't go backstage. I didn't want the London people to know that I was interested. Equally important, my appearance would make the group's availability a public issue; other companies then begin making offers.

Ten Years After had a very successful show that night. It was clear that they had a star's aura about them onstage and Alvin, in particular, brought the crowd to its feet several times. Critics might throw brickbats at them, but the group's appeal was solid and massive. Sometimes commercial judgments require you to forget about the critics, whose criteria for evaluating artists can be quite different from yours. Capitol Records, for example, has made millions on Grand Funk Railroad; the reviewers said they were terrible. Warners has done extremely well with Black Sabbath; the reviewers turned up their noses. I didn't have quite such a hard decision to make. Ten Years After might occasionally be flashy and guilty of excesses, but they were highly professional musically and, most important, they radiated that indefinable electricity. I decided to sign them—and it turned out to be the right decision. Their first Columbia album went gold; and after that they averaged several hundred thousand copies per album, giving the company a handsome profit.

# 3

Dave Mason was signed in 1972. Brian Rohan called me one day when I was in California to say that Dave wanted to leave Blue Thumb Records. Dave felt that Blue Thumb had materially breached its contract for financial reasons, and he was especially incensed at their threat to release an unfinished tape as an album. He planned to visit with two, perhaps three, record companies before signing a new contract.

As I always attempt to do when considering a deal, I went a few weeks later to see Dave perform at New York's Academy of Music to get a current appraisal of his situation musically. This is vital. You never know when an artist is changing direction—for the worse. But Dave was very impressive. His unique blend of intricate guitar work and stylized composition made him very exciting. He wasn't a superstar, but he was an important talent with a great deal of promise for the future.

In these situations when an artist comes around to talk, you usually spend two or three hours with him; little or nothing is planned ahead of time. You don't negotiate; you talk about music, or listen to the problems he may have had with his last company, or discuss what kind of things Columbia can do for him. It's understood that he'll be talking with other company presidents as well —basically you're sizing each other up and getting impressions of what the relationship will be like. During one visit to the company, Dave met John McLaughlin; our artists often roamed through the building just to keep in touch. And Dave was tremendously impressed by the chance to meet other artists like this and exchange ideas. After McLaughlin left he looked at me and said, "I've just got to be *here*. I really want to be with you on this label!"

I eventually signed him, though the signing involved some very unhappy exchanges with Paramount, which distributed Blue Thumb, including the threat of a lawsuit. When they finally released the tape that Dave had thought was a demonstration record, he got violently angry and told every concert audience of his to *avoid* it. He didn't want to be judged by what he considered an inferior product. Relations between him and Blue Thumb reached the absolute nadir and it was not helping either him or Blue Thumb. We finally worked out a settlement. Dave was free to record with Columbia, but Blue Thumb would get a lump-sum settlement plus an override on the first two albums.

# 4

Basically, talent raiding involves finding out who is available and then deciding whether you believe in the artist's future. It was clear, for example, that we could use some additional middle-of-the-road talent. To make room for some of our new rock acquisitions, we had earlier decided not to bid again for certain artists already on the roster. Most of these were middle of the road: Robert Goulet, Steve Lawrence and Eydie Gorme, Tony Bennett. We had room for a big new star and Liza Minnelli came to mind immediately. She was a brilliant, multimedia, bravura performer— but she hadn't broken big in records. Stevie Phillips, Liza's manager, told me that Liza's contract with A&M Records was about to expire. What was astonishing was that she didn't care about a guaranty—wonder of wonders! She was making all the money she needed from motion pictures and club appearances.

All we ask, said Stevie, is that you *guarantee* high-level chart success. If we don't have that success, we want to be able to get out!

Now, no one can guarantee that sort of thing, but it seemed obvious that Liza had the goods and we had the promotion and merchandising clout to make chart action reasonably predictable. We agreed to this kind of deal, and began getting the papers ready. Before they were signed, the movie *Cabaret* was released. It was an instant hit; Liza made the covers of *Time* and *Newsweek* simultaneously. She was suddenly the toast of show business —which usually means that prices go up. But Stevie held with the original agreement. We want success with you, that's all, she said, and the contract was signed.

It remained only to find the best repertoire for her. Liza and I met one day in my office and she asked my thoughts about this. I felt that she was doing too much specialty material. She needed to branch out, to acquire more of a contemporary image. It would be wrong to go too *far* in this direction, for she had to bridge the gap between middle-of-the-road and contemporary audiences. But I thought that for recording she had to get away from total dependence on Broadway and theatrical material.

She agreed to this, and seemed very happy to have a direction to follow rather than releasing records on a hit-or-miss basis. As it happened, we really lucked into the first album we released, *Liza With a Z,* the soundtrack album of her acclaimed television special. It was an immediate hit, climbing quickly into the charts' Top Twenty albums and selling more than three hundred thousand copies. Her follow-up album of contemporary songs also sold well. Liza was now a recording star and she was delighted.

Talent raiding isn't as brutal as it may seem. You rarely *steal* artists; they usually shop at two or three companies when they are unhappy with their current label. Money is most often not a factor. Invariably the artist believes that he is not selling as well as he should or is not as big a star as he should be—he's not being advertised or promoted enough. I got calls constantly: Connie Francis is available; Sammy Davis, Jr., is free; you can have Diahann Carroll; The Four Seasons are looking. The trick is to know whom to pursue—whose future is ahead of them rather than behind them. A creative evaluation is necessary, and poor judgments can be very expensive.

Tony De Fries, then manager of Mott the Hoople, called in early 1972 and said that the group was coming off its contract with

Atlantic. They were selling only fifty to seventy thousand albums per release and wanted to change labels. Tony had a demo of a song from an album the group was recording. It was produced by David Bowie, the big rage of London. The song was "All the Young Dudes" and it was great. It had style, a sense of identity and the performance and production were first-rate. The group had never really broken in this country, but with Bowie producing their album, and with material like this, I felt they could make it. So I acquired still another English group. "All the Young Dudes" came out as the group's first single and it immediately launched them bigger than they had ever been. Now they are headliners selling several hundred thousand albums a release. They have a magnetic presence both onstage and in their music that can make them one of the world's top groups.

Earth, Wind & Fire, a progressive rock group, was under contract to Warner Bros. Their signing involved slightly more skulduggery than usual. The group's producer, Joe Wissert, called. He and the group's managers, Bob Cavallo and Joe Ruffalo, thought that Warners didn't understand where the group was going musically. They were black but they didn't play straight rhythm and blues material. They needed to be helped to find their own special category, and they didn't feel that they could get this help at Warners. A great review in *The New York Times* of the group's appearance with John Sebastian at Philharmonic Hall earlier in the year had piqued my curiosity. I agreed to see them.

The audition was arranged secretly. If word ever got out that I was seeing a group, the current label invariably made it very difficult for them to leave; so we met at a small, hot studio in Los Angeles. As soon as they started to play, I was knocked out. They were all good musicians. Maurice White, the leader, came out of a strong jazz background and had high standards. They also understood the importance of sex appeal and showmanship; their movements onstage practically choreographed a story by itself. I felt that their music would cross all the artificial barriers, appealing to blacks and whites equally. I was suffocating from the heat but I wouldn't leave. It was worth the trouble.

We bought the group's contract from Warners and also got their first album for about a total of one hundred thousand dollars. From the beginning we tried to capture both the black market and the progressive FM audiences. The promotional campaign worked. They had had two albums out on Warners averaging about eighty thousand in sales. Their first Columbia album did in excess of three hundred thousand; the second was certified gold and sold over six hundred and fifty thousand copies and their third was certified gold shortly after its release in early 1974. Earth, Wind & Fire is now a major group.

# 5

As a group, Lesley West, Jack Bruce and Corky Laing never achieved superstardom, but their signing was hotly contested; and the battle showed record-industry competition at its fiercest. West is one of the finest guitar players in music, first gaining fame with the group Mountain. Bruce is one of the world's ranking bass players, though he remained somewhat in the shadow of guitarist Eric Clapton during his days with Cream. And Laing is a fine drummer, also beginning with Mountain. Now that Mountain and Cream were split up, it made a great deal of sense for them to join forces. In fact, their tour across America was booked and sold out on the strength of their names without their having recorded an album together. There was a great deal of excitement about the group; the bidding soon narrowed down to Columbia and Atlantic.

Bud Prager, who represented West from his Mountain days, called me one day to suggest a meeting to discuss a contract. The terms he proposed at the meeting were fair and I accepted on the spot. The problem was that Prager had to get the consent of Robert Stigwood, who represented Jack Bruce. Stigwood was the very successful producer of *Jesus Christ Superstar* and the well-known manager of Cream and The Bee Gees; he was both a personal and business friend of Ahmet Ertegun, their relationship going back to the days when Atlantic distributed Cream in the United States.

Ertegun, meanwhile, was making a spectacular pitch for the group. He visited them backstage during a Los Angeles gig and suggested a trip to Las Vegas on the Warners company plane to see Elvis Presley. They readily accepted, and for the occasion he rented them an entire penthouse floor at Caesar's Palace. The company plane took the group back to Los Angeles, and then took Prager across country to New York. Wow—this was old-time-movie spending and I was flabbergasted! All I had done was lend a phonograph to Lesley for his country home and send him some of the newer Columbia classical releases.

But despite the substantial pressures Prager was getting from Atlantic, he wanted to stick with our deal. Stigwood finally called me from London to set up a New York meeting. We had lunch a few days later, and he was extremely friendly, saying that his ties with Ertegun would not interfere with his business judgment. He knew that both West and Bruce wanted to go to Columbia, and as far as he was concerned the deal was 99 percent closed . . . except for clearing up some problems of foreign rights.

That last 1 percent worried me. Stigwood went directly to California and had a series of meetings with Ertegun. I soon heard that they were plotting to set up an independent label through Atlantic for Stigwood, and The Bee Gees *and* West, Bruce & Laing would be on it. From there he returned to England. It looked bad. Clearly Atlantic would prefer to make a label deal with Stigwood rather than lose West, Bruce & Laing altogether.

Fortunately, Bud Prager was steadfast and was the entrée to West and Laing. He called to say that the group would be making its first New York appearance that spring. He planned to host a party at his home; considering all the attention Ertegun had paid to them, he thought that I should be there—no other record executive would be.

I agreed to come. But I was also scheduled to preside at the Record Industry Association of America's annual Washington, D.C., dinner that night. This was an extremely important public relations occasion, attended heavily by senators and congressmen; I was Chairman of the Board of the Association. I could hardly miss the event.

Still, I wanted to meet with the group. The result was an evening possible only in the jet age. I went to Washington for the predinner cocktail party and the dinner; then I made a speech and gave out the Association's annual cultural award to Congressman John Brademas of Indiana. As soon as the spotlight focused on Brademas, I walked quickly to the back of the hall and into a waiting limousine, which took me to the New York shuttle plane. At La Guardia airport I was met by another limousine and driven to Bud Prager's home on Manhattan's Central Park West.

It worked beautifully. A few people at the party wondered

why I wore a tuxedo—but this also made my extra effort obvious, for it soon became known that I had to be back in Washington the next morning for a 9:00 A.M. board meeting—another limousine and shuttle routine. Shortly after that, Prager flew to London and took the firm position that he and Lesley wanted to go with Columbia or there'd be no group; it was finally settled.

West, Bruce & Laing have had no runaway success, though they have had important sales and chart albums. The group was a guaranteed sellout in its major city appearances, but they never developed the musical rapport needed for continued recording successes. They then split up, and the original group, Mountain, re-formed for a comeback, this time on Columbia. At any rate, the chase was fun, and Columbia certainly didn't *lose* any money.

**6**

Frequently I am asked in interviews what the new sound in music will be. I can never answer that question; industry executives don't determine that, artists do. That, of course, is the point of creative genius—to initiate trend-setting music. But as an executive I could appraise musical *direction,* and that I watched closely. In 1971 two areas impressed me with their growth potential—one involved the fusion of jazz with rock, the other was the explosive crossover potential of black music.

After John McLaughlin formed the tremendously successful Mahavishnu Orchestra, other progressive musicians began approaching us. I became interested, for example, in an exceptional group of jazz artists called Weather Report. Like McLaughlin, they wanted to fuse contemporary progressive music with more traditional forms. Several members of the group were consistently on top of the polls in *Downbeat* magazine, the jazz bible. Their verbal descriptions of what they wanted to do musically were exciting; I didn't have to hear them play. These were brilliant names—Joe Zawinul, Wayne Shorter, Miroslav Vitous—and they represented quality and virtuosity to me. It was enough to know that they were moving in the right direction. They asked me at one point to write the liner notes for their album. I had done this only once before for an artist—Tony Bennett—but I felt so good about the project that I did it for them. This, in turn, was seen by Jon Mark and Johnny Almond of the group Mark Almond, which was under contract to Blue Thumb but also unhappy. Jon came to New York and called me at the building on Washington's Birthday, 1972, to say that he wanted to come to Columbia; he was so impressed that I would have the interest and take the time to write liner notes for a brilliant *progressive* album that he didn't want to negotiate anywhere else.

Another artist who had long interested me was Herbie Hancock. Despite his years of experience, Herbie was still young, good-looking and charismatic, and he was valiantly attempting to take his audiences to new musical frontiers. His commercial success to this time was only modest, but as 1973 approached I believed that time and the direction music was now taking would be more and more on his side. David Rubinson, formerly a Columbia A&R man and now a well-regarded participant in the San Francisco music scene, was interested in his career, and that bode well. I also believed that something was really happening with black artists from a progressive music background who were exploring contemporary music. We concluded negotiations with Brian Rohan and signed Herbie. And his record career really proceeded to take off. His second Columbia album reached the Top Twenty of best-selling *pop* albums in the spring of 1974, selling several times the highest amount he had ever achieved before.

# 7

Around this time I also noticed that the entire market for black music was shifting. *Billboard* lists the Top Two Hundred albums each week, and as I read this and other trade papers, I noticed that more and more of the top-selling albums featured rhythm and blues music. There suddenly seemed to be a greater receptivity to R&B crossovers. The *Shaft* album was the first really dramatic example of these market changes. But Diana Ross and The Supremes also had best-selling albums now; before, they had sold mostly singles. The Temptations' albums also were moving into the Top Twenty, and Curtis Mayfield of *Superfly* fame was hitting strongly. I asked for some market research on this, and it became clear that black audiences—mostly singles consumers until now—were buying more and more albums. This was also a time when Hollywood was discovering audiences in the inner cities. Most important, the trend seemed to be involving the white audiences as well; they were more inclined to get into rhythm and blues music and black themes. Until now, the area had been dominated by Atlantic, Motown and Stax Records; Columbia had barely scratched the surface.

Black music was an obvious extension of our talent search. We were not really equipped, however, to jump right into it. I'd largely ignored the market during my early years, primarily because of its emphasis on singles. During Columbia's history, it had had a few black A&R men—Clyde Otis, Tom Wilson, Billy Jackson and Esmond Edwards—but very few successful black records had emerged. The company's black performers at that time—Johnny Mathis, Mahalia Jackson, O.C. Smith, Ronnie Dyson—had appealed equally to white audiences, if not even more so. Sly Stone was an exception; his singles always jumped to the top of the R&B charts, but he was selling across the board too.

It became clear that we couldn't get into the rhythm and blues field by ourselves. Our promotion staff didn't know the territory. Black radio was also becoming increasingly militant; black program directors were refusing to *see* white promotion men. I met with my promotion staffs at our regional conventions and asked this very question. Can you effectively relate to rhythm and blues stations? They always said yes. But I kept asking them: Shouldn't we at least hire black men to deal with R&B stations regionally? They said it wasn't necessary. I didn't think they were being candid with me—or at least honest with themselves. Promotion men by nature do not like to admit defeat. They *always* feel they can do a job better than anyone else . . . which is nice, unless you happen to be dead wrong. And I felt that they were.

I finally asked Ron Alexenburg and Steve Popovich, Columbia's crackerjack top promotion men, to hire some new men to deal regionally with R&B stations. If we were going to get into black music, it was obvious that we had to have black promotion men. Promotion men take records to the radio stations; they must develop relationships with program directors. If a record is ripe to be added to the black station's play list, but is not quite a sure thing, it is ridiculous to have a white man trying to convince the program director to put it on.

The next problem was that of signing artists. I encouraged the in-company A&R men who happened to be black—Billy Jackson and Esmond Edwards at the time—to start looking. With a difference: we didn't want just hit singles. I felt that Columbia could best stay on top of the industry by building durable careers rather than just seeking out hits. If you are going to release a hit single, why not launch a career rather than just settle for a novelty hit?

But not much happened. It became clear to me that we needed outside help. It was about this time that Kenny Gamble and Leon Huff called. They were producing records in Philadelphia under an exclusive contract with GRT Records; they were easily one of the country's most successful black producing teams. We met and talked, and they said that they were unhappy with their GRT deal. They had signed originally when GRT—among other tape companies—had had a great deal of money to spend. But even with that money they still hadn't built successful artists, and the latter was far more important to them.

We began talking immediately about building careers. Earlier, they had made plenty of *single* hits but had never really produced artists with album appeal. They wanted this badly, and they also wanted the kind of merchandising and promotional efforts that could build careers for their people. So we agreed to sign; they managed to get out of the GRT contract relatively quickly— probably by buying themselves out of it—and we closed a deal with a seventy-five-thousand-dollar budget for fifteen singles and a smaller number of albums at twenty-five thousand dollars each. By every yardstick of independent producing deals, this was modest. But from Gamble and Huff's viewpoint, money mattered considerably less at the time than the chance to be associated with a quality record operation which would give maximum exposure to their productions. Not long after the signing, Gamble and Huff exploded. Within nine months, they sold ten million single records: Billy Paul, Harold Melvin & the Blue Notes, and The O'Jays all hit with Number-One R&B records that went straight to the top of the pop charts as well. The artists had substantial album sales as well. *Me and Mrs. Jones* led to a gold album for Billy Paul; albums for Harold Melvin and MFSB did very well, and The O'Jays sold seven hundred and fifty thousand albums off their "Backstabber" and "Love Train" hits.

Then I got a call from Al Bell of Stax. He was in New York

and called to set up a dinner date. His company, based in Memphis, was doing extremely well with such artists as Isaac Hayes, The Staple Singers, Luther Ingram and Johnny Taylor. But he had seen how well Gamble and Huff's Philadelphia International label was doing with Columbia; he wanted to make a deal.

Al's problem, despite creative success, was cash flow. He had established an independent distribution system, but the distributors were giving him serious credit and collection problems. Nor did they give him the exposure in retail stores that he wanted. He was spending too much time worrying about sales and distribution when he wanted only to be in the studio with the artists.

He asked whether Columbia would be interested in acquiring 50 percent of the company. I explored this with Columbia's lawyers, but they saw antitrust problems. We made a national distribution deal instead. Stax would continue to do its own creative work; also promotion and advertising. But they would use Columbia's sales and distribution forces. We would sell their records to Sam Goody or rack jobbers—or whatever—and handle the credit and collection problems ourselves, an impressive addition to our salesmen's line!

I had benefited from an important lesson learned years earlier. An artist can be extremely gifted and yet remain unsuccessful if he or she records the wrong music, or gets an image that confuses potential audiences. The best example of this was Columbia's painful inability to break Aretha Franklin. Aretha had been signed by John Hammond in about 1960 and then produced by him—and a whole series of A&R men—without success. She was recorded by both black and white producers; everyone knew she was a brilliant talent. But nothing much happened. She was very young then and needed professional guidance; yet no one found the right songs for her. She had a hit, for example, with the old Al Jolson-Judy Garland song "Rockabye Your Baby," strange as it may seem.

It was most embarrassing, then, when she went to Atlantic and became an absolute giant. Jerry Wexler took her right into the church. He established a milieu based in gospel that used songs with infectious, driving melodic hooks—and she was indelibly stamped as one of the all-time greats. Columbia at that time simply didn't have the A&R intuitive feel to capitalize on Aretha's talent. Though I was a corporate attorney when she recorded for Columbia, the lesson greatly affected my thinking when I wanted to sign black artists and producers like Gamble and Huff. Who would the producer be? What kind of material would be used? I used this sort of thinking in signing The Isley Brothers in 1973. They were self-contained, producing themselves, and were right in the forefront of black music's excitement. They hit the top of the charts with a gold single and a gold album almost as soon as the contract ink was dry.

Back to raiding—and one very big coup. Toward the end of 1971 and during 1972 I kept hearing great word of mouth about Pink Floyd. Kip Cohen knew the group's manager, Steve O'Rourke, and he arranged for O'Rourke to meet with the two of us. Once again, it was a case of a group being unhappy—this time on Capitol. They were not selling what they thought they should. Their concerts were sellouts; their record sales didn't reflect it. O'Rourke met with Kip and me a few times to get a feel for our outlook. Then he attended our weekly singles meeting to see the company in operation. It worked like a charm. Columbia was what he wanted and he agreed to come to terms right then.

It was the end of 1972: the contract would take effect at the beginning of 1974, and the group wanted about two hundred and fifty thousand dollars advanced on signing.

It was a big decision, for the time lag and the advance up front were considerable. Most of my business advisors were against it. They hadn't heard that much about the group and they felt this was a dangerous precedent. But here is where creative judgment comes in. Pink Floyd was a progressive music group of the highest quality, which also could have Top Forty hits—a very rare combination. When that clicks, you get sales of the Jethro Tull variety—well into seven figures. I considered that the downside risk was small and the upside potential great. If I waited any longer Capitol would know that something was up and they would start bidding competitively, so I followed my instincts and we signed them. With their very next Capitol album, Pink Floyd became one of the world's biggest groups. The *Dark Side of the Moon* album sold over two million copies and stayed around the top of the best-selling album charts well into 1974. This was a giant acquisition.

It all sounds, I realize, like an unbroken record of phenomenal successes and acquisitions—similar to what had happened right after Monterey. Well, it was—and it would be foolish to be coy about it. One can't assume, however, that it is all so simple. *Every* company is looking for major artists, and well over a dozen have millions of dollars to spend for them. They go about this in different ways. When tape companies like Ampex and International Tape tried to get into records they invariably went the producer route. They made million-dollar deals with independent producers who they thought would bring them top artists. They lost every penny they invested. It's one thing to be a producer-arranger trying to make a hit record—and it's another to be an entrepreneurial talent scout. These are two separate and distinct abilities, as the tape companies sadly learned.

On the other hand, the actual bidding for artists can be expensive; the stakes are high. RCA lost a fortune when it paid over a million dollars for Paul Anka *after* he had peaked. The company also paid too much money several years later for Jack Jones, Mama Cass Elliot, and then for The Kinks and Wilson Pickett. MGM lost its money on its Righteous Brothers acquisition and also on its deal for Steve Lawrence and Eydie Gorme. These companies didn't have other good acquisitions to make up for the bad, and got hurt. Warners, in contrast, did extremely well by luring The Allman Brothers Band (although it was from its sister label, Atlantic) onto its roster, and it won a hard-fought victory over us for Seals and Crofts, which paid off very handsomely for them. This more than offset their current loss on Tony Joe White, who ironically was another victory for Warners over us in the negotiating wars.

We also got hurt on two acquisition deals: The Rascals and Delaney & Bonnie. The Rascals were one of the best groups ever to come out of New York. Their string of hits was one of the biggest in rock history. I agreed to pay them two hundred thousand dollars an album, but right after the signing, a key member, Eddie Brigatti, left the group. He and Felix Cavaliere had been the group's leaders and we were only protected if more than two members left, or if Felix departed. So we had to record them without Brigatti. They did only two albums for Columbia, averaging sales of about one hundred thousand copies each, and then they broke up. So the loss was about a hundred thousand dollars per album. History repeated itself with Delaney & Bonnie. We bought their contract from Atlantic when they were already a major act and arranged a seven-year artist deal for six hundred thousand dollars. The annual cost of eighty thousand dollars looked good. But after only a few months they split up—both maritally and onstage. They gave Columbia only one album each, and were dropped. The company never got a real shot at what they could do together.

# 8

Last we come to the artist who most symbolized talent raiding's rewards and problems: Neil Diamond. Neil was one of my earliest signings during this phase, following closely on the Ten Years After agreement. His contract wasn't scheduled to take effect until 1973, but the images of money and power which accompanied the 1971 negotiations blew the deal all out of proportion. I paid four hundred thousand dollars an album for Neil for ten albums—exactly what Warner Bros. offered him, and not very different from what they paid to Dionne Warwicke. It was more than a million dollars *less* than Atlantic paid for The Rolling Stones, and at a much lower royalty. And it wasn't I who went to Neil; he contacted me through his attorney, David Braun.

I had been thinking that soon we would have to find a candidate to replace the sales volume Andy Williams had been generating; an artist who could appeal to a broad spectrum of fans, yet one who leaned toward contemporary music. Diamond fit the bill. Neil was beginning then to emerge from a Top Forty image. He'd had a long succession of single hits, but now he was acquiring a reputation as a performer and writer. When Braun called to say that Neil had about eighteen months to go on his MCA contract, I was very receptive. Here was someone who could very well emerge as a giant talent, a Presley or Streisand, a "superstar."

The image, obviously, was not lost on Neil. He felt that he showed enough promise to ask the kind of money that would ensure his future. Like Johnny Winter, he planned to negotiate with a limited number of companies: Columbia, Warners and MCA.

This actually was my second shot at Neil. I'd negotiated a contract with him five years earlier when he was leaving Bang Records. Columbia had concluded a deal with his manager, Fred Weintraub, who at the time was a part-owner of The Bitter End nightclub. When I thought that the deal was closed, I sent Neil a telegram saying how delighted I was to have him joining Columbia and how I looked forward to working with him. Nothing was signed. Then he went to the West Coast and signed a reported two-hundred-and-fifty-thousand-dollar deal with MCA, including an offer to make a motion picture. I was very upset. Weintraub and I had shaken hands; I didn't think it was fair to take another offer—even if the money *was* greater. I was so angry that I threatened that no Columbia artist would play The Bitter End for a long time. When I simmered down I didn't try to enforce this, however.

During those early meetings, I was quite impressed by Neil's grasp of the business. He knew about music, he also knew how record companies worked. If his voice ever fails, he could easily become a successful record executive. But he was also supremely confident in his talent; no question in his mind that he would become a great star.

My anger over the MCA deal subsided in good time, and I found myself inadvertently following his career. In 1970, I saw him perform at a NARM rack-jobber convention. It was clear that his talent was growing. He took absolute command of the stage. The performance was powerful. I asked one of my aides to go backstage and say hello—and Neil in turn asked if I would like to come back myself. We were not personal friends, but the greeting and a few minutes of conversation served easily to break the ice for the future. I said that I hoped our paths would cross soon again; it may have been one reason why Columbia came into the picture when Neil was shopping around.

This time, Neil didn't want extended negotiations. He wanted everything settled in a few weeks. He wanted all three offers at once, so that he could make his decision quickly—an unprecedented move in the record business. Contract negotiations often take from six months to a year, or longer.

I submitted an offer roughly equal to Warners' earlier bid for Donovan (which I hadn't yet matched): about two and a half million dollars, or two hundred and fifty thousand dollars an album for ten albums. I thought that the offer was solid and respectable; it was the highest one I'd ever made. A week went by, and David Braun called. He had Warners' offer—it was four hundred thousand dollars an album, a total package of four million dollars! After a moment of silence, Braun added: "Neil personally likes you very much, and he likes Columbia. MCA has not made an offer, but Neil isn't going to wait. Money is money, and he feels that he shouldn't have to take any less from Columbia than from another company. He knows that you have the resources to match Warners, and if you won't, he'll view it as a lack of faith in him as a recording artist."

I thought quickly about this, and I answered Braun on the spot. We'd match the Warners offer, dollar for dollar, penny for penny, I said. Let Neil make his decision with absolutely no dollar differences between Warners and Columbia. A few days later, Braun called to say that Neil had chosen Columbia. I felt great.

# 9

The Diamond deal brought into the open a lot of questions about big money and the industry's increasingly "Big Business" image. I've always felt unjustly pilloried in this area. I backed off from many deals with unreasonable price tags—Tony Joe White and Dionne Warwicke, for example, both of whom went to Warners. With Dionne, I didn't even enter the bidding; she is a fabulous artist but the deal seemed too big a risk. And a year earlier, The Rolling Stones also made an approach, right in the middle of their intensive negotiations with Ahmet Ertegun.

I knew that Ahmet was spending a great deal of time with Mick Jagger, flying back and forth to London and wining and dining the group at length. When their business manager, Prince Rupert Loewenstein, called to say that the Stones were interested in hearing from Columbia, I picked up the phone and called Jagger in London. He came to the phone immediately. I said that my style was different from Ahmet's. I traveled sometimes, but I couldn't spend a lot of time socializing with him. Nonetheless, would he consider Columbia? Mick was very direct. This is business, he said; the decision will not be based on social considerations. I'm told Columbia is the best company in the business, and I know of your reputation. Please bid. I feel very good about the possibility of coming with Columbia.

I was delighted. I made a short pitch on the phone, talking mostly about our merchandising and promotion capabilities—since the Stones' creative worth was obvious—and he suggested that I speak with Prince Rupert about the money deal. This was about a year before the Neil Diamond deal.

Prince Rupert was equally direct—the Stones wanted between five and six million dollars. They wanted a staggering royalty rate as well. I had to think. With The Beatles going separate ways, The Rolling Stones were likely to become the most important rock group in the world. But I also knew that they hadn't been selling up to their prestige. Their most dramatic appeal was onstage. They were selling seven hundred fifty thousand to a million units per release—less than half the sales of Chicago, or Santana or, earlier, Blood, Sweat & Tears, and nowhere near Simon & Garfunkel. The money precedent was just too risky. What would I pay Chicago when they came to renew—or Santana?

One's image is a key factor in stories involving big money. Ertegun, with the help of his tape and foreign licensees, met the Stones' unprecedented price; the money publicity caused hardly a ripple. Joe Smith and Mo Ostin of Warners were spending as much money as Columbia, if not more; yet their "Big Spender" image was somehow diffused, perhaps because two faces were involved. Ahmet Ertegun shared the limelight at Atlantic with Jerry Wexler. RCA and Capitol *always* seemed to be willing to outspend Columbia, but many artists didn't want to go to them, money notwithstanding. MGM, as I've noted, had offered a substantial amount of money for Bob Dylan several years earlier. I was hardly the record industry's only money mogul—but I always seemed to get that kind of attention when I made a deal. It used to bother me a lot, but there was nothing I could do about it.

For one thing, the concentrated talent-raiding campaign meant that Columbia was always involved. And I was always there. I had no partner, no alter ego for this purpose. We had a terrific organization and many exceptional people, but when it came to closing the deal, the artist or manager demanded my presence and my involvement. They got it; I became a Big Spender.

Ironically, for all the artists mentioned in this chapter, there were only a few "million dollar" deals made. Ten Years After, Neil Diamond and Pink Floyd. These three deals will stand the test of time. The others were within every company's grasp. But we were right there, at the right time and with the right image.

One important point: talent raiding—and the enormous success we enjoyed from it—never altered my original feeling that a record company's prime function was finding talent. My career spanned far more fresh signings than "raids," and in this I take pride. Not that a raid doesn't require as much creative judgment; it does, and the stakes are higher. But the thrill of discovering and launching a Joplin or a Santana or a Winter is unforgettable and just can't be duplicated by anything else.

# 10

Except for press speculation about the money involved, my experiences with Neil Diamond were always very gratifying. Our contract was kept secret for nearly a year to avoid embarrassing MCA—but even the secret signing was memorable.

Neil wanted to have a joint signing on the West Coast. When the time came, his then manager, Ken Fritz, said that Neil was at a recording studio in Los Angeles. The papers were there, and he asked if Elliot Goldman and I would drop by. When we arrived, Neil, his wife Marcia, his producer Tom Catalano, and David Braun were in the control room listening to the latest album he was recording for MCA. We listened to several songs and they sounded great. For Neil has an emotional urgency in his voice that, coupled with his enormous writing talent, makes his songs very compelling.

When the songs ended, he suggested that we go into the studio itself, which was dark. When the lights flicked on, I was shocked to see a small mid-Victorian stage setting: an antique desk and chair, quill pens and antique lamps. Neil and Marcia had obviously gone to great lengths to convey the special significance of the occasion. It was a beautiful moment. A lot of money was involved—but also a vitally growing career. It felt awfully good taking that quill pen in hand.

Neil and I also became good friends. Somewhere within our Brooklyn backgrounds, the fact that our wives had both recently given birth, and love of music itself, we found it very easy to spend time together. When he came to New York, or if I went to Los Angeles, we often got together—once in Los Angeles we went to a health food store he liked and ate sandwiches and soda in a parked car while talking for hours about music and his career

. . . hardly a typical executive and star relationship. He talked often about classical music, how he would like to try writing in that medium, or perhaps scoring motion pictures or Broadway musicals. But he was also keenly aware of his strengths in the contemporary area. Hit records had gotten him this far; he had no intention of forgetting them. I was glad about this. It's fine— and almost necessary—for a creative artist to stretch out from time to time to explore the extent of his talent, but it's prudent always to remember his roots.

Neil made an extraordinary appearance in the fall of 1972 at New York's Winter Garden Theatre, booking it for two weeks and selling out completely as a one-man show. The performance was stunning. The lighting and stage effects created dramatic tension, and his rapport with the audience was awesome. The rock group behind him was excellent and the stage had steps ascending to the ceiling with performers and musicians sitting on various levels. I was overwhelmed by the show. It confirmed my feeling that those skeptics who had questioned my acumen in signing him a year and a half before the end of his contract would be proven wrong. The show got excellent reviews—except for one. *Rolling Stone*. And the way the review was written enraged me. The critic called the performance hokey, saying that it was over-staged and badly done. I can't take issue with a reviewer's opinion; but this one seemed on a vendetta because he went on to say that the house hadn't sold out (which it had), that it had had to be "papered" (wrong again—tickets were being scalped) and that Neil was paunchy, which he clearly isn't. Even though Neil was still under contract to MCA, I wrote to *Rolling Stone* to set the record straight. The letter was printed without comment. I later learned that Neil had refused to give Jon Landau, the reviewer, an interview before the opening night show. He'd given a few to other reporters, so Landau, presumably, had a grudge—his reporting on other occasions has been incisive and accurate.

Neil's interests do not stop with music. He has worked as a drug-clinic counselor and given his time and money to countless charities. His opening night concert at the Winter Garden, for example, was a charity benefit sponsored and attended by the Kennedy family. During the same engagement, Janet and I accompanied him and Marcia to a McGovern-Shriver benefit at the Shriver estate outside Washington, D.C. Ethel Kennedy sent the family plane to pick us up in New York, and then met us at the Washington airport in her car for a rather fast-paced ride to the grounds, which were open to thousands of McGovern fans that day for a picnic at ten dollars per person, with Neil's performance as a bonus. It was a warm, wonderful afternoon. At one point Neil asked Janet, who has sung opera professionally, to join him onstage and play the maracas: quite a sight, indeed. We also lunched privately with the Kennedy family before Neil's performance, and Eunice Shriver provided a tour of the Kennedy memorabilia inside the home.

Neil and I frequently talked after that about his future plans. He became involved in the *Jonathan Livingston Seagull* movie and asked me to meet director Hall Bartlett so that I might share his excitement. I was skeptical. This was to be his first Columbia album—and a soundtrack album's success has always depended on the quality of the movie. I couldn't help but think that my reputation was also squarely on the line in this deal; I felt very vulnerable because of the publicity over the signing. But Neil was reassuring, saying that he was going to write at least one solid hit and an album score that would hold up independently of the movie. Because of the book's massive sales, he saw the album as an enormous opportunity.

Bartlett screened about twenty minutes of silent footage for me, and I had to agree that the photography was truly beautiful. Neil wanted my enthusiastic backing and he got it.

What happened next was incredible. Despite massive advertising and promotion campaigns, the movie totally bombed. It got terrible reviews (nearly all the critics—except, enigmatically, *The New York Times*—panned it), and author Richard Bach's lawsuit to stop its showing until it conformed more closely to his book provided the finishing touch. Yet Neil's album went straight to the top of the charts—*without* a hit single. Precedent should have dictated exactly the opposite; but within three months the album's sales approached over one million copies. It was certainly a testimony to Neil's talents—and appeal—as an artist and performer.

The business world can be exciting, but the real drama of music lies in dealing with artists. One of my major regrets at leaving Columbia is that I can no longer be directly associated with Neil Diamond's career.

# Ten

*1*

When I entered Columbia's executive offices, the music industry was led by RCA, Capitol and Columbia. Which company was in the top spot depended on the particular year's record star. Capitol jumped ahead of the rest with The Beatles in 1964 and 1965. When RCA had The Monkees, *The Sound of Music* and *Hello, Dolly!* they were number one. Columbia's basic strength was its Broadway catalog and Mitch Miller's Sing Along albums. Our market share during the period 1964 to 1967 fluctuated between 11 and 13 percent. But a radical change took place when we hit it big between 1968 and 1970; the troika was shattered and our share soared to 22 percent—a giant bite out of the industry pie and something of a shock to our competitors. We became larger than the next two labels combined.

The opposition's basic problem was their failure to take the rock revolution seriously. Both Capitol and RCA lost considerable momentum here, falling headlong from the top rung of the ladder. It was ironic: both companies had signed pioneering rock acts. RCA had Elvis Presley and later signed The Jefferson Airplane. Capitol had The Beatles. The upshot of their indecision—whatever the reason—was that the industry's number one spot came up for grabs. New forms of creativity were asserting themselves; the companies which identified with them best moved to the front.

After Columbia, the company which caught on the fastest was

Warner Communications. The merger of the Warner-Reprise labels with Atlantic Records initially made Warner Communications the fourth-largest company in the industry. Then Warners began gearing up for a major entry into the rock field. The Warner-Reprise labels signed Jimi Hendrix and The Grateful Dead, and Atlantic signed Cream and The Bee Gees. Following that, Warner-Reprise added James Taylor, Joni Mitchell, Jethro Tull, Black Sabbath and Alice Cooper. Atlantic signed Iron Butterfly, Crosby, Stills, Nash & Young, and Led Zeppelin. The combined strength of the two companies became extremely formidable—then Warner Communications bought the Elektra label, which gave them Judy Collins, The Doors and eventually, Carly Simon and Bread.

Capitol meanwhile was riding with The Beatles. They had acquired Quicksilver Messenger Service and Steve Miller, and then signed The Band and Grand Funk Railroad, but their penetration into the rock world was relatively modest considering their size. RCA never really got seriously into rock at all. After The Jefferson Airplane, they signed a number of amorphous rock groups, used the disastrous merchandising idea of "Groupquake," and that was about it. During the seventies, they did break a few top artists, including Harry Nilsson, John Denver and David Bowie, but their loss of momentum by this time was severe. Both companies remained so-called major companies because their overall strength included strong country and classical artists and an extensive catalog. But it was rock that rose up to account for more than 50 percent of the industry's retail sales, and this made all the difference in the changing industry structure.

Columbia flew off to a very substantial head start. We got solidly into rock, and our artists were breaking all over the place. Most of the industry's executives had come into power in the late fifties or early sixties and didn't understand what was happening around them. Styles changed. Executives grew sideburns and longer hair, and some even wore stack-heel boots and dressed in bell-bottoms—but these were mere trappings. Many didn't understand the music—or the artists—they were dealing with. They also had personnel problems. There are scores of young men in the industry who appear at your door each week and *sound* as if they know a lot about music. They've grown up with rock, they read *Rolling Stone,* they *talk* knowledgeably. But they rarely have that special feel for the creative process; they don't know, in short, how to come up with hit artists.

Yet companies were hiring these people and giving them lots of money to spend. The results were calamitous.

Warner Communications avoided these problems and moved rather quickly into second place. Their top-executive roster included Ahmet Ertegun, Nesuhi Ertegun and Jerry Wexler of Atlantic, and Mo Ostin and Joe Smith of Warner-Reprise—the most powerful array in the industry. When Elektra was acquired in 1970, they obtained Jac Holzman, a brilliant pioneer of the industry who was only thirty-eight years old. A&M Records also showed a definite feel for the changes taking place. Jerry Moss did a tremendous job of taking his company from the period of Herb Alpert's enormous strength with The Tijuana Brass to an entirely different medium. At first, Jerry had simply extended the Alpert image by acquiring such acts as Sergio Mendes, The Sandpipers, Claudine Longet and Chris Montez—a contemporary yet moderately middle-of-the-road image which worked quite well for a while. Then Jerry, who is widely regarded as one of the industry's most astute and sensitive leaders, saw that times were changing. Through his English contacts and the invaluable assistance of his lawyer, Abe Somer, he acquired Cat Stevens, Humble Pie, Joe Cocker and Procol Harum; A&M's image abruptly changed.

By 1970, the industry's profile was considerably different. Columbia was number one, and Warner Communications had the second spot. Capitol and RCA were struggling for the number three position, with A&M coming up strongly. Between 1971 and 1973, the race between Columbia and Warners became much closer. A&M, with its acquisition of Lou Adler's Ode Records (Carole King, Cheech & Chong) moved abreast of Capitol and RCA; and London Records, an American distribution arm of the English company, British Decca, scored with The Rolling Stones, Tom Jones, Engelbert Humperdinck, Gilbert O'Sullivan, The Moody Blues and Al Green, growing to the size of a major label.

All this led to a lot of reshuffling among presidents of companies. Capitol has had four presidents in a seven-year period: Alan Livingston, Stanley Gortikov, Sal Iannucci and its current one, Bhaskar Menon. RCA went from George Marek to Norman Racusin to Rocco Laginestra to its current president, Ken Glancy. None of these men is by any means a slouch and each can point to accomplishments, some of them substantial. But life in the mercurial world of contemporary rock music was a difficult adjustment for most. Every one of them has moved on to a more suitable assignment and has performed with much distinction. Menon and Glancy have enjoyed successes in record operations outside the U.S. and are now hard at work to accomplish the same here.

Some smaller companies did well. ABC-Dunhill, under Jay Lasker, had good results, especially with Three Dog Night and Steppenwolf, and later with the tragically ill-fated Jim Croce. Decca was in real trouble until MCA's current president, Mike Maitland, took over. Decca had long been one of the industry's majors, but too much dependence on catalog and too little creative flair, had caused them to lose position drastically. Under Maitland, MCA restored some of the luster with Elton John, Neil Diamond, The Who and *Jesus Christ Superstar*. With *Superstar* having run its course and with the loss of Neil Diamond, MCA now has the strenuous task of both replacing that volume and maintaining the impression that it is a "hot" company. This is important when you are trying to build up your roster; for artists shopping contracts around talk constantly about "hot" and "cold" companies. Clearly, it is best to be hot. Artists tend to assume—logically enough—that your success with other groups means that you'll do well for them. In contract negotiations, on the other hand, companies with relatively few best-selling artists argue that they can give the fullest possible attention to your career. We can *concentrate* on you, they say.

After 1968, I rarely came up against Capitol or RCA in negotiations. Warners and A&M more and more became the major competition. And the negotiating battles were intense for what we thought were key artists. Not that the money kept escalating. Most contests were won or lost on the basis of who sold his company the best—who convinced the other side that the group would be happiest, and sell more, on his label.

A&M and Warners argued, of course, that Columbia's size would minimize an artist's chances of breaking through. *They* were small; *they* could pay closer attention to the performers they signed. You'll get lost at Columbia, they said. It was all claptrap. I pointed out that Warners' and Columbia's monthly release sheets were equally long—and that theirs was far more internally competitive. Their roster was nearly all rock, whereas Columbia's included country, jazz and middle-of-the-road albums. But Warners very cleverly managed to project a "small company" image; the ads were almost clublike, and they made it very hard for me to argue that Warners was *really* a gigantic complex.

My primary argument against all this was career longevity. It was no accident, I said, that The Byrds were still considered a major group—without having had a hit single in a long, long time. Our merchandising campaigns constantly emphasized their major role in contemporary music, their identification with Dylan songs and their introduction of folk rock. As a result, they stayed in business long after ceasing to be a chart-busting group. The same was true with Blood, Sweat & Tears. The group could split up, change personnel or drop off their lofty sales peak—but we helped keep them alive through carefully planned promotion and advertising techniques. We never let the public forget their early greatness or their pioneering influence on contemporary music. By contrast, I argued, Iron Butterfly had had one giant hit, "In-A-Gadda-Da Vida," and quickly disappeared. This was not to say that Ahmet Ertegun didn't run a crackerjack ship; just that Columbia was *better* at ensuring an artist's longevity.

I had the same problems negotiating against A&M, which had built up an unassailable small-company image. They had offices in the old Charlie Chaplin lot, near Sunset Strip, and the grounds were filled with warm, friendly people. They are also one of the last truly independent large record companies. But they had endured cold periods, mostly after Herb Alpert, Sergio Mendes and Chris Montez faded. And so I would tell an artist: Yes, you can have hits with A&M—but how long will you *stay* at the top.

The small-company image worked best, of course, for hot labels. I rarely had to worry about it when competing against companies in trouble. Artists usually assumed that a company was cold for good reason.

The other part of the selling process—aside from money—involved impressing the artist with Columbia itself. I always started with a tour of the tenth floor, where our album-cover artists and designers worked. The department projected a gilt-edged approach to things (displays of awards and citations on the wall—that sort of thing) and it never failed to impress visitors. I took artists and managers to our singles meetings so that they could see the scrutiny each record got before it was released. They were also free to interrogate any and all department heads. I never took the position that our track record spoke for itself; they could dig into our operations as deeply as they wished.

For example: Terry Ellis, co-owner of the Chrysalis label, met with Columbia people in 1972 and poked around the building for nearly two weeks. He knew Warners well, from his Jethro Tull dealings, but wanted to see what Columbia was like. He talked to *everybody*; this time, unfortunately, we did not get the label, mainly because we were outbid. Warners agreed to give him a very high royalty rate and, as a bonus, made it retroactive for a current best-selling Jethro Tull album; the bonus offer amounted to more than half a million dollars and Ellis and his partner, Chris Wright, could hardly refuse. But his tour of the company convinced this careful businessman that we were not the typical large company steeped in bureaucracy, and if the money offers had not been so disparate, the outcome could have been different.

Artists had become increasingly sophisticated in their assessments of companies. When The Grateful Dead's contract with Warners was nearing completion, for example, they made it known to me that they would consider coming to Columbia—*if* they didn't go into business for themselves. We had a good relationship with them because we'd already signed New Riders of the Purple Sage; both groups had the same manager, Jon McIntyre, and they used a lot of the same road people. And Jerry Garcia sometimes played for both groups.

The life-style of the Dead and the Riders was—to say the least—informal. When the Riders or individual members of the Dead came to New York to see me, I felt oddly compelled to be defensive about the structural coolness of Black Rock. Warners had bought a Manhattan brownstone for its East Coast headquarters. I found myself telling the group members that I felt a little vulnerable—but also that Columbia had to accommodate a much greater variety of artists; homey, funky brownstone offices weren't Vladimir Horowitz's style, for example. To my surprise, they thought this was very reasonable. When it came to business, they had nothing against efficiency. Their lives were communal and basic; but their approach to commercial problems was crisp. Jon McIntyre arrived promptly at meetings, and took notes during all of them. If he said that he would call you Thursday at 4:00 P.M., he did . . . exactly on time.

I eventually agreed to go to San Francisco in November, 1972, for a "family" meeting of the Dead. Jon picked me up in San Francisco. Paul Baratta, head of West Coast contemporary A&R, and Mike Klenfner, head of FM promotion, were along, and we all drove into Marin County. I was soon ushered into a large conference room with an oval table and confronted with about twenty people; some were musicians, some were not. Everybody appeared to have decision-making power, and I was *bombarded* with questions for three or four hours—right down to the kind of vinyl we used in our records and whether or not it could be made purer. It was an incredible cross-examination, exhausting and exhilarating at the same time.

The "family" was never hostile, but they had an interest beyond Columbia. They'd been researching the possibility of going into business for themselves: recording, distribution, advertising and promoting—*everything*. Ron Rakow, a business-advisor member of the family, was doing a detailed study of the problem. The Dead wanted, in short, to stop signing with companies that gave them only royalties while hassling them about the need for product.

As a business executive, I found this a very threatening idea. While it was very exciting for them, it could be a bad precedent for the industry if it worked. I tried to raise a number of business considerations I felt they should be aware of.

For when artists hit big—as the Dead had done—they often feel that they can put a few people together to run sales and promotion and thus keep the profits for themselves. Normally they'll get a 10 percent net royalty. But there are obvious problems and the Dead were approaching some of the issues a little idealistically—for example, originally they were going to sell records through Good Humor men or door-to-door salesmen. To their credit, they wanted to explore everything that was non-traditional, with the important objective of helping to spread the wealth around. Only when they were convinced of the impracticality of alternative distribution arrangements did they discipline their imaginations and devote their attention to setting up a strong independent-distributor network. If this system works for them, the precedent will strike at the very heart of the record business. Corporate profits rise and fall on the sales of hot artists; if they decide in droves to set up their own companies it could restructure everything drastically. I wish us all luck.

# 2

Signing artists—and then keeping them happy—is the most difficult and dramatic part of the business. You have to make judgment after judgment based on fragmentary information. And this begins during the earliest negotiating stages. No artist is going to give you *exact* information about his past sales or current creative strengths. You have to research the matter as best you can, and make decisions based in part on instinct.

I became fairly adept, for example, at using the *Billboard* charts to dig into an artist's past. This involved measuring how high his most recent albums had climbed, how long they stayed in position, and then making a graph of their sales patterns. You rarely had actual sales figures; understandably, companies don't pass them around. So you used the charts as a start. But an appraisal of current and future vitality is also important. I always tried to see an artist perform, sometimes twice. I *always* saw a new artist perform, but this applied to established artists on other labels as well.

Looking at a group which had recorded before, you had to check up on its personnel. If an artist hadn't released an album for a while, say a year, you looked to key talent agencies for information. A lot could have happened in that amount of time. In a group, the lead guitarist might have found a guru; the drummer might be having drug problems; someone in the brass section might be thinking of forming his own group; or a key soloist might be quitting. The talent agencies can also tell you if the act is currently playing to full or half-packed houses; this tells you whether they have momentum or are declining. Mistakes in this area can be costly. Many companies have substantially overpaid artists because they did not have a pulse on what was happening. This is what the advance-money game is all about; you are making a judgment based on all the facts about the artist's future—and then laying money on the line to back it up.

Care and attention is another problem. When I traveled to California, artist relations became almost a science. A large number of Columbia artists lived out there, and I had to be scheduled to the "nth degree" for those trips. Sometimes it seemed as if the entire West Coast roster was lined up outside my hotel room, calling in on the phones, waiting in the lobby, sending tapes, expecting a great deal of attention. Business started each day with breakfast and ended with drinks in the early hours of the morning; the entire day was scheduled into fifteen-, thirty- and sixty-minute meetings. I always had at least one and perhaps two colleagues in adjoining hotel suites answering telephones and talking to people who had arrived and had to wait.

Each artist, manager, producer or lawyer had to have my complete attention, if only for fifteen minutes. No unnecessary distractions; no telephones or messages or sideshows. It was practically a game of musical chairs. I usually took a bungalow at the Beverly Hills Hotel. Artist managers Larry Larson and Todd Schiffman might call from the lobby; I'd go there and give them my undivided attention for half an hour in order to avoid interrupting a business meeting in the bungalow. Back in the living room, Brian Rohan had arrived to introduce me to Lee Michaels. Thirty minutes with them, unscheduled (they'd come down from San Francisco), which set everything *else* back. Another call from the lobby; Jim Messina has heard I'm in town and he would like to talk about his career. I ask Elliot Goldman to meet him in the lobby and take him into an adjoining bedroom while I finish with Brian and Lee.

Sly Stone might call next and say he had tapes he wanted me to hear. At that point, I might ask Jimmy and, let's say, Richard Perry and Harry Nilsson, who had become close friends of mine and were waiting to go to dinner, to come into the living room so that we could all listen. I would also be scheduled for supper late that night at Abe Somer's house—he was always a gracious host to me when I was in Los Angeles—drinks with Andy Williams to discuss who would be his next producer, and a visit to our recording studio to listen to Roger McGuinn play the latest Byrds album. By that time, I'd already had breakfast with Lee Colton, a prominent music-business attorney, lunch with Jerry Rubinstein, a highly regarded business advisor, and meetings over more cups of coffee than I could count. If it were Sunday, and it was sunny, I might try to do some of this at poolside.

Listening to tapes in this situation always presented a problem. Artists can be incredibly insensitive about the work of *other* artists. An artist's heart is in his music, so I always tried to give a tape my fullest attention—whether I liked it or not. The crazy thing was that the other artists didn't do this. One artist would be playing a tape; other artists would be chatting on the far side of the room, perhaps even making snide comments. I couldn't run my hotel room like a dictator, so I rarely said anything about this— but it was exasperating! If I knew someone well enough, I might say, come on, let's get into the music, or whatever. But most of the time when someone talked, I just got tense and felt bad for the artist whose music was at issue.

It's a great feeling, of course, to have friends and other artists around when you listen to something brand-new. A new acetate might come in of, say, Paul Simon or Chicago, and I'd want to turn people on to it. If everyone really likes it, it can be a tremendous experience. Other times, I should add, people don't care for a new record, which can be awkward.

I held a number of auditions at the hotel. If the artist played a guitar, I might listen to him right in the bungalow. If he or she played piano, we went to a rather unlikely place called the Rodeo Room, which happened to have the hotel's only piano. It was an L-shaped ballroom of sorts laid out in semibaroque splendor, bar on one end, a large window overlooking the pool-cabana area at the other. When I took an auditioning artist into this setting, I usually apologized for its inappropriateness; this is *not* typical of Columbia Records, I said. I felt foolish; you could tell that a Bar Mitzvah or a wedding reception was about to take place. The artist would sit down at the huge grand piano and start to play and I'd sit near him—and suddenly workmen would come in to move furniture. I'd try to get them to stop, but they had "orders." With luck, I could get them to stop for twenty minutes or so. It was a ridiculous place to hold an audition.

I was never passive during auditions. I knew that the artist or manager would be watching me, and if I liked him, enthusiasm would be written all over my face. I doubted that it would shoot up his price; negotiations involve business considerations, and if the terms are right, the deal goes through. There was no reason to hide my emotion—especially if I liked what I heard. By contrast, I didn't waste time if I wasn't impressed. After the fourth or fifth selection, I would cut things off as politely as I could. I'd simply tell the artist and his manager that I didn't think he was ready to make it at this time. If you beat around the bush, it comes off mealymouthed. I'd add that he should go other places; I could be wrong. But I was firm in saying that the artist didn't reach *me*.

During an audition I always looked for uniqueness, originality . . . a special identity. Naturally, the specifics varied depending on the type of artist involved. If he was a writer-performer, my attention mostly centered on his writing talent. If that is great, the public has a way of adjusting to—even making an asset out of—an untrained voice, e.g., Bob Dylan, James Taylor, Randy Newman, etc. So I listened closely to the artist's songs, their structure, lyrics, the sense of identity they had, and what *I* felt in turn. I wanted mainly to gauge the artist's feel for melody and lyrics. Could he write a chorus? Were the lyrics too bubble gum—or too sophisticated? If social commentary was involved, were the thoughts fresh and worth listening to? If the writer has primarily a lyric skill without melodic strength, he has to have something terribly unique to say, as Dylan does. But it's getting harder and harder to break *these* artists despite the fact that the underground press normally gravitates to them with glowing reviews. Bruce Springsteen, an artist we signed in 1972, is a good example. He's received tremendous critical acclaim for his fascinating use of words and his lyric ideas. He is building a small cult, but it's been difficult to break him commercially. Bruce is so unique that even without a hit I know he will make it, but without that trademark single, it's a slow build. This problem applies to Loudon Wainwright III as well. His strengths are his whimsy and humor. His writing is funny, fanciful, often cutting, but his only "hit"—"Dead Skunk In The Middle Of The Road"—is a novelty song and doesn't give a true indication of how compelling a talent Wainwright is. He has yet to find that combination of melody and lyrics that can really launch him.

Sometimes the writer-performer breaks only after other artists have hits with his songs. If enough songs become hits by other artists, then public curiosity about the writer gathers steam and there is a readiness to accept a different kind of "voice." This happened to Dylan *after* Peter, Paul & Mary hit with "Blowin' In The Wind" and The Byrds scored with "Mr. Tambourine Man" —and to Laura Nyro after The Fifth Dimension hit with several of her songs. It's ready to happen to Randy Newman and Paul Williams also, two brilliant writers who should be—and will be— stars.

I'm not one of those people who feel that *only* the writer can meaningfully interpret his own songs. The ability to perform other people's songs is a separate and distinct talent—and it can affect an audience and sell records. Carole King, for example, has a gigantic following both for records and concerts, but it was Barbra Streisand, performing some of Carole's great songs, who lifted a McGovern youth audience at the Forum in 1972 to its feet time and again. Janis Joplin's version of "Me and Bobby McGee" had meaning and insight not found in Kris Kristofferson's rendition. The same is true of Judy Collins doing Leonard Cohen's classic, "Suzanne." *Both* versions are haunting; hers, however, reached a larger audience.

But when it comes to auditions of these nonwriting individual performers, you have to be extremely careful. It's very difficult to break an artist who does not write his or her own material. It can be done: Tom Jones, Liza Minnelli and Bette Midler are good examples in recent years. But the talent has to have a unique kind of magic capable of radiating electricity—or involve a special combination of looks, voice and personality that lends itself to hosting a weekly television show, the best way to break this kind of artist. Andy Williams, Glen Campbell and Helen Reddy are illustrative of this. If the artist doesn't have any of these qualities, the company is under a tremendous burden to produce a succession of single hits that will keep the artist in the public eye. And when the string runs out, so does the artist. No steady album audience is waiting to hear the artist do other songs, as with a Sinatra or a Mathis.

In this age of rock music, most of the auditions involve groups. And many of them are good. But you have to be able to distinguish the competent talent from the star. You have to start with a base of virtuosity and then have at least the ingredients of showmanship, audience appeal and, it is hoped, charisma. There are just too many good groups today and more than competence is required. I have always looked—and looked very hard—for people who could contribute new musical forms or new ideas. Blood, Sweat & Tears, The Mahavishnu Orchestra and Earth, Wind & Fire are all good examples of this. Where innovative talent is coupled with song sense and an identifiable sound, you have a super group—like Chicago or Santana.

Some auditions particularly stand out in my memory. Dr. Hook & the Medicine Show had theirs in my New York office.

I'd heard about a movie starring Dustin Hoffman called *Who Is Harry Kellerman (And Why Is He Saying Those Terrible Things About Me)?* Its songs were written by the tremendously talented humorist Shel Silverstein, and they were performed by the group. I got a tape of one of the songs, "The Last Morning," liked it and called their attorney, Fred Gershon, to request an audition. It was an unusual afternoon. Dr. Hook and his entourage were not at all put off by the Black Rock building, my office, the fact that I was the President of Columbia, or anything else. They pushed the couches against the wall, pulled the coffee table to one side, cleared off my desk—and got into the audition with a vengeance. The Silverstein songs were witty, irreverent and incredibly funny. Dr. Hook had an eye patch. The rest of his group guffawed and danced around in jeans and rough, country-style clothing. It was a great audition, with singing and laughter and dancing on the coffee table, and the banging of spoons and knives in time to whatever they were doing. One group member sat on my desk; others jumped and moved all over the room. I offered to sign them on the spot.

The meeting with Edgar Winter was also auspicious. We eventually went to the room where I'd auditioned Laura Nyro (and would audition Dave Loggins a few years later), but Steve Paul, Edgar and I talked in my office first. I felt a little awkward; I didn't want Edgar to think I was interested in him just because he was Johnny's brother. So I asked about his musical ideas—and he turned out to have very definite plans. He wanted to try "progressive things." He was very strong in rock, he said, but first he'd like to try something innovative—and then he described plans which sounded distinctly *un*commercial to me. But he added that he wanted to get those radical tendencies *out* of his system; if they were commercially successful, fine, he'd keep on working in that vein. If they weren't, he'd go immediately to rock 'n' roll, where the money was. We then went down the hall from my office to the conference room, and he played the piano. I was very impressed with his singing—a throaty roar that shifts suddenly to a high falsetto and back again. He also had very good delivery, good timing and excellent taste.

I agreed to put him on Epic. When his first album came out, sure enough it contained lofty progressive music that got tremendous reviews . . . but sold only twenty thousand copies. True to his word, Edgar then formed a group and got strongly into rock. After hard work, a lot of touring and some exciting albums, he now has one of the country's top rock acts, and is a giant seller for the company.

I remember for another reason one particular audition-meeting held outside by the Beverly Hills pool. The California trips often stretched over weekends, so when the weather was good it seemed perfectly reasonable to conduct business from a poolside cabana. One problem was that Ahmet Ertegun did the same thing. We often found ourselves watching each other across the water— and occasionally having awkward moments as a result. A key manager might be quietly negotiating with both of us—at the same time—and not know that I was in town; he'd drop in to see Ahmet —and find *me* in the next tent. I'd pop up and say hello, and he would look a little sheepish and make a point of coming by *my* tent afterward.

Ahmet was always very gracious about this. I was talking at the pool one day to David La Flamme and two other members of It's A Beautiful Day just after I had auditioned them when Ahmet walked by. We were always tremendously competitive in the talent-acquisition wars—but he stopped and said, "Look, I don't know who you are, but you are talking to the best in the business. You can't do any better than to entrust your musical lives to him." Then he walked away. The group was impressed, and I was more than touched by this tribute.

# 3

The pool provided many colorful moments. The most dramatic of them belonged to Sly Stone.

Sly was in one of his worst periods—no product, but he wanted money, and it was a continuing problem. I like Sly; he is one of the true geniuses of modern pop music, and I wanted badly to keep him on the label. But I was hearing terrible stories about him, and he was becoming difficult to defend. The tales of excessive drug use and not showing up—or arriving hours late— for concerts were legion. Worst of all, he wasn't writing any music.

Sly was one of the giants of the late sixties. He could bring twenty or thirty thousand people into a stadium and drive them wild with songs like "I Want To Take You Higher," "Dance To The Music," "Everyday People" and "Hot Fun In The Summertime." But when he had started out, his audience had been more limited. David Kapralik, then head of A&R for Epic, had brought him into the company, and his first hit was "Dance To The Music." It started on the R&B charts and crossed over to pop, but it wasn't followed by significant album sales. Sly's albums then sold around a hundred thousand copies, disappointing considering his singles success. He seemed to have mostly R&B appeal. He had played the Electric Circus in the East Village, but Fillmore audiences didn't seem to be able to make him out. I wanted to break him in the underground.

Sly had a close relationship with Kapralik, so I asked them both to lunch one day. Sly at that time had made no compromise to the Fillmore mentality. In an age of blue jeans and T-shirts, his stage act included costumes, unusual hairdos and stylized body movements. He was a dedicated musician, and I knew that he was serious about his work. But I thought this glitter was a mistake; this was not the age of costumes (not yet). I thought that he should make some concessions. You look too much like a Las Vegas act, I said—the kids don't know how to take it.

He disagreed. They *will* know what to make of it soon, he said. I have a definite idea of what I am trying to do, and I want to stay with it. Maybe the kids will be put off at first, but they'll get into it. I understand what you are saying, I respect your opinion—but I want to keep doing things my way, and I hope there are no hard feelings. Sly was polite—and firm. I had to go along with him. As it turned out, of course, I underestimated him; I had really missed the genius behind the satin and sequins. His appeal soon began to spread and right after he electrified everyone at Woodstock, his career soared. He captured the Fillmore crowd, the R&B crowd, the Top Forty audiences and became one of the great popular artists of the day.

As often happens, Sly also began to live very well. It was different during his earlier days, when he worked seven days a week. One Sunday, in fact, he was stopped by a CBS security guard as he was trying to take his guitar out of the building to go to a rehearsal; he had to call me at home so that I could vouch for him and establish his credibility. And whenever I saw him coming out of a recording studio, he was literally running to another appointment, looking intense and preoccupied. He was dedicated to becoming a success. And now that he was successful, he was into exotic cars and jewelry, expensive homes, private planes, glittering women . . . and, apparently, drugs. I didn't mind giving him advances; he was making plenty of money for Columbia. But I began to wonder after a while. . . .

A record company has no more right to interfere with its artists' lives than a book publisher has to tell its writers how to live. But I got to thinking: if he's *really* got a habit, maybe I should be doing more as a human being! You can't be a preacher about this; but was I *hurting* him by giving him advances at all? It was a difficult problem. Publishers don't hassle alcoholic authors; and it was questionable whether I should interfere with Sly's life. If his records attempted to be drug propaganda, that was one thing, and I would stop it. But it was valid music.

We spoke about this several times. I told him that he had to *deal* with his problems. You're just not producing, I said; it's a tragic waste and it could ruin your life. But nothing seemed to change. Finally I decided to withhold his advances until I got product. This seemed a legitimate business decision to me. But it led to several unhappy conversations. He called me one Sunday from California, for example, and asked for a change in his contract so that Columbia would pay for all his studio time. But he was spending hundreds and hundreds of hours at the boards—and producing nothing. I wouldn't do it. Finish the album, I said; then I'll give you the money you need.

Throughout this period, Sly always had an excuse for missing concerts. The plane was late, or he was given the wrong time, or a member of the group was sick. He never admitted that something was wrong with him; he always insisted that he was in complete control of himself. He even changed managers a few times in attempts to get money. We finally decided to suspend his contract. He was so far behind schedule that I was getting worried that his contract would expire and he'd sign with someone else for the large advance he was seeking.

Sly in the meantime had bought John and Michelle Phillips's sumptuous home in Bel Air for himself and his growing entourage. The mortgage payments were huge, and he began feeling financially pressed. He called me one Saturday at the Beverly Hills Hotel and said, I must see you. I'm coming over and bringing my lawyers along. I have to talk about our situation. I said fine, I'm at the pool. Call me when you arrive and we'll go to my bungalow.

His lawyers arrived first. We were talking casually in my pool cabana when Sly arrived thirty minutes later and called from the lobby. You really have to picture the Beverly Hills Hotel pool scene: Arabian yellow tents, Hollywood-style, laden with entertainment people, starlets in bikinis, old men with money; show business names popping off the paging system; an elegant liquor carriage for easy access to drinks; heads turning constantly. I told Sly that I was in my bathing suit; I'd meet him at my bungalow. No, he insisted, he'd come down to see me.

It was an unforgettable sight. To reach the pool, you have to sign in at a turnstile bar and then walk down a series of steps. Suddenly everyone's head turned toward the turnstile. Sly had appeared in a black and red satin jump suit, high heels and a basketball-sized Afro. He walked down the stairs with studied grace . . . slowly . . . in measured paces . . . like a panther . . . followed by every eye at the palm-fringed pool. He was practically floating; a number of people recognized him and a distinct murmur of excitement arose. He finally reached my cabana, and we attempted to talk business.

It was soon obvious that we couldn't. His original purpose had been obliterated by whatever he was into, and he was in no condition to deal with the logic of finances and contracts, with or without lawyers. However, his mind was hardly blank. When am I going to get the money, he asked? When you deliver the album, I answered. You're gonna get it without fail on Monday, he said. (He *always* said it was coming the following Monday.) Then you'll get the money on Monday, I answered. At this point, between royalties and advances held up by the contract suspension, he had about two hundred and fifty thousand dollars coming to him.

Sly paused. Then he looked up. "Man, I've got a great idea," he said. "Why don't you write out the check right now and postdate it to Monday. I won't be putting anything over because I can't cash it till Monday, you dig?"

I could never be angry with Sly (whose nickname fits him perfectly) and I had to laugh; I also had to say no. However, I didn't have to wait long, since he *did* finish the album two weeks later, and came in a much better state to my office in New York to play the tape. It included the incredible hit "Family Affair," which sold over two million copies, with the album itself selling over a million.

Sly has always been ahead of his time. The "Family Affair" album, for example, was a departure that worried me at first. But, as always, Sly knew what he was doing musically. His use of rhythms and lyrics is extraordinary; and his drawling, stoned singing style, his low energy working its way through the instrumental tracks, is irresistible. Some of the songs on his subsequent album, *Fresh,* have the old driving beat; the force of others catches you almost . . . unaware. I'm convinced that Sly has considerable staying power. And it looks as though his head is returning to the right place. Once that happens, he'll likely be in the front ranks of music for a long time.

# Eleven

## 1

I've just talked of auditioning new artists. These stories, running from the time of their discovery up to their breaking out, often involved a test of judgment and evaluation. But I must add that raw luck is sometimes involved; and occasionally everything falls apart. Let's begin with Loggins and Messina, where I was lucky.

Jim Messina called one day. He had helped form Poco, a solid group I had signed two years earlier, and he'd been a member previously of Buffalo Springfield. Jim was calling to say that he didn't want to stay with Poco any longer, and he wanted to talk about it. Another breakup. I felt that Poco had the potential to become a major group. They weren't selling outstandingly yet, but they were building fast. I'd just heard their newest "live" album, which Jim had produced, and I thought it was tremendously exciting, possibly a breakthrough. I was taking a train to Philadelphia that afternoon on business, and I suggested that he meet me at the station and ride down.

Jim was touring with Poco at the time, and he had a fairly common musician's dilemma. He was tired of Holiday Inns, and tired of being away from his lovely wife, Jenny, who was studying acting in Los Angeles. He wasn't making much money, and he was having disagreements with the group. I gave him the usual arguments. The group was making a name for itself and big money was around the corner, I said. Why get tired of traveling *now* (he was about twenty-three and he'd already spent quite a few years with traveling bands)? Maybe he and the rest of Poco could work out their differences, I said hopefully.

But long before we pulled into the Thirtieth Street Station, I realized that Jim had clear ideas about his future. He wanted to go out on his own; for the interim, he asked for a staff producing job in California. I said that I'd give it to him. But I asked him to ponder the decision for three or four more weeks, cool off and get back to me. Jim thought about it during that time, and decided that he still wanted to leave. He also sent me a well-organized budget detailing everything from rent to carfare expenditures, suggesting that he needed a slightly larger salary. A bright, well-disciplined young man—how could I refuse?

I had a tape at the time that I liked from an unknown artist named Kenny Loggins; his brother, Dan, who had recently managed some retail stores for our Discount Records operation, had submitted the tape along with Don Ellis, who also came from the Discount Records retail-store operation and later became head of Epic A&R. Jim was searching for an artist to produce, and he listened to Kenny's tape. He liked it and said he'd be willing to try him. After that, I heard nothing else from them for a few months.

Finally, Jim called to say that the album was ready. But he wasn't sure how to "handle it." Kenny was a little inexperienced, he said, and he wound up singing on it to help Kenny out. "Our voices worked well together," he added, "but this isn't what I want to do. I plan to make a solo album. So we've called it *Kenny Loggins With Jim Messina Sittin' In.*"

The tape *had* something . . . a special sound, bounce and feeling. "Don't you want to call it 'Messina & Loggins' or 'Loggins & Messina'—or *something?*" I asked. Jim said no; he wanted to preserve his option to make albums alone. He agreed to tour with Kenny just for the first round of dates, but he didn't want to continue after that.

"It'll be embarrassing if this album takes off," I argued. "In effect, you'll be breaking up right after the first record." But Jim stuck to his original idea.

From their very first date at the Troubador, Loggins & Messina tore the house apart. Word of mouth spread amazingly fast; their album began moving steadily up the charts. They did everything they should—playing important free gigs for exposure, visiting radio stations in each key city and cooperating with the record company in every way. Their first tour was with Delaney & Bonnie, and soon it was extremely difficult for Delaney & Bonnie to close behind them. Kenny and Jim created enormous excitement—infectious, melodic, basic rock 'n' roll that brought audience after audience to its feet. They worked very hard, crossing the country again and again, moving from second bill to headlining act, working six and seven nights a week.

Jim called me after a while to say that they would soon finish recording a second album. He *still* wanted to use the "sittin' in" concept. I thought this was silly. "You're getting second billing," I argued, "and you are *not* an added attraction. The group is now clearly 'Loggins & Messina'—why maintain the fiction that you are on the verge of leaving? Make a commitment, and stay. Forget the solo option; it will keep."

Jim said he'd think it over. He finally called me back and agreed to commit himself to Kenny for the foreseeable future. Loggins & Messina was off and running. Their first album went gold; the second sold even more. Their third album was gold immediately after release and now they've already packed Madison Square Garden as headliners. Thanks to the luck of the draw (not to mention their enormous individual talents) Loggins & Messina are now among the best groups America has produced in the seventies.

# 2

Obviously not every new and talented group finds success. The same principles of critical judgment and promotion nonetheless apply to breaking any group, so it might be instructive to review two which haven't yet made it. The first is The Rowan Brothers. I signed them after a Rodeo Room audition in 1971 and I had high hopes. They were young, good-looking and, most important, their music was excellent—lush melodies, appealing lyrics, beautiful songs. I was very excited.

The brothers lived in San Francisco. They came to me with a manager and two engineering and production people who also worked as backup musicians—all in the same package—and I knew that David Geffen was wooing them as well. At one point he gave them a thousand dollars to live on while they made up their minds between Asylum and Columbia. I kept the pressure up and agreed to give them a two-year contract rather than the usual deal of one year with four one-year options. It was a strong commitment to make for a brand-new act, and this was decisive in persuading them to go with Columbia.

The problems we had might add up to a textbook case in how to kill a promising career—that is, how the artists might kill it themselves. For a start, it was clear that the boys needed more professional guidance than they were willing to take. This is not an uncommon problem. New artists often tend to value the purity of their music—and of their ideas—far more than considerations of professionalism or, God forbid, commercial success. My first suggestion was that they work with Roy Halee, the San Francisco producer who has done so well with Simon & Garfunkel.

But they made it clear that I was buying a five-man unit; the brothers had only two votes. The producer, manager and engineer were equal partners. In short, they planned to produce and manage themselves. I reluctantly accepted this, thinking that I'd give them the benefit of doubt for a while. This was, after all, a totally inexperienced group; I assumed that they would drop the manager or producer or whatever else was necessary after a few fumbles. Then we'd get down to business.

It didn't happen. Their manager, for openers, talked as if they were the most important group since The Beatles; they *were* good, but this is extremely dangerous thinking. It sets up comparisons that new, untried artists are bound to suffer from— whether you speak of your act in the same breath with The Beatles or Bob Dylan or The Budapest String Quartet. It creates critical and public expectations, in fact, that can work actively *against* a new group. For when critics hear an act ballyhooed as the "best thing since The Beatles," they often (rightly) assume that they are about to be hyped. And from a strictly professional view, this approach means that the manager isn't disciplining his group well. The best-thing-since-The-Beatles doesn't have to work very hard; success is assured. The *fact* is that new groups always have to pay their dues, including the once-new Beatles.

Yet the brothers' San Francisco-style innocence was quite beguiling. They wrote wistful, lovely ballads; melodic, flowing songs that I thought had big potential. And then they went into the studio. We heard nothing for several months. The administrative people in A&R naturally kept trying to find out what was happening. It is their responsibility to monitor recording costs. But the brothers were using an outside independent studio and the flow of information was spotty. We asked for something to hear but were told that nothing was ready. We knew the brothers were working hard, that *they* were satisfied with their progress— but recording costs were rising . . . dangerously. The costs soon reached fifty thousand dollars. Although we were protected contractually against excessive studio costs (an overrun on the first album decreased the amount they could spend on the second), this was hardly reassuring. I saw the increasing costs not only as a mounting economic risk but also as a sign of other potentially serious problems. I finally called and said that I wanted to listen to what they'd done.

"We've finished a few numbers," they said, "and we'd like to entertain you." I flew out to San Francisco with Kip Cohen and we were taken to a charming house outside the city. As we rode in the car, their manager made it clear that he had *big* ideas. I was going to hear incredible, magnificent songs! This group had to be launched with as much ceremony as a moon shot! I listened quietly . . . and got worried.

The brothers were warm, unassuming hosts. We sat around at first listening to other artists they were into, and then we had a marvelous home-cooked dinner. Afterward, Kip and I went into the den to hear their tapes.

I was terribly disappointed.

I didn't hear the arrangements, composition or production that good records require—they were wasting a lot of time. I was very upset. The evening had been very nice; but fifty thousand dollars' worth of production had amounted to *nothing*. I had to be straight about it; no more smiles. The Rowan Brothers were in danger of failing altogether. I told them flatly how unhappy I was. And I asked, "Please, let me bring in some professional production people to finish the job." It was a very depressing scene for me—and for them. I learned later that they wrote a song the next day, based on the experience, which included a line about doing "the best you can." Then they went back to work.

To their credit, the boys themselves turned the album around. The songs were special and their production efforts eventually resulted in a strong, distinctive sound. But it also cost a fortune—the most expensive album for an untried act in Columbia's history.

Now, the task of breaking the group out had to be faced. There are several ways to do this, which usually involve trying for a hit single, public appearances, or creating underground audiences through FM play. I wanted to try all three, as we had with Loggins and Messina. It was necessary to use all avenues since FM radio wasn't breaking artists the way it had in the middle and late sixties; also, new groups who are into melodic songs aren't sophisticated enough for FM-ers, who are usually much more receptive to progressive newcomers. First we released a single, but it didn't break through. This is the quickest route; also the most difficult. The competition among singles is enormous; tip sheet writer Kal Rudman once compared breaking a single by a new artist to getting a bill through a hostile Congress. The brothers' single was a good one; it just didn't survive the competitive wars.

That left public appearances, the most tried-and-true route; also the slowest and most tiring. We introduced the brothers first in San Francisco. Their performance received excellent reviews and generated substantial press. But the handling of their publicity left a lot to be desired. In one *Rolling Stone* interview, their manager bragged (stupidly, I thought) about the amount of studio money spent. On top of this, all of our advertisements included a quote from Jerry Garcia of The Grateful Dead: "One of the most important new sounds since The Beatles. . . ." It was simply too much; no group can live up to its notices under such circumstances.

Nonetheless, the album was received very favorably and got considerable FM play. Public appearances, however, would clearly have to be the key to success for The Rowan Brothers. They had to play all the half-baked clubs across the country, appear five or six nights a week and settle for second billing until word of mouth could spread sufficiently for them to be able to fill a house by themselves.

They wouldn't do it. They made one or two appearances, including a short stint as opening act for The Grateful Dead; and they got good press reaction. But somehow, possibly because of their overenthusiastic management, they refused to take any outside direction. After the Grateful Dead gigs, they said they wouldn't be an opening act ever again.

The fact was that they had a lot to learn about stage presence, image, opening and closing their act, progression of songs . . . and so on. These are crucial elements in creating the kind of "don't-miss" word of mouth comment that club owners, taste-makers and critics will pass around and in so doing ensure an artist's future.

I flew into San Francisco at one point and asked them over to my hotel to talk about this. Again I argued for personal appearances—but they were pretty much on the same wavelength as their manager. I don't know who was influencing whom, but they were convinced that they couldn't win over fans as an added attraction. Audiences are rude to unknown artists; they don't listen to opening acts. The brothers felt that they just couldn't take these situations. They weren't smug, nor particularly aggressive. They simply believed that it wasn't the best way for them to break out.

Their album sold twenty to twenty-five thousand copies. It's impossible to know if they would have broken out with touring—but at least they wouldn't have been such a quick flop. Two singles were released from the album. They made a few station visits, but compared with Loggins & Messina, they were not at all cooperative in utilizing and capitalizing on all the platforms we wanted to provide. We *brought* them to the altar; we let the public know they were something special; we even adopted (wrongly, I think) some of their manager's ideas in our ad campaigns (the Garcia quote). We set them apart from the pack of struggling new artists through publicity and promotion. But we needed *their* cooperation as well, and we didn't get it.

# 3

Pamela Polland is another talented artist who didn't break. And, worst of all, she was quite willing to do *all* the legwork necessary to make it happen.

George Daly, Columbia's A&R man in San Francisco, asked her to audition for me. She was already a local celebrity there, known for a soft, husky singing style and the warmth of her personality. Pamela had—and still has—the ingredients. She is a talented writer, an attractive person—fresh-scrubbed and wide-eyed—

and she was willing to work hard. She was also extremely popular with her colleagues; her refreshing candor was contagious. She had become a friend and counselor to many local artists by the time I met her.

We hit it off immediately. And what was unusual was the loyalty she came to feel for the company—she became a sort of Good Will Ambassador. She felt that she'd found a creative home at Columbia, and she never hesitated to tell other artists and industry people how happy she was. This helped us considerably in signing other San Francisco artists.

Sadly, Pamela's warmth and concern for other people hurt her own career. George Daly wanted to produce her, and my initial reaction was that he lacked the experience to work with a totally new talent. He had a musical background, and he had performed briefly with a group; but he hadn't produced an album on his own. I wanted to put Pamela in thoroughly professional hands. It was not a time in her career to take chances.

But she fought hard for him. "He's very talented," she argued, "and great producers have to start *somewhere*. He has to have a first album, and I'm willing to let it be mine." So I reluctantly agreed to it; George, after all, had recommended Pamela to me. As a compromise, I asked them to record three cuts and submit a sample to me.

I got ten instead (the number of which bothered me greatly). They weren't bad; but they weren't great. I suggested some cuts and editing. Pamela took all this with her usual grace, and went back to work. Still, things didn't improve measurably. I finally asked her to go down to Nashville and record part of the album with Norbert Putnam, a highly-regarded independent producer. The final album worked well—but there was no solid single to break out. So the only hope was to tour. She began working places like The Bitter End and The Cellar Door, but it became clear that she was not going to emerge from these appearances either. Her reception was good and she built a small coterie of devoted fans, but her warm, San Francisco flower-childlike aura wasn't electric enough to create the required word of mouth.

At this point, she was in trouble. She was getting a "nice" reaction, but nothing *urgent*. Her album, moreover, didn't lend itself easily to FM support; the medium was getting more and more progressive, and her music, by contrast, was pleasant and melodic. She was caught at an unfortunate midpoint between FM and AM audiences.

The solution, of course, was a hit single. To that end, we asked her to record a second album. She was introduced to Gus Dudgeon, who was the producer of Elton John's brilliant albums. He liked her a lot and arrangements were immediately made for her to work with him in London, where studio costs are much cheaper.

But this time *I* made a mistake. For I accepted Dudgeon without knowing whether his strengths complemented Pamela's. I should have looked, for example, at his specific contributions to Elton John's albums. Arrangements? An ear for hit singles? Technical skills? I investigated none of this. I was guilty of the superficial approach that tape companies took during the late sixties, when they read producers' names on successful albums and then called up and handed them hundreds of thousands of dollars to bring in artists. No background checking, nothing. "Just bring us hit artists," the tape companies would say. "We've read about you [on the backs of album covers], and it all sounds very good to us."

The approach cost them millions and millions of dollars.

If I'd thought about it, I would have realized that Elton John is very much a part of the making of his albums. I met Elton, for example, when he was in New York for a Carnegie Hall appearance in 1972. At the time, I thought that he might enjoy hearing several relatively new Columbia artists (David Bromberg, Loudon Wainwright III, Edgar Winter) and I took their newest albums along for the visit.

"I've already got them," he said. It was Thursday; the albums had been released on the previous Monday. "How could you have them *already?*" I asked in disbelief. Elton said that he read the trades every week and always went down the list of new releases. If he was curious about an artist, he bought the album right away. He opened up a trunk in his living room to show me hundreds of cassettes and eight-track tapes. I was amazed. It became instantly apparent why Elton John has hits so consistently. He knows where contemporary music *is;* he hears its changes, and he knows his audience. He can make outrageous departures from standard repertoire and still have hits because he keeps his finger on the public pulse. This does not compromise Elton's giant musical talents; his feeling for the public pulse simply makes him bigger. I also met Elton's lyricist Bernie Taupin shortly afterward; he has the same curiosity that Elton has and is tremendously aware. They make a fantastic combination.

So I sent Pamela to London without any specific idea of whether Gus Dudgeon had contributed more than great technical skills to Elton John's efforts. She finished the album and returned to New York in early 1973. I'd already heard excellent word of mouth but it only made my disappointment that much greater when I heard the record itself. The sound was great; the production superb. Dudgeon was indeed a master at that. But the songs were almost all abstract; they didn't showcase her basic strength. Pamela's talents lie in the Carole King direction—good, solid, down-to-earth songs. This album went off ethereally. There was just no single at all.

This left us almost no opportunity for radio play. Pamela's songs still weren't progressive enough to get substantial FM attention; and I knew already that touring wouldn't create the word of mouth she needed.

"Where's the single?" I asked.

"I don't know," she said. "Gus said we would find one. I just assumed he had one in mind."

I met Gus in London for the first time shortly afterward, at a birthday party for Elton John. I liked him at once and felt comfortable enough to analyze Pamela's album with him. "Where's the single?" I asked.

He looked at me silently for a moment. "I don't think there is one," he candidly answered. "I just worked with the songs Pamela showed me and didn't encourage her to write more."

The problem was clear. Gus was making an error that the large majority of producers make—even some great ones like him. He somehow separated the business and creative functions of a producer where they really should be joined. He thought that he'd done the creative work; I was supposed to take care of the business side. And Pamela, regrettably, hadn't been experienced enough at that point to keep the single concept in mind when she worked in the studio; she had left this up to Dudgeon. Now it was too late for me to do anything.

I had no choice but to take the album off release. "There's no point in bringing this out without a single that will help it break," I told her. "Without a single, it *won't* break. It won't help your career at all."

Pamela was quite upset, though again sympathetically. She realized—belatedly—that she and Gus should have thought more seriously about this. I asked her to write more material, hoping for a single breakthrough before we released the album. She needed a solid, trademark hit for herself; then the album would sell extremely well, ethereal songs or not. She went off to do that, but Columbia dropped her a few months after my departure. I hadn't heard the new songs; they apparently didn't make it.

# 4

Our campaign to break The Rowan Brothers may have been more intense than the effort made for most new artists, but the techniques in all cases are similar. The idea is simply to get the artist and his music right to the public. During a tour, for example, an artist will go from city to city, and the local promotion man will line up interviews and press conferences. The artist might talk on the air with a local FM disc jockey, then drop by the AM station to see the program director, hoping to persuade him to take a shot at the single. The objective is to build relationships with local press and radio people—always a slow process—which will spread to local fans.

Solid roadwork won't always launch a talented artist immediately. But if he is really good—particularly in his writing—a company will usually stay with him, perhaps through a second, third, even a fourth album if necessary. We waited for Edgar Winter's second album, and RCA waited quite some time for Harry Nilsson to break. Warner Bros., in turn, has waited a few years for Randy Newman. Columbia at this writing is sitting it out for Loudon Wainwright III and Bruce Springsteen.

Another example is Mac Davis. He took two albums and several singles to break. Mac, as it happened, came to me with impressive writing credentials; he'd written hit songs for Elvis Presley and Kenny Rogers & the First Edition, and had appeared on a number of television shows. He played his new songs for me in my hotel suite and they were good; I signed him. He then cut two albums for Columbia; neither did much. So I advised him to cut only singles—until one broke. He did that, and sure enough, "Baby, Baby, Don't Get Hooked on Me" sold a million copies and took him to the top of the charts. If you believe in the artist, the answer is to stick with him.

But sometimes artists can fail to break, and you know it's over before it starts. Frequently, coming to grips with actually recording can cause them to stray from the musical ideas that moved you to sign them in the first place. A company has a right to expect that an artist will record the kind of music he played at the audition; sometimes he doesn't even record any of the songs he performed at the audition. For example, I signed Genya Ravan in 1971. She was very good and very earthy. But by the time she entered the studio, she'd changed a lot of her musical thinking. Her backup group had changed, and she was having an identity crisis as well. She appeared on "The Johnny Carson Show," for example, wearing an evening gown and talking about her long-suppressed desire to play engagements like The Persian Room. This was ridiculous. Here was a funky singer in the Joplin tradition, with a throaty, powerful voice. Joplin would no sooner have played The Persian Room than appear in films as Snow White. It was not her image. Nor was it Genya's. Yet here was Genya—even before she had an image—diffusing it in just the way that Blood, Sweat & Tears set themselves up for a fall by playing Caesar's Palace.

Obviously, you sign a group—at least in part—on the strength of the songs you hear. Sometimes you later find out (however incredible it may seem) that they don't even want to record them on their first album. They have newer songs which are closer to the "real" group. Then the album comes out and it doesn't make it commercially. In effect, you have a new group on your hands. You call them and say, "I'd like to listen to some of your new songs." They play them, and you don't like what you hear. So you come to a parting of the ways without waiting for a second album at all. They have irrevocably strayed too far from the promised package. And then when they insist on *total* creative control, the decision becomes clear.

If the artist gets out of the studio in reasonable shape, the booking of his engagements will then become very important. He has to consider performing at what are called "taste-making" clubs. These are places where particularly "in" critics hang out; also where music people like to go—and where an act can get the word of mouth it needs. Booking is a talent agency's and manager's joint problem; unfortunately, you often find that new managers know less than the acts themselves about what they should do. And this is a shame, because it is the manager who ultimately makes key decisions about his artists' appearances. Should they go the club route? The Bottom Line, Reno Sweeney or Max's Kansas City in New York? The Cellar Door in Washington, The Main Point in Philadelphia. The Quiet Knight in Chicago? Or should they tour as an opening act for a bigger group—thus getting exposure to larger audiences?

Which headliner will best draw the audience you need is also a vital point to weigh. I sometimes think of the unfortunate artist who was booked to tour with comedian Soupy Sales. What a waste of time! Soupy's audiences are *not* the people who will create effective word of mouth for a rock act. Loggins & Messina used the "opening act" formula with really great success. You take a talented group, a really good first album, and then you put them on a bill with, say, Billy Preston and Delaney & Bonnie, as Todd Schiffman and Larry Larson did with Kenny and Jim. By the end of two months' touring, Kenny and Jim were launched. All the same ingredients could have been present for The Rowan Brothers—but their management recommended against touring, and that hurt.

I hate to belabor the point, except that it's really a pity to see a talented act fall by the wayside, temporarily or permanently. Everything *has* to be in place to complement and support the artist and his songs: production and arrangements, savvy management, the right bookings, coordinated promotion and company support. A hit single can change everything, of course. Randy Newman has everything but that, and when he gets one, there'll be no stopping him. The same can happen to The Rowan Brothers. But the key elements are talent, timing, hard work—and a little bit of luck.

# Twelve

## 1

There is hardly any tougher task in records than the search for the hit single. It is the industry's equivalent of jungle warfare, truly survival of the fittest. Despite the key role a single can play in launching or sustaining careers, artists—particularly in the rock age—tend to lose perspective here. They (and the critics) often say that the approach is too commercial. You can't always compress good music into three-minute emotion-grabbing ditties for the AM radio audience, they argue. It limits the creative process; it lacks musical sophistication. It puts the emphasis on money rather than art.

And so on.

The fact is that hit singles are not always crass tunes designed to manipulate the market; they *can* be banal, but often they are the product of exceptionally fine writing—nothing to apologize for. The reason to care about singles—if one is needed—is that they get your work before the largest possible public. They break out new artists; and they help established artists stay in the public eye, frequently gathering larger numbers of fans. If an artist has important, interesting (or simply entertaining) things to say, single hits will keep him in front of the audience he deserves to have.

Single hits have an obvious commercial value to the industry. For they lead directly to large album sales. Record companies can make some money on the sales of 45 rpm records alone—many survived this way in the fifties and early sixties—but real profits are in albums. The industry became more and more album-conscious when music changed so radically in the late sixties; prior to that an "album" meant the single hit plus ten cuts laid down in a hurry when the single reached the charts.

Artists are considerably more album-oriented now. Some can survive solely on album sales without making the singles charts at all—The Grateful Dead and The Mahavishnu Orchestra are examples—but the artist must be very special to pull this off for any real length of time. For all artists benefit from the stimulus of the single hit. As noted in Chapter Four, one hit can raise album sales by several hundred thousand units and two or three big hits can carry the sales of an album well above a million.

The ability to have single hits is frequently the most important factor determining whether an already established group with a strong following will reach superstar status. Poco has been an important headlining performing group, but without a hit single they've never reached the front ranks; Loggins & Messina reached it—they've had a consistent string of singles success. The Mahavishnu Orchestra has been a trendsetter and headliner. But its music has never been played on AM stations and so it hasn't achieved the great success of Jethro Tull or Pink Floyd, two progressive music groups which have hit with singles.

Companies can rise and fall on an executive's ability to recognize winning singles. This is usually a question of "ears"—your intuitive song sense. I have no idea where mine comes from. I can't read music, and I know nothing about its structure. I have a "sense" of music, however; I tend to get into melodies instantly, perhaps because of my early training in singing. But my "ears" are really a question of disciplined, intensive immersion in contemporary music. Each time I hear a record my mind factors out (unconsciously) the ingredients involved that might—or might not—make it jump on the charts.

This is something you *feel*. Something happens in your chemistry, your blood, when you hear the record—a tingling, a certain electricity, a sense that audiences will grab onto this song and take off with it. I remember hearing Lynn Anderson's "Rose Garden" in Nashville. I flipped out; the crossover potential seemed obvious. Billy Sherrill, head of our Nashville A&R, was quite surprised. He thought that it was a solid country hit, the kind that might sell a hundred to a hundred and twenty-five thousand copies; but he wasn't convinced of its crossover possibilities. He shook his head at me. He wanted enthusiasm from New York, but he didn't expect *this*.

"Rose Garden" went on to become one of the decade's biggest singles, selling millions of copies all over the world. It also sold more than two million albums worldwide.

A hit single is a question of musical ingredients—they've all got to be in place and they've got to complement each other. You start with the "hook," a basic, repetitive melody or lyric line that grabs hold of the listener. In lyrics, the safest theme, naturally, is love or lost love. The hook doesn't have to be lyrical, however; nor does it have to be about love. It can be a strong dance beat, or a particular musical riff that becomes overpowering as the song progresses. Ideally, the lyric *and* melody combine within the hook to make this line something nearly impossible to forget. But hooks come in all sorts of rhythmic, melodic and lyrical shapes and sizes. Think of hit instrumentals and the riff from Dave Brubeck's "Take Five," or the repetitive guitar line from Edgar Winter's "Frankenstein," or the strong appeal of "Love's Theme" by the Love Unlimited Orchestra.

When I hear a song, my mind works like a computer. The "hit" ingredients register in it, and they are shunted off to various preprogrammed compartments for analysis. Voice is terribly important. Certain kinds of voices *don't* lend themselves to Top Forty play. A song sung by Diana Ross—"Touch Me In The Morning," for example—might be a hit, while Eydie Gorme would have trouble getting on the charts with it at all. Eydie is a terrific singer, but Top Forty audiences resist voices that they identify with middle-of-the-road music. Diana's voice has a catchy, youthful pull to it that teenagers immediately relate to. Eydie grew out of MOR music with the big, dramatic ballad. She is every bit the singer Diana is, but her style is resisted by Top Forty programmers.

The voice—and its reputation—can lead to chart hits for simply technical reasons. One is a question of air play. If Top Forty audiences like a particular kind of voice—or know the artist from past hits—they will call the station to request a record again and again, thus ensuring the repetitive air play that is so important to breaking out a single. An artist like Carly Simon with consistent Top Forty hits gets automatic air play; unknown artists, in contrast, have to come up with singles that will make it without benefit of a prior audience identification.

When I hear a song, I'm instinctively going over a checklist. Is it bubble gum? That might have made it a few years ago. Now records need stronger lyrics; a strong melody alone usually won't do it. Maybe the lyrics are really powerful; but what if there's no *melody* to hang your hat on? The problem, of course, is to see *all* the ingredients. Many records that might have been hits five years ago, for example, won't make it now; you always have to keep the marketplace in mind and update yourself. By contrast, an infectious rhythm-and-blues record has a much easier shot at the charts these days, whereas five to ten years ago AM audiences weren't so receptive to these sounds.

So you are thinking of voices, arrangements, melody and lyrics—and, above all, of the hook. All these must fit together, though you can't be too inflexible about this. You might hear a song and think: "Wow! That melody is so strong it doesn't matter that the lyrics are weak. It's a hit; no question about it!" In one way, your judgments are born of the excitement and enthusiasm of good music. They also, by necessity, must be cold and calculating. I don't know, for example, that I could go into a studio and make a hit record. My track record with hits is based largely on my ability to view a song from on top—which is a cold, objective place. An artist sometimes gets too close to a record; perhaps he'll get carried away by one particular part of it and forget the other ingredients. Artists are often not the best judges of their singles. As a result, singles decisions were usually made by me or two or three other members of the company.

I usually listened to singles in my office. Sometimes I'd get so turned on I'd call up Steve Popovich or Ron Alexenburg and tell them to come to my office immediately. When you really like something, you want to spread it around; it's extremely exhilarating to hear something you *know* is going to be a hit. There is little to compare with the excitement of hearing a record you believe will be known in Hong Kong or Buenos Aires ten weeks later.

# 2

After the record is recorded and ready for release, the next job is to break it out. This involves securing air play on Top

Forty radio—no small problem. Each major city has one premier station, and at least one other trying to challenge its supremacy. The objective is to get the city's top station to "go on" the record. Each of these stations, in turn, is engaged in a hotly competitive ratings game. Rock listeners are avid dial twisters; the station worries about packing its air time as fully as possible with the strongest, most compelling sounds. If a program director goes on a new song, he wants to be convinced that it is a chart-climber of major proportions.

New York's WABC is the epitome of the best and worst of Top Forty radio. Like most big-city rock stations, it has an extremely tight play list. Programming selections are changed by their astute director, Rick Sklar, only once a week, and the station rarely has more than twenty records (plus an occasional Golden Oldie) on its list. So when you consider that perhaps a hundred new singles are released each week—and the average big hit stays on the charts for at least ten weeks—it becomes clear that breaking out a new single is monumentally difficult. On the other hand, WABC plays its Top Twenty list again and again, all day long. This provides the repetition needed to sink a melodic or lyrical hook deeply into the listening audience's mind—and pocketbook.

The question is how to *reach* WABC, or its equivalent in other cities. An artist with a previous track record—George Harrison or Elton John, for example—has the surest entry. These names will get automatic exposure. The radio station knows that an audience already exists for them—and thus will not worry about ratings. In fact, they might *lose* listeners if the competition goes first with such a single. Without a superstar behind a single, however, your task is considerably more difficult. You have to "work" the record very hard.

To start a record, there are certain stations across the country—KILT in Houston, KLIF in Dallas, KJR in Seattle and WOKY in Milwaukee, for example—that have more flexible play lists. These stations add seven or eight new singles a week; your promotion man's job in this case is to gather a fund of information about a particular single and try to convince the program director at, say, KJR, that the station *should* add this song. Perhaps other stations have already gone on it, or one of the tip sheets speaks highly of it, or it simply has the right *feeling*. You argue that the station will *benefit* from adding the record; after all, they really have no other reason for doing it.

The campaign begins when the record is released and mailed to radio stations all over the country, both Top Forty and "secondary." You also might mail it to country and middle-of-the-road stations, depending on your judgment of its appeal. Turning that idea around, you also make judgments about where to mail middle-of-the-road and country songs if you think they have crossover potential. You'll mail Streisand and Andy Williams to Top Forty stations almost automatically, also new Charlie Rich. On the other hand, country, jazz or MOR singles that look good, but are not surefire crossovers, will go only to markets you hope will be responsive to them. When we began promoting Lynn Anderson's record "Rose Garden"—an exception to this—I told the promotion department to mail it to all Top Forty stations *and* have the men in the field take it to the major stations in their area by hand. Usually, with a country or R&B or MOR single, you work it first in its primary market area; if it does well there, you try to cross it over.

Radio stations, meanwhile, subscribe to "advisory" publications—better known as "tip sheets." The big ones are *The Gavin Report* and Kal Rudman's *Friday Morning Quarterback*. Each has a different approach. Bill Gavin is the more direct and scholarly. Rudman's writing is colored by a natural enthusiasm and a variety of highly emotional, upbeat predictions. Rudman also works as a promotion man—so you have to read his sheet with some degree of sophistication. To put it in a different perspective: if Gavin is the Walter Cronkite of the advisory services, then Rudman is the Walter Winchell.

Each of these sheets lists the major and secondary radio stations around the country and what they are adding to their lists; also what is rising and falling in various areas, and things like the "pick of the week" or "sleeper of the week." It is possible through these sheets to keep reasonably on top of musical trends around the country. The radio stations use tip sheets and other information to keep current. They also call local record stores to see what is selling, count their own telephone calls and listen to promotion men argue for various singles. No one wants to be left out; and everyone wants to be . . . slightly ahead of the competition. Not too far, however; no station wants to be more advanced than its listeners. That would hurt ratings.

The station thus keeps track of a record's progress so that it can make a fairly rational judgment about whether to add it to its roster. The program director might be looking closely at ten different singles during a week when he has one slot to fill on his roster. Perhaps he sees that one of them was picked by KILT in Houston last week and numbered 28; if it *stays* 28, he'll assume that the record is not particularly strong. If it jumps to 16, something is happening. And if this particular program director's demographics are similar to Houston's (meaning that he has the same kind of audience), he'll think seriously about adding that particular single to his list.

From the record company's point of view, the idea at the beginning is to build up a single's credibility. For this, you depend on your field promotion men, who are part of an up-to-the-minute commando operation that involves constant telephone calls, teletype messages, transcontinental skull sessions and enormous tension every day. Columbia's and Epic's operations each have about eighteen local promotion men in the field, four regional promotion men and a national promotion staff in New York. In New York, the singles are charted on large status sheets; their movement—or lack of it—is the subject of constant strategy sessions. Each record in turn is given its individual analysis. You first have to decide a record's status. An "A" record requires the full-time work of all promotion men in its area, which could mean anything from the Boston area to the entire United States. A "B" record can be put aside until all "A" records are getting appropriate attention; it will be moved onto the "A" column if other "A" records in a particular region are covered.

By looking at these status charts in New York, you can see at a glance what stations around the country have gone on a particular record. Additionally, you can pick out trouble spots and concentrate your promotional energies in specific directions. You also can make decisions about the *next* move on a record, depending on the regional appeal you think it might have. Your promotion men also know about regional tie-ins; a record that makes it in Atlanta, for example, will probably do well in New Orleans despite the geographic distance between them. From these same charts, you can tell when a single has begun to peak (or skyrocket). If a record goes up to number 8 at WRKO in Boston, for example, and then drops to number 11 the following week, you know that it is in trouble. When a record begins to descend, it rarely turns around. After Boston, the record will probably start dropping in other regional areas, so you'll deploy your promotional forces accordingly.

# 3

A promotion man's job, basically, is to convince a program director to add the singles that his company is pushing. To that end, he will gather up the information favorable to the single and feed it to that director—trade charts, Gavin and Rudman, reviews, press clippings, reports of secondary stations that have gone on the record, whatever word of mouth he thinks appropriate. His first move will be to take the single in to the program director and play it for him . . . *if* the director will let him, which sometimes will depend on their personal relationship, and also on what the director has heard about the song already. Once the director hears the record, he'll react in one of several ways. He'll be knocked out. He'll say, "I like it; this will be one of six records I'm considering for next week's list." Or he'll hate it. In the latter case, he'll *still* have to go with it if he becomes convinced it's going to be a major hit. No program director will flatly refuse to go on a record, unless he objects to its lyrics. This is the time to lay all your research on him. (It's *always* time for that, anyway.)

The competition can be very hectic. If we are pushing hard on a particular single, our promotion men will be calling us all day long from places like Miami and Cleveland to report their progress. California promotion men are three hours behind New York, so they will be calling halfway into the night; there were days when Popovich and Alexenburg literally slept overnight in their offices to keep up with a particular record. Steve lives about fifty miles from Manhattan; he drives back and forth to work pushing buttons on his car radio to see if his singles are *really* getting the action described on the charts. His car radio is able to pick up stations quite a distance away. And when a "push" single broke onto an important station, he always called me immediately—sometimes at home. I got as excited as he did.

Next comes the problem of "spreading" the record. If a Loggins & Messina record breaks out in Boston, it is not automatic that Denver or Philadelphia will pick it up. Other stations might choose to wait and see how well it does in Boston. If it moves up slowly, the others may decide to hang back; or they might not be terribly impressed with the station that started it. WMEX in Boston, for example, is a good station—but the top station in the area is WRKO. The Boston promotion man, therefore, will automatically go to WRKO armed with tip sheets and his most persuasive smile (or wail) and try to get WRKO to take on the record as well. At this point, personal relationships can be a factor. The promotion man might go so far as to say that his job is at stake. He might start calling record stores to see how the single is selling and then use that fact, if the news is good. He might fly the artist in to meet personally with the program director. If the artist is good at promotion, as Mac Davis and Bobby Columby are, this can help a lot. Basically, he'll try anything he can think of, obviously within reason and the law.

In the end, it all comes down to the viability of the single itself. The program director can be swayed in various ways; his final decision, however, will involve his *own* neck. In short, will the single help or hurt his station's ratings? His job depends on these decisions.

Records break out in other ways, some happily, some not. You might find that a single dominates the air waves in Denver, but for some strange reason flops in Dallas and Detroit. Or it might move too *quickly* through one of those markets. It might shoot up—and off—the charts in New Orleans before we can "spread" it anywhere else—which is terribly frustrating. It is also possible to have a "turntable" hit, which means that the single breaks onto the charts all over the country—but doesn't sell in the stores. The nicest surprise, of course, is a "switchboard hit." "Brandy" by Looking Glass, for example, was a routine Epic release which nobody was working particularly hard—when we heard that a small Southern radio station's switchboard was lighting up like a Christmas tree. A disc jockey had simply liked the cut and decided to put it on the air; and the local audience response was overwhelming. As a result, "Brandy" became a national concentration record and it climbed to the top of the national singles charts, selling over a million copies.

In addition to the facts provided by the promotion men, the trade charts are also an important source of information to radio stations. Precisely how these charts are assembled is never quite known; they are usually a combination of private surveys, radio station programming lists from selected Top Forty and secondary stations, and store sales reports in key markets. If a record is getting good store reports, the trade papers might start it at 90 with a "bullet." (The bullet means that the record is moving with strong, upward momentum.) Then, if things are going well, it might go to 78 with a bullet. But if store sales don't increase, it might go only to 75 the following week and lose its bullet. This indicates that you are in trouble. The radio stations will see this as a loss of momentum. Stations frequently *say* they are not terribly influenced by the charts, but that's not really true. An effect is felt. A record that loses its bullet one week can still be saved, but two weeks without a bullet leaves only true believers among the stations playing it.

Timing is terribly important. In a large company, you are juggling a dozen or more different balls to keep upward momentum going—and spreading—in eight or ten different places around the country. Record promotion is so key, in fact, that I decided in 1972 to initiate a major upgrading by changing the Director of Promotion's title to Vice-President. Steve Popovich thus became a Vice-President of Columbia Records at the young age of twenty-nine; Ron Alexenburg became a Vice-President at twenty-nine also, but his responsibility had been broadened to encompass not only promotion but also sales and distribution for Epic and all the custom labels. Both men have enormously taxing jobs; in some cases the tension is so great that marriages run into trouble, gray hair appears and calm gives way to mania. Ron and Steve—easily two of the most dedicated men I've known in the music business—avoided silver hair, divorce and madness; but each gained a lot of weight from the constant snacking that tension and strange hours will induce. Steve's trademark after a while became a can of low-calorie Tab.

In any given week, the promotion staff watches about a hundred Top Forty stations. There are also separate charts for country and R&B singles (which you are also watching, mostly for cross-cover potential). During that time you'll be working an average of fifteen single records and the same number of albums, trying—in the case of the singles—to coordinate the progress of each record in regional patterns. A typical Columbia promotion week, in short, involves fifteen records multiplied by a hundred radio stations—not to mention country, R&B and FM promotion, local concerts, album promotion and special events.

Occasionally, your promotion men are overburdened with "A"-category records. This necessitates either slacking off on singles releases, or hiring an independent promotion man. In the latter case, a company will hire men to work in Atlanta or Chicago (or wherever) for perhaps a hundred and twenty-five dollars a week for a guaranteed minimum of four weeks. The man is supposed to work alongside your promotion people. This is usually done with a record you have a particular *feeling* for—but that may be slightly off the beaten track and need special attention. You want to be sure that it doesn't get lost. The problem, of course, is that the independent promotion man might be handling fifteen or twenty different accounts—the record might get just as lost with him as with your promotion staff.

Promotion often resembles a military campaign. Steve and Ron seem to be generals deploying forces over a vast battle terrain, mounting attacks, retreating, then attacking in other areas; they chart wins and losses and territory gained at New York headquarters, evaluate intelligence (the charts and tip sheets and promotion reports) and send soldiers (the field promotion men) into various skirmishes or to make counterattacks. The stakes are very high. Thousands of singles are released each year; only a few hundred make it into the charts—and make money.

The goal, simply enough, is to have each record tested. The promotion man can't do anything about quality—the point is to get the record heard in the marketplace. If it fails after that, the Promotion Department isn't to blame. Naturally artists, their managers and A&R men tend to see things differently. An artist and his manager are always kept informed of a single's progress. But sometimes—all too often—it doesn't get any play and gathers no momentum; it is impossible to spread it out.

The artist always says, "My God, it didn't get tested properly! You lost it! The company never paid any attention to it!" I usually tried to make sure that we weren't excessively vulnerable to this charge. But 98 percent of the time the cries still come and you have to ignore them if you feel a thorough effort was made. Obviously some records are worked harder than others—but that's always the case where emphasis and direction have to be given. For real creative excellence among a week's releases sticks out and demands your attention. It's inevitable that you'll devote more energy to some records than to others.

# 4

This brings me to the subject of "payola"—paying someone at a radio station to play your records on the air. Does it exist? Is it an established practice?

I have to say that *I* never saw it. In fact, I personally never even heard anyone *propose* it as a promotional device in all my time at Columbia. I recognize that, as a company president, I would have been unlikely to have heard about any dealings in payola that might have taken place at the various promotional levels. Payola (or anything resembling it), nonetheless, was strictly forbidden at Columbia. To erase all doubts about this, we sent a letter from CBS President Frank Stanton each year to the entire distribution force. Payola is *illegal,* it said; anyone found engaging in it will be fired immediately.

So it was heartbreaking when stories began circulating in 1973 speculating that my termination might have something to do with payola. CBS publicly denied this—repeatedly. But when these stories began appearing in print, CBS had the New York law firm of Cravath, Swain and Moore conduct an exhaustive investigation of Columbia. The firm found no evidence that payola had been used by anyone in the company, and the company filed a report to this effect with the United States Senate Subcommittee on Patents, Trademarks and Copyrights.

I can't say categorically that payola doesn't exist in the industry. Occasional rumors make it impossible to dismiss the question summarily. But I submit that if payola is practiced today at all, its use has to be extremely limited. For one thing, many radio play lists are so tight that records are programmed only *after* they become hits elsewhere. Rock stations are engaged constantly in tense ratings wars. A station keeps its ratings up by playing either the established hits or records that the program director is sure *will* be hits. He has little leeway to put maverick records on the air and thus risk a "tune out" by the listening public—leading to lower ratings.

Moreover, public taste controls airplay far more than most people assume. Consumers buy records because they like them; and they call radio stations to request records they want to hear. If a record is ever put on the air through payola it won't last unless it's a *good* record. And if it's a good record, it will be able to get programmed on its own merits.

I've described in this chapter how promotion works. It involves open, hectic and often bitter competition; also frantic hard work, considerable ingenuity, boyish enthusiasm and tireless attention to detail by both record companies and radio stations. For a promotion campaign functions effectively only when the record itself has the elements of a hit. Even then, it takes an organization of hardworking and informed field people using split-second timing and a great deal of energy to get the record moving up the charts.

# 5

The trade papers unquestionably have the industry's most sought-after information—the charts. *Billboard, Cashbox* and *Record World* all publish on Monday, though chart information is available to record companies the previous Wednesday, which gives you an advance reading on records you are particularly concerned about. Among the three, *Billboard* has the most sophisticated chart system, occasionally involving outside consultants, statistical surveys and market research; still (like the other trades) they get hundreds of calls each week from artists, managers and promotion people saying how *tragically* they erred in the week's list. It's inevitable.

As I've noted, the charts are assembled through cross-section samplings of record sales, radio station lists and, to no one's surprise, periodic educated guesses. The trade papers often change their specific sources of information so that record companies can't find and try to influence them. The lack of real facts, however, leads to problems—especially if *your* record is involved. Still, the charts are the best thing we've got.

Except in one area. If a strong MOR artist releases an album that will have steady—but substantial—sales over a long period of time, it won't be reflected accurately in the charts. By contrast, Dawn might release the single "Tie A Yellow Ribbon 'Round The Ole Oak Tree" and have an album based on this hit zoom up the charts behind it. The album, which is usually marketed after the single has been out a few weeks, will last as long as the single—and then frequently disappear. But in the meantime, it will see a lot of chart action—possibly going to the Top Twenty—based partly on the fact that it moved from zero to four hundred thousand sales so fast.

Ray Conniff, on the other hand, might sell four hundred thousand copies of an album over a period of four years but never pass number 90 on the charts. The steady sale doesn't produce the bullets. A Dawn album following a weaker single—"Candida," for example—might sell only two hundred thousand copies, yet still quickly jump to one of the chart's Top Thirty positions because of its singles momentum. Its life might be only ten weeks, though. The result is that you can't always make accurate judgments about an artist's strength from the charts. In the long run, Ray Conniff is likely to sell many more albums than singles-oriented groups who nonetheless surpass Ray on the charts.

The industry tends to be snide about the trades; they are everyone's whipping boy when things go badly, and your best friends when you want some puffery (or a nice picture) put in. The fact remains that they are vital to the industry; *everyone* reads them. Bob Altshuler, head of Columbia's Publicity Department, handled our relations with them, aided by a staff of five or six people in offices in New York and Los Angeles. This involved a lot of give-and-take trying to keep them informed and up-to-date, and in turn getting appropriate space when *we* wanted something.

Now and then I had to square off with the trades myself. Most of the time I let Bob handle these problems; *Cashbox* and *Record World,* for example, are usually reasonably sensitive to company needs—they are more open to print the stories and pictures you send over. Within reason. *Billboard,* however, cloaks itself in what it calls "higher journalistic standards," sometimes seeing itself in a *New York Times* mold. I really applaud their idealism in doing this, but unfortunately it leads to problems, because *Billboard* frequently falls short of its goal.

It isn't that *Cashbox* and *Record World* are slaves to the industry; more to the point, George Albert, Marty Ostrow and Irv Lichtman, who run *Cashbox,* and Bob Austin and Sid Parnes of *Record World,* are very affable, easygoing people who understand a trade paper's role in the industry and have no hang-ups about it. *Record World* in recent years initiated a series of in-depth interviews with industry people and began to add music stories and columns; as a result, it's clearly now making up the lead that the other two older trades enjoyed. *Billboard,* however, remains the most read and the most complete paper—also the most vexing.

We came to blows—so to speak—over Janis Joplin's last single, "Me and Bobby McGee." *Billboard* always reviews singles, often predicting whether the record will reach the Top Twenty, or Sixty, or One Hundred. Their reviews sometimes can be used if you are trying to convince station directors to go on a single. Out of sixty singles released in a given week, *Billboard* usually predicts which two or three will reach the Top Twenty, which four or five will make the Top Sixty and which others will get into the One Hundred; they'll also list some "possibles." Beyond that, they barely acknowledge a single's existence.

As I've noted, "Me and Bobby McGee" had a very emotional effect on me. I insisted that it be the album's first single release; and I asked that our promotion men be instructed to hand-carry it to all important radio stations. I also requested that a two-page ad be taken out in the trade papers; and I wrote my own personal feelings into the ad copy for this first release after Janis's death. It mattered a lot to me; I wanted the last tribute to Janis to be tasteful—and flawless.

Then I heard that *Billboard* had reviewed the single as "also possible."

I was stunned. I felt that the song would be a giant—in fact, the ad called it an "instant classic." I'd never telephoned a reviewer before; this time I got on the phone.

I asked what the basis was for an "also possible" review.

"Janis's last single didn't do very well," the reviewer said. "She's primarily an album artist—her singles don't usually get on the charts like those of Stevie Wonder or Three Dog Night." I realized that this was true; Janis had a number of trademark songs, but none of her singles except "Piece Of My Heart" did exceptionally well. She was known through her concert appearances and extensive FM play.

But I felt that it was unfair to review *this* single on the basis of her history. This record was different; it was beautiful and moving; it couldn't miss. "And besides," I said, "I have a *personal* statement in your paper *right now* saying that this song is an instant classic. I'm embarrassed to be calling you; I don't want to tamper with reviews."

So I asked for one favor—that they omit the review altogether. It was the one time *Billboard* did this kind of favor for me. They certainly must get countless complaints and bitches every week over chart positions and reviews, and it is to their credit that they resist them. But in this case they decided to make an exception.

The rest is history. "Me and Bobby McGee" did indeed become a standard, indelibly stamped on the public's memory. It was the only time that I ever tried to interfere with *Billboard*'s critical judgments—and I was glad that it didn't prove an embarrassment to either of us.

**6** ═══════════════════════════════════════════

Columbia had a weekly singles meeting when I took over in 1965, but it was mostly the preserve of the A&R staff. The meeting was rather bland; the point was to acquaint a select few people with the week's releases.

I knew that this would have to be expanded. A really *tight* company should have creative matters on its mind all the time— even in the sales departments. Sitting at the top of a company, you realize in short order how few people really know what is going on. The singles meeting was a weekly chance to change this. I wanted as many people as possible to know what my priorities were, and to be familiar with my short-term objectives and immediate concerns. I also wanted everyone to feel a vital part of the company, and only if they were well informed could this come about.

So I asked that all department heads—and as many key assistants as we could fit into the room—be required to come to these meetings. If nothing else, it is very impressive for an outsider (or an artist we want to sign) to be talking to, say, the head of Merchandising and find out that he's totally up-to-date on the progress of current releases and creative matters. Then I expanded the agenda of the meeting itself. Key album cuts were played, new singles were discussed, and important problems were aired, if they lent themselves to public discussion. I brought in newly signed artists so that the company could meet them and perhaps hear them perform; I invited managers, press people and others I hoped either to impress or with whom I wanted to begin a relationship. The meeting became a colorful, frenetic session that showed the company at its best. It became the subject of numerous articles in such magazines as *Esquire* and *The New Yorker,* and in the underground press, and after a while an invitation to attend became a highly sought-after prize.

Columbia's meeting was held each Wednesday at eleven o'clock in the twelfth-floor conference room, which has a large rectangular table and pictures of Columbia's and Epic's major artists on the walls. Epic's meeting was on Monday. About twenty-five people sat around the table, and forty or fifty more took chairs against the wall. All the product managers were present, and also people from Business Affairs, Advertising, Publicity, National Promotion, Sales, International Distribution and, obviously, A&R. I sat to the right of the head of the table; Marvin Cohn, then top administrator of A&R, would sit at the head of the table, announce the new records and signal the engineer in the control booth to play them.

The meetings lasted at least two hours, and I frequently programmed them to accomplish specific purposes for that week. I might announce a new signing, or recommend a key advertising campaign, or set in motion a particular press and publicity build-up. As the music played, it was fascinating to watch so many people react, collectively and individually: heads nodded and bodies rolled rhythmically back and forth if the record cast the right spell; or faces suddenly looked uninterested, even bored, if the music wasn't going anywhere.

After the records were played, the Promotion Department reported on the progress of each single and album currently in the marketplace. If there were problems, we discussed whether to focus more attention on a single—concentrate a particular region's efforts on it, take a trade ad, or hire an independent promotion man just for that record. The status of forthcoming major albums was also described by the product managers so that we could get a feel about the releases over the next two or three months.

In short, the meeting came to be a terrific pulse-taking session. It also was a great showcase. Steve O'Rourke, manager of Pink Floyd, came to one meeting after I'd learned of the group's dissatisfaction at Capitol. He was tremendously impressed by the enthusiasm and professionalism he saw, and it made my negotiations for the group much easier after that. The same was true when Billy Joel's manager saw the company in action at a meeting and observed the individual attention given to each record.

I had to be a *little* careful about the approach to each meeting, however. If an artist up for signing was sitting in, I passed the word that people should avoid discussing the *full* range of Columbia's repertoire—the larger-company image problem again. I sometimes altered the day's program slightly if there were visitors I wanted to impress; if the singles selections seemed a bit thin, I might resurrect some of the stronger titles from a few weeks earlier. There's nothing more demoralizing than to listen to five new records that you know are going to flop; after that, it's time to hear from Chicago or The O'Jays.

At these meetings I used sales figures and the pictures on the wall in the same way. Every picture had to be of an identifiable star—Joplin, Dylan, Simon, Streisand, Cash, Horowitz—so that visitors would *feel* the company's career-building success. Steve Popovich would always read the latest sales figures of our best sellers, *Bridge Over Troubled Water* or the second Blood, Sweat & Tears album, even if everyone had heard them the week before. This would invariably invoke gasps when sales of three or four million were mentioned. And when an important manager or lawyer was visiting, the promotion heads were alerted ahead of time to mention records or artists the visitor might be connected with. Nothing could be worse than to slight the clients of a key industry figure.

I was told that these meetings caused some anxiety among my executives. I never fully realized it, but my rapid-fire, pointed questions led many department heads to spend Tuesday nights boning up on odds and ends in their fiefdoms. I never intended this *precisely;* the questions were spontaneous, and they emerged out of my personal curiosity as well as out of a need to use this forum for gathering information that might not otherwise get through my office door. I never liked calling anyone on the carpet; on the other hand, a little homework never hurt anyone.

The most important part of the meeting, of course, was the

playing of the singles themselves. I always watched people's faces, looking for spontaneous reactions. A really strong single took over the room completely. Heads bobbed up and down, fingers moved and shoulders rocked; even John Hammond, one of the industry's truly venerable men, would lean back and burst into a joyous smile if he liked what he heard. But the crowd at the long table could be a hard audience. It took a very strong record to get them going. In the opposite case, of course, I saw blank expressions and aimless table-strumming, and heard the rustling of chairs. It was all part of the scene.

The singles meeting, in sum, was a picture of a tough, professional, spirited group of men and women who cared deeply about music and were willing to be thoroughly immersed in the frenzied pastime of breaking records and building artists. I loved it.

# 7

The final step in promoting a record is advertising. In some ways, this is a record company's most essential job; you can make a mess out of an artist's career very fast if you create the wrong image for him. You *have* to transmit his creative sense correctly; if you don't, you can hurt the company's image as well as his.

Much of the industry hurts itself with "group" merchandising. Companies take out ads saying, in effect: "These are our September releases" and show between ten and fifteen album covers in the ad. This is a real turn-off. Consumers are unlikely to buy an album just because it is part of an amorphous group of unknown names. And from the artist's point of view, why would he want to be advertised that way?

The primary thrust of an ad campaign, logically enough, is to motivate consumers to purchase one or more albums by a particular artist. But how? The simplest thing is to print a picture of the album cover over an announcement alerting the artist's fans that the new release is at hand. But this is the easy way out. There is considerably more to it. Assuming that the cover reproduces well—which isn't always true—you've got to take a great deal of care with ad copy. One or two highly readable lines *must* communicate the essence of what an artist is all about.

What would motivate *you* to purchase this album? You must always ask yourself this question. If this ad showed a Warners release, would I go out and buy it?

There are other, more subtle questions. You must have a feeling for the artist's previous level of public acceptance. If you underestimate it, the ad will seem to approach hype. Bob Dylan and The Beatles, for example, need no introduction. Advertising can—and should—provide direction, charisma and momentum for most artists. Some music companies, of course, avoid ad copy aimed at salesmanship; they fear turning off the contemporary consumer. They reproduce the album cover alone and say nothing. In most cases, this is a waste of money.

I've been called aggressive because I don't like to follow this approach—even though the low-key, subtle style of life among underground audiences seems to demand it. It seems to me that consumers *can* be jogged a bit. I believe, for example, that you can get away with heavy or flamboyant ads like ". . . in the tradition of Bessie Smith," or ". . . the year's most important new artist!"—*if* you've got the talent. Your creative judgment has to be totally on target. If you are wrong, you risk charges of overhype that can help to obliterate a new artist's career (as with The Rowan Brothers).

But if you're right, the ads will heighten interest enough to begin building the career of a superstar. I believe you should take that chance.

This usually involves a negotiated compromise with your ad department, which tends to think in more subtle terms for contemporary artists. I eventually reconciled myself to ads which provided motivation but didn't put the company terribly on the line. The best copy involved quotes from appreciative critics, perhaps a pungent short statement from us, and a picture of the album itself. If someone *else* (say, in *Rolling Stone*) said that this was the "heaviest lyric-writing to come along" or "the album to watch this year," I'd use it. This always took the onus off the company. If a critic felt that this artist was something special, he could be as flamboyant as he wanted; I liked it.

Other times, of course, I wanted very few words. The average record consumer spends little or no time studying an ad, however carefully you've worked on it. You've got to get the message across fast and succinctly. The ad also has to reflect more the artist than Columbia. Columbia should be faceless—except to convey a general image of quality. For it is the artist who sells. The names of Columbia artists—Chicago, Liza Minnelli, Leonard Bernstein, Miles Davis, Andy Williams—mean something specific to most consumers. The images are individually defined, and this is no accident.

Trade advertisements have a different objective from consumer ads. Mostly, you are trying to impress the industry, massage a particular artist's ego, or create some word of mouth that will spread to the public through promoters and disc jockeys. In those cases, you might put sales figures or assessments of chart strength into the copy. Some companies' trade ads, however, are ridiculous—a double-page spread showing the company's entire release sheet for one or two months. I think these are such a waste! Many of the artists on these "laundry lists" are unknown outside their own companies, and the *known* artists can hardly fail to be offended at being lumped into such things. Beyond that, the ads project nothing except a shotgun approach to merchandising. The point of a trade ad, I feel, is to project images of strength and momentum.

I became quite involved in the preparation of ads as time went on—but almost always when I was personally responsible either for the artist's signing or career development. In those cases, I keenly felt what image I wanted projected, and I would spend considerable time with Bruce Lundvall and Arnold Levine, the talented head of Columbia's Advertising Department, going over a proposed ad or a campaign for these artists. The translation of an artist's music and personality to the public must be handled with extreme sensitivity and taste. From the copy written, the picture used—indeed, the whole design—the artist is on view for all to see, and impressions about him can vitally affect his whole future. The importance of this was constantly emphasized and we tried very hard not to lose sight of it.

# Thirteen

## 1

A revolution inevitably leaves someone or something behind. In music, pop vocalists and middle-of-the-road composers had to give way during the sixties to more contemporary writers and performers whose product was first called Rock, and was later expanded to become the broader form known as Contemporary Music. This was not an easy transition for many of them. Prior to the sixties, they had ruled the airwaves; *they* were the culture heroes and objects of worship by emotional audiences and swooning fans. And then the era began its decline.

At Columbia, the fifties belonged to Doris Day, Jo Stafford, Rosemary Clooney, Frankie Laine, Johnny Ray, Tony Bennett, Guy Mitchell, Percy Faith, Ray Conniff and Johnny Mathis. It was the era of Mitch Miller—who was not only the well-known Sing Along conductor but also head of Columbia's A&R. Mitch would define once and for all what A&R really meant, signing all these artists and choosing the repertoire they would record. It was a time when a company's head of A&R was the all-powerful figure, and Mitch became the most powerful in the industry.

Only Mathis, Bennett, Conniff, Faith and Mitch himself remained significant record sellers into the sixties, and as rock made its presence felt fewer new MOR artists broke through to replace the older names. Columbia's two biggest acquisitions of the early sixties who kept MOR momentum going were Barbra Streisand

and Andy Williams. We had an occasional hit with Robert Goulet or a decent-selling album from Jerry Vale or Eydie Gorme. But Andy and Barbra soon became the King and Queen of middle-of-the-road music for Columbia—and the industry.

As we approached the second half of the decade, the decline in middle-of-the-road momentum became noticeable. Mathis had left the company to go to Mercury Records for a large guaranty and royalty (where he had no chart success at all). The Sing Along concept sang itself out and became only a memory. And Top Forty was becoming almost exclusively rock-oriented. Broadway writers were writing fewer and fewer hit songs. Tony Bennett's great streak in the early sixties, which had included "I Left My Heart In San Francisco," "I Wanna Be Around," "If I Ruled The World" and "Who Can I Turn To," was now in jeopardy. New vitality was needed. MOR albums needed a new approach.

I began studying the material Conniff, Faith, Williams and Bennett had been recording; a distinct pattern emerged. Only Williams was really keeping current. He was open to the new, younger writers that were emerging. He kept in touch with composers like Burt Bacharach, Jimmy Webb, Paul McCartney and John Lennon. Andy is a thorough professional; he always understood that Records was a distinctly different medium from Television. He knew that his weekly television show added hundreds of thousands of sales to each of his albums, but he never rested on that. He realized that his television show also benefited from continued success with single records. As his career progressed, he first had his own big hits with songs like "Moon River," "Days Of Wine And Roses" and "Can't Get Used To Losing You." He was then the quickest to realize that being the first to record the Academy Award-winning song gave him the closest identity with the song. If that was not possible, he would still be the first on the market with the song as the title of an album. This led to his great-selling albums "Dear Heart," "Call Me Irresponsible," "The Shadow Of Your Smile" and "Born Free."

Movie songwriting then got bogged down for a few years. Academy Award songs didn't have their former appeal, and Williams had to look elsewhere. He had the right instincts. He went to the writers of today, not for rock songs, with which he might feel uncomfortable, but for contemporary songs that had universal appeal: "Alfie," "Michelle," "Yesterday," "You've Got A Friend," "How Can You Mend A Broken Heart?" "MacArthur

Park." These songs were often hits for other artists, but Andy's fans wanted to hear him sing them too. He would continue to look for his own trademark songs—those he broke as singles for himself—and he would find them: "Love Story," "Love Theme From 'The Godfather'," "Music To Watch Girls By." But his sales were greatly aided by his staying attuned to the fast-changing record market.

I urged Andy to include only the most well known of contemporary songs in his albums. I had carefully studied the sales of his albums and it was a matter of mathematics: sales increased in proportion to the number of identifiable titles on the album cover. It became almost a formula. I figured out that each well-known title in an Andy Williams album was worth between 5 and 10 percent of the album's sales. Three *unknown* songs, for example, might hurt sales by 15 to 30 percent. Other packaging elements such as cover art, or an album's title, also affected this. It was clear that the best of Andy's covers showed him in close-up, with his blue eyes prominent. A black and white cover or one that had him looking too hip or mod would hurt. Cover art could affect about 20 percent of potential sales; the pull of a title had approximately the same value. If the cover and title were strong, the rest of the album—that is, the song content—totaled a 60 percent variable.

It became possible, therefore, to be quite calculating about middle-of-the-road albums. Naturally the approach was criticized as manipulative; when the formula became apparent, I encountered hostility and misunderstanding. A&R men felt threatened by it, radio stations were hostile and some artists thought it forced them to become commercial machines. For A&R men, the approach seemed a threat to their creative judgment; MOR albums limited to current hits narrowed both their prerogatives to select the music for their artists and the approaches they could take in producing it. The radio stations feared an avalanche of the same songs, making their programming more difficult. They were quite vocal about this—but I knew that the problem was being exaggerated. Besides, our primary job was not to service radio stations, but to sell records.

The most important consideration, of course, was the artist's feelings. Ray Conniff was extremely hesitant to use the approach. His audiences were not into current songs, he continually said. And his albums tended to sell over periods of five to ten years; if he put contemporary hits in them, they might have a shorter life. Nonetheless, I convinced him to try this—and he walked away from his middle-of-the-road competition. His sales became considerably greater than those of Lawrence Welk or Billy Vaughn or others of a similar musical reputation. The life of his album sales was not shortened at all. Conniff eventually became the most exacting practitioner of the principle, even demanding exclusivity of titles for his albums.

Percy Faith, like Conniff, worried that his catalog sales would shrink if he turned to "covering" hits. More important, this offended his artistic sense. I *cannot* go into the studio and do this, he said. I've got to put my own writing into these albums. The money doesn't mean that much, but my artistry does. I can't go into the studio and just cover hits by other people. I've got to spread my *own* wings!

I understood; and I tried not to be too heavy-handed about this. It isn't really a question of money, I said, it's your *career* that's at stake. If you have a hit single, your album will sell. But if you don't—which is likely—you'll be a "has-been" unless you get into current writing. If you want to get on the charts, you'll have to try this. We eventually worked out a compromise. Percy did two or three albums "my" way, and then recorded an album "his" way. The contemporary albums outsold the other better than two to one. In fact *Today's Themes for Young Lovers* tripled his ordinary sales and eventually became his number-one catalog seller as well.

The formula became so obvious to me, particularly since rack jobbing had come to dominate the industry. Albums now appeared in plastic skin-wrapping. As a result, record consumers couldn't play an album in the store. MOR consumers now looked at the cover to see what titles the artist was performing—the more current and identifiable the titles on the album, the more likely they would be interested enough to buy. Eleven hits on a Percy Faith album clearly had more pull than, say, five.

The issue came into sharp focus when Andy Williams wanted to record an album of original songs produced, and, in some cases, written by Mason Williams. It was to be a "concept" album—which was always a turn-off in the MOR market. The artist might be deeply into the idea, but the public rarely understood. Andy said that he wanted to do a range of songs extending from "birth to death," a musical way of talking about life. He was very enthusiastic about this, which made my job even more difficult. For he was one of our top artists, and a drop of five or six hundred thousand from his normal million-or-so sales mark would make a visible dent in profits. This was toward the end of 1970; I was beginning to worry about how Andy would do without weekly television exposure.

It's one thing for a *contemporary* artist to do a concept album, I said, but without a single hit your air play will be only middle-of-the-road stations. The concept won't get *across* in a skin-wrapped album. If a single breaks out, the album will do well. If one doesn't, you'll be left with an album of mostly unknown compositions. Believe me, the sales will be shockingly low!

As I've said, Andy is a pro. He thought this over and suggested a compromise. One side of the record was to feature the Mason Williams "concept"; the other would have songs like "Bridge Over Troubled Water" and "Raindrops Keep Fallin' on My Head." I really didn't want to do it. Sales would be affected badly even by this, but he felt so strongly about this "concept" that I went along with him. We titled the album *Bridge Over Troubled Water*—but, true to form, it had exactly half the sales of an album *filled* with current hits. The point was not lost on Andy.

It seemed such an obvious way to increase sales; ironically, I found that only Columbia was doing it. Other MOR artists were recording current hits but they were also using albums to attempt to break out new singles or simply showcase unknown compositions. I didn't advertise the formula—no point in sharing your secrets—but I couldn't believe that no one else was practicing it. One reason may have been that other companies couldn't deal with the internal pressures the formula caused. I had to *keep* answering questions. My sales people and A&R men, radio programmers and artists kept coming back again and again; I'd spend hours and sometimes days talking to managers and the artists. Fortunately Jack Gold, who was head of Columbia West Coast A&R and who also produced albums at one time or another for Conniff, Faith, Nabors and Streisand, understood the idea thoroughly and was very useful in helping me translate it into actual practice. Bruce Lundvall, the head of Marketing, also saw the value of the approach and ably shared the burden of it. We had to make sure the key point communicated to the artists was that these albums were no substitute for trying for a hit single every ten weeks. That's where creativity of the A&R man and the artist could be tested. If the song was unknown and could be a hit, try it as a single. Don't waste a valuable album-cut space for a failure that would hurt sales. If the single became a hit, then it would be the title of the next album; if not, then leave it alone.

As commercial as the approach seemed, I felt that it also had artistic merit. For this down-the-line approach contributed enormously to the longevity of many artists. More and more, Columbia became the predominant middle-of-the-road label. Because of it, Jerry Vale regularly outsold Jack Jones or Sammy Davis, Jr.; Ray Conniff added years to his career, outlasting Billy Vaughn; and Vikki Carr had a whole new recording life open up when she joined Columbia after leaving Liberty in 1970.

Another artist who enjoyed "new life" was Johnny Mathis. Mathis had been *the* pop vocalist for about six years, beginning in 1956. A whole generation danced and romanced to "Chances Are," "It's Not For Me To Say," "Wonderful, Wonderful," "The Twelfth of Never," "A Certain Smile," "Misty" and "Maria," among others. In fact, his album *Johnny's Greatest Hits* still holds the record of having been on *Billboard*'s best-selling-album charts for the longest consecutive period—eight *years.*

As I mentioned earlier, Mathis had left Columbia to go to Mercury around 1963. His contract was for three years; his success there was minimal. I had always been a strong admirer of Mathis's unique style and I successfully campaigned to get him to rejoin Columbia. I then studied his Mercury albums and saw that most of the songs recorded were not major copyrights. Without single hits there, I wasn't surprised to see his sales drop to a hundred thousand. We got to work immediately and applied the "formula." Albums like *Love Is Blue, Those Were The Days* and *Love Theme From Romeo and Juliet* included songs such as "Little Green Apples," "This Guy's In Love With You," "By The Time I Get to Phoenix" and "Walk On By." Every song had been a blockbuster hit and Mathis fans returned in droves, followed by a host of new ones. His sales tripled and the three albums he recorded each year sold about one million units altogether.

I took a very active interest in Johnny's career. His voice was ageless and he was still young. When he started in 1956, he was only eighteen years old. When he rejoined us, he was twenty-nine. I first showcased him to the entire Columbia organization at the sales convention in Puerto Rico in 1968. His magic was still there. Then I introduced him at the NARM convention so that the

entire industry—manufacturers, distributors, rack jobbers and retailers—could see his youth *and* artistry. His performance sparkled;
he received a cheering, standing ovation.

I was constantly trying to reach the new record buyers for him.
I felt that today's youth should know of him and get into his voice.
So I asked him to incorporate some of the best rock songs into his
act; and he did, using Santana's "Evil Ways," George Harrison's
"My Sweet Lord," the Carpenters' "We've Only Just Begun" and
Carole King's "It's Too Late." All this helped to expand his audi-
ence. Then, as 1970 was drawing to a close, I decided to take a
gamble.

I had become closely identified with contemporary music. I
was also working very hard with our middle-of-the-road artists,
but because my participation was mostly behind the scenes, it was
not very visible. The signing of artists like Joplin, Blood, Sweat &
Tears and Johnny Winter got the publicity, not the contemporiza-
tion of such performers as Williams and Mathis. Yet Columbia's
MOR roster was considerable; our investment here was substantial. And these artists had millions of fans. Why should a Mathis or
a Vikki Carr play only to Waldorf-Astoria audiences of five hundred at a time—with a prohibitive price tag of about seventy-five
dollars for a dinner for two and an evening's entertainment? Why
not take over Madison Square Garden and put on a show for
eighteen thousand people? Contemporary groups could fill it; I
thought that Mathis and Carr could also.

We announced the evening in a *New York Times* advertisement: Columbia Records Presents Johnny Mathis, Vikki Carr,
Percy Faith with an orchestra of 60. The local New York promoters raised their eyebrows at the risk—our gamble involved
almost one hundred thousand dollars. Despite the fact that the
artists were performing for no fee, there was no way that we could
make any money. But the cause was a good one—to bring excitement to MOR music.

We followed the *Times* advertisement with posters all over
the city and radio-time buys on New York's middle-of-the-road
stations. The MOR disc jockeys took up the cause. This was their
music and they were delighted that we were really getting behind
it. I was told that if I gave New York radio station WNEW an
interview, we'd get an hour's special. I agreed, and the station's
well-known disc jockey William B. Williams talked with me about
the event and then played only Mathis, Carr and Faith records for

an hour. Ticket sales mushroomed. Two days before the concert, we were assured of a sellout.

We left nothing to chance. We brought in the finest engineers and sound experts to make the vast, unpredictable Garden into a beautiful sound chamber. We installed a revolving stage, bathed in colorful lighting, so that everyone would see well. I acted as master of ceremonies and introduced each artist. It was a memorable evening in every way, as was the gala midnight supper held at New York's glittering Rainbow Room to celebrate the occasion.

Mathis rejected one last idea I had for him. It was 1972 and I was very impressed with the hit records Thom Bell had been producing with the R&B groups The Stylistics and The Spinners —both of whom sang very much in the Mathis tradition. I arranged for Mathis and Bell to meet and then do an album together. I felt that although Mathis should continue to please his current fans, most of whom were white, he should also be exposed to larger black audiences. R&B and Top Forty were blurring into each other. Black stations would program Mathis now, given the right record. He should also perform more in the black community. "You're going to laugh at this idea," I said one day, "but I think you should play Harlem's Apollo Theatre for a week."

"For a *week*?" he said. "The *Apollo*? I'd have to do seven or eight shows a day!"

"Why?"

"I played the Apollo when I started out. You *had* to do that."

I laughed. It was no longer true. The bill would have been more like two shows each night, perhaps three on the weekend— about the same as he did at the Waldorf-Astoria. But Johnny didn't think that I was serious, and I never got him up to One Hundred and Twenty-fifth Street. It's too bad. He would have done beautifully.

# 2

I had considerably less luck with Tony Bennett. Tony hadn't been happy with his sales since the late sixties. He was extremely successful in nightclubs, a headliner all over the world. He used to call me from engagements in London, Rome or Las Vegas to say how *well* he was doing—why weren't his albums reflecting that?

The answer was obvious. Musically, Tony was looking over his shoulder. His repertoire was dated, and the public wasn't buying it. All the advertising in the world—or sellout audiences at Caesar's Palace—wouldn't change this. I tried constantly to convince him to use more contemporary writers, but he resisted. I knew that the audiences were out there; Tony's appeal is enormous. Album-buying audiences, however, want current songs they recognize.

The best writers in the world, Tony kept telling me, were Gershwin, Richard Rodgers and Harold Arlen; he may have been right. The best performers were Judy Garland, Al Jolson and Jimmy Durante. Again, he certainly could make a case. He felt that his artistry was linked to them and he did not want to compromise it. I respected this. But my obligation was also to make Tony aware of the tastes of current record buyers. Material written a number of years ago was not selling records today. And, in fact, as great as Garland and Durante were, they were never the record sellers that their place in entertainment history would indicate they should have been. Tony had been a top seller, but now his sales were slowing down and he needed advice—albeit unwanted.

I wasn't asking him to sing songs he felt *uncomfortable* with. That would have been silly. But there were hundreds of strong contemporary titles to choose from; how could he not find eleven songs that met his standard? He wouldn't budge. I met with Buddy Howe, who was Chairman of the Board of CMA, a large talent agency that booked Tony's live engagements, to ask his help. Buddy agreed with my objective, but he was having his own disagreements with Tony and couldn't help. Then Tony's sister, Mary—who sometimes acted as his manager—called to say that Tony was so emotionally distraught over the problem that he was literally throwing up just thinking of recording this unfamiliar repertoire.

I felt terrible. I shouldn't be having conflicts with such a unique artist, who was clearly one of pop music's all-time greats. Yet he kept calling to complain about sales; and this would inevitably lead to arguments about whether he should be recording an album of Rodgers and Hart or Lennon and McCartney. "I fully respect your artistic integrity," I said, "but if you keep accusing us of not promoting you enough, I have no choice but to put on my business hat. You have to *update* your repertoire. With all the music written today, it's inconceivable that you can't pick eleven songs to fill out an album." Finally, at long last, after opinions from all his advisors became unanimous, Tony agreed to try an album of contemporary songs.

Once he got into the project, he really liked it. We found several good, relatively current titles, songs by The Beatles and Burt Bacharach, among others. Tony even called to say how pleased he was. In fact, he was so happy with the album that he asked me to do the liner notes. I'd never written liner notes before (this was about 1970), I'd avoided it mainly out of fear of being besieged by other artists. Nonetheless, this album had involved such a great deal of effort by us both that I decided to do it.

With current repertoire, Tony's album sales jumped substantially. Another such album would have built on this larger base if Tony hadn't suddenly backed off again. He would put two or three contemporary songs into each album, but he basically returned to his original thinking. In a sense, I understood. Tony's recording career had been enormously successful. His artistry was clearly defined—he just couldn't change.

At this point we became distant from each other. He called a few times with the usual complaints, and my answer was always the same. After a while the conversations ceased; we were both exhausted. But I would never have stopped making our recording studios and label available to Tony, even with all the travail. He deserved tremendous gratitude for his contributions to the company over the years. And his ability as a vocalist has never become impaired. His inimitable phrasing of a lyric, his soulful reading of a song, leave him with few equals among singers. Our business problems never caused me to cease respecting him as an artist.

Tony eventually got a good offer from MGM Records and left Columbia in 1972. He continues to sell out clubs and concerts everywhere. His record sales are still the same.

# 3

Barbra Streisand also had difficulty in adjusting to the changing music scene. She had been the industry's best-selling female vocalist during most of the sixties, selling around a million copies of albums that included such great standards as "Happy Days Are Here Again," "People," "Second-Hand Rose," "He Touched Me" and many more. Then she went to Hollywood and achieved movie stardom with *Funny Girl*. The soundtrack of that album sold well over a million copies and she was riding high.

But she began to lose touch. She became immersed in motion pictures and was no longer close to the world of music—which was changing fast. Her albums *What About Today, Je M'Appelle Barbra, A Happening in Central Park* didn't make it. She was recording a lot of material written by her Hollywood friends whose writing wasn't in vogue at that time. Her sales fell to one-third of their former strength, settling at about three hundred and fifty thousand copies per release.

I began talking with Marty Erlichman, still her devoted and skillful manager. Streisand had begun her career as a teenager; she was in her late twenties now, the same age as many of rock's hottest writers and performers. It seemed obvious that she should be performing their music instead of Broadway and Hollywood tunes. Erlichman agreed and said he'd try to talk to her. But he struck out. I asked for a shot at it myself, and he arranged for me to meet with her on the set of *Hello, Dolly!*

She was shooting a scene when we arrived, and I watched for about thirty minutes before we went into her dressing room-cottage to talk for nearly an hour. I'm not trying to "commercialize" you, I began, but your album sales will continue to decline unless something changes. You have to contemporize your image. The problem, of course, was that Streisand—like any good artist—valued her individuality; she didn't want her image altered at all. She was also a little insecure and worried that she might not have too much to offer contemporary rock audiences; I disagreed. A performer of her magnitude could bring entirely new meaning to modern songs. I didn't want to be heavy-handed at this meeting; I hoped only to lay the foundation for a change of thinking. I could see that she was more unsure of herself than adamantly opposed to the idea.

Abstractions didn't do the trick. I decided to propose actual songs to her. I had become friends with Los Angeles producer Richard Perry, who had been on the Warner Bros. A&R staff. I had always admired Richard's productions. They indicated great promise. But the artists he worked with didn't give him much room commercially; his first real success, ironically, had been with

Tiny Tim. Richard was very sensitive with all his artists, and he had a fine contemporary feel. He showed it when he produced a beautiful album of Ella Fitzgerald singing Beatles material. But neither that album nor the one he did with Fats Domino sold well. Nevertheless, I believed in him and I approached him about Streisand; naturally he was dying to produce her. It happened that he—like Streisand and myself—came from Brooklyn. He felt they could communicate easily, and he started gathering songs. This was to be his big professional chance.

Richard brought about ten songs to me. We listened to the tape and cut the selections to five, including a few by Laura Nyro. Then I told Erlichman about Perry, and he arranged for Streisand to meet him. She loved the songs and was convinced on the spot.

This precipitated a tremendous change in Streisand's career (and Perry's also—he picked artists much more carefully thereafter, going on to produce the great Nilsson-Schmilsson album, the "You're So Vain" classic album of Carly Simon and Ringo's giant album that included "Photograph," "You're Sixteen" and "Oh My My"). The album's title song, "Stoney End," was a huge hit, and the album went gold. She was on AM radio again, gathering in hundreds of thousands of new fans. Her older fans may have been a bit shocked at the new repertoire, but they loved her anyway and they adjusted. We got the album on FM radio too, since much of its material was written by composers known to FM audiences. She also incorporated several of the songs into her stage act, winning a new cabaret audience as well. It was clear that she could do contemporary material extremely well. We were careful, of course, not to stray *too far* from her nucleus of middle-of-the-road fans. This was her musical base, and we wanted to keep it intact while gathering in the younger fans. With her enormous talent, it was no problem to mix John Lennon, Laura Nyro and Carole King material with Burt Bacharach and Jimmy Webb songs and keep everyone happy.

Changing and broadening Barbra's musical horizons wasn't motivated by money alone. She'd already made the million-dollar guaranty we had fought so hard over a few years earlier. She had earned 65 percent of that merely from sales of the *Funny Girl* album. It was more a question of her potential; her audience was *larger* than Broadway. One vivid test of this was a performance she gave in 1972 at a McGovern benefit at Los Angeles' Forum Theatre. James Taylor and Carole King, the two hottest names in contemporary music at the time, were also appearing. Taylor had just had two big hits, his own song "Fire and Rain" and what was to become a standard, Carole King's "You've Got A Friend." Carole was riding high, with one song after another from her *Tapestry* album becoming a standard and pushing that album to rival Simon & Garfunkel's *Bridge Over Troubled Water* as the best-selling album of all time.

There was one very difficult moment when Erlichman called to say that Lou Adler had suggested Streisand not close the show; he thought that Carole King should do it. Adler's suggestion was logical: the audience that lined up the night before tickets went on sale was completely youthful, likely to be more into King and Taylor than into Streisand. Yet Streisand is a "closing" artist—a superstar who *always* closes the show—and Erlichman felt that this might be a slap in her face. I agreed with his instinct to take the risk with the young audience.

About eighteen thousand people packed the Forum. During the first set King and Taylor performed individually and then together; they did very well. A delay followed because a large orchestra had to assemble to back up Barbra; the audience began to fidget. But as soon as the loudspeaker announced her and she came onstage, it was clear that everything would be fine. She was greeted with a thunderous ovation. After that, she had the crowd in the palm of her hand. This was a *live* audience and she was a performer without peer. It was one of popular music's legendary concert performances and the evening belonged to her. The press and word-of-mouth comment was so phenomenal that we released a live album; it went gold immediately.

One lesson learned when "contemporizing" an artist: be careful of the media. The *Stoney End* album's advertising campaign was aimed, logically enough, at young audiences. We spent nearly a hundred thousand dollars advertising in underground papers, rock magazines, *Rolling Stone,* and on all the major FM stations. "Barbra is as young as the writers on the album," we said, and we listed their names in large, bold type. Fine—except that it convinced Erlichman and Streisand to go all the way and try to capture the *Rolling Stone* crowd as well. She agreed to an interview which led to a story titled "The Jeaning of Barbra Streisand." *Rolling Stone* has made a tremendous contribution to contemporary music, but it also consistently takes a snide attitude toward "establishment" artists; a lack of purity is assumed, I suppose. This story was no exception; Barbra was pictured as an old-style movie-star type living in the glittering Hollywood Hills and incongruously wearing dungarees. It didn't match, and the magazine hammered this home.

Still, Streisand was able to mix both worlds of music as few other artists could. She had a hit with Laura Nyro's "Time and Love." Then she followed it up with one by Carole King, "Where You Lead" and included this in an album with impeccable performances of Jimmy Webb's "Didn't We" and Burt Bacharach and Hal David's "One Less Bell To Answer." Streisand's talent is awesome. Occasionally she shows poor judgment. Her television special "Barbra Streisand—And Other Musical Instruments," was weak musically and in turn led to a bad soundtrack album. But she bounced back with her big hit "The Way We Were," which showed again that she could still do it—and do it brilliantly—on her own terms.

## 4

Country and Western artists were another group that felt somewhat disenfranchised by rock's dominance. It was not entirely the same problem. They had their own fans, but I had to let them know—regularly—that I fully appreciated their music. I always went to Country Music Week, for example. Office pressures kept me from going to Nashville more than two or three times a year, so I tried to make up for that by participating heavily in that week's activities. At first, it was difficult for me to get into the music. Most people I knew had grown up in rock or jazz; they couldn't take seriously country music's often simplistic lyrics. Fortunately, Columbia's and Epic's top promotion men, Ron Alexenburg and Steve Popovich, were avid country fans. Thanks to them, the lines of communication to Nashville were kept fully open at all times.

Columbia had the city's top creative talent, Billy Sherrill, as head of its Nashville A&R. Billy is a tremendously successful writer and producer. He has a long, impressive string of hits behind him in both areas and he has an extremely keen sense of competition—a fierce ambition to see that Columbia is number one in country music. It was *his* love for that music that soon infected me. I never became a dyed-in-the-wool fan; but I did learn to understand the music and its broad appeal. With increased exposure, it became easier to look for the emotion-tugging hook or melody that put everything together and somehow made you look into yourself.

I felt like a fish out of water during my early visits to Nashville. The fans are the die-hard, lasting loyalists, and many then seemed to come from another time in American history. Women sometimes wear beehive hairdos, and men dress in Stetson hats and cowboy boots. Country Music Week is extraordinary. Grand Old Opry runs the festivities, and thousands of fans flood into town to get as close as possible to their favorite artists. The town is filled with "hospitality" suites; these in turn are jammed by eager fans.

The artists meet them head on, appearing at the receptions in spangles and sequins, shaking hands and signing hundreds of autographs. At each performance, people rush to the stage to take photos; you can make a fair estimate of a performer's importance by the camera clamor. A moderately prominent artist draws twenty-five to thirty amateur photographers; Johnny Cash drew hundreds. A country performer is very important to his fans, and he has a well-defined, almost "family" image to them. Artists tend to last a long, long time; and this isn't because of looks, sex appeal or public relations. It is the songs they sing. An empathy can build up between fans and a performer that lasts years because of the emotion the performer projects to his audiences.

Nashville sociology is also different from the rest of the music world. Despite their natural competitiveness, people there are enormously friendly; there is relatively little label-switching. It is like a small town, polite on the surface, relatively closed to outsiders. There *is* a large amount of combativeness underneath —but it is hidden by camaraderie and very prescribed and orderly ways of doing business: no arm-flailing, hype or get-rich-quick impulses are supposed to be visible. The town revolves around music; most of the music companies and publishers have their offices within a small geographic area comparable to several city blocks. There is also a ruling aristocracy made up of important artists, some industry executives, leading publishers and a few people connected with Grand Ole Opry.

Minnie Pearl is a member of it. I met her during one of my early visits and got a good lesson in Nashville politics. An A&R

producer named Bob Johnston was running our office down there at the time. Bob had been a staff producer in New York; he had had some success with Patti Page and had supervised an album that Simon & Garfunkel had recorded, but his track record wasn't distinguished at the time. This was before he was to gain recognition for his work with Bob Dylan, Johnny Cash and Leonard Cohen. Bob was always very up, an enthusiastic type. He was skilled at artistic hand-holding and usually said the right thing in difficult studio situations. He had been sent to Nashville to replace Don Law, who for a long time had been a "dean" of Nashville, responsible for such signings as Johnny Cash, Ray Price and Marty Robbins. When Law retired, it was difficult finding the right person to fill that spot. Bill Gallagher finally settled on Bob; I had no one else to suggest, so I gave my consent. It was a bad assignment.

Johnston went down to Nashville to bring Columbia back to first place in country music. In the previous two or three years the label had slipped—relatively few emerging artists had been signed by Law compared to RCA's success with Charley Pride or Capitol's with Merle Haggard, Buck Owens and Sonny James. Johnston had a large task ahead of him and he plunged right in. Rather than go about his work quietly, building up a record of imposing artist signings, he kept giving interviews saying how he was going to shake up Nashville; how things had gotten encrusted and fossilized and how he was going to create waves and change everything. This must have scared the hell out of the ruling establishment, and Minnie Pearl was apparently chosen as the person to tell me.

She casually walked over to see me at an annual dinner given by Broadcast Music, Inc. It looked like a chance meeting—but it couldn't have been. She was very polite—it was an "honor" to meet me, Columbia had been wonderful to Nashville, the company had built up a great tradition . . . and other courtesies. Then she got to the point. Bob Johnston wasn't the kind of person who succeeded in Nashville; he was shaking up established ways of doing business and rubbing a lot of people the wrong way. The town was . . . *noticing* this. What a terrible thing it would be for Columbia's great name if the company became known as a . . . disruptive force on Music Row.

She talked in friendly, almost milky words. The emotions seemed genuine. It was quite refreshing to get a dressing-down in such a warm, personal way. I was far more used to the cool, impersonal ways of New York. After that, I looked carefully at Bob's operation. In contrast to what he was saying in the press, very little was happening creatively. I concluded that most of the artists he was signing had very little potential. And so I asked him to give up this executive post and return to producing, this time under an independent producer's contract with us. The problem for now was solved.

I gave Billy Sherrill, who was successfully handling A&R for the Epic label and had built that label up practically single-handedly with artists like Tammy Wynette and David Houston, responsibility for Columbia as well. After that, Columbia did extremely well in Nashville. I loved Billy's high standards for artist signings. He told me he waited for that "special tingle" in his spine and then he knew he had something unusual in tow. He didn't have to elaborate. I used to wait for the same thing in myself. I knew he'd do beautifully for the company. His low-key demeanor also belied a prankish sense of humor and a fierce pride to excel. And excel he did. He signed them, he wrote their songs and produced their records. Tanya Tucker and Barbara Fairchild emerged as important new talents as a result. Tammy Wynette remained on top with one hit after another, and her album of *Greatest Hits* sold over one million units. He brought in Glenn Sutton to join him in A&R, and then they both persuaded Lynn Anderson, Glenn's wife, to leave Chart Records and come to Columbia. Within a few months she recorded "Rose Garden"; it became an international hit, selling over three million copies worldwide and over one million albums in the United States alone. Again leaning on a spouse's influence, he convinced Tammy Wynette's husband, George Jones, to join Epic, and proceeded to have a separate streak with George alone and then one with George and Tammy together. Finally Charlie Rich joined the giants of country music with records like "Behind Closed Doors" and "The Most Beautiful Girl In The World."

It was a tremendous accomplishment and we all watched with awe and pride. Country music was playing a larger and larger role in the company's overall picture. To Sherrill's record, add the fact that Johnny Cash had emerged as a cult personality and was selling millions of albums; and then that Ray Price's record of "For The Good Times" became a national best seller, leading to sales of one million albums and a whole new career for him and Don Law, who continued to be his producer. It became necessary to make the entire company much more conscious of country music—more understanding of the whys and wherefores of its appeal. We sent our top Marketing people to Nashville—the advertising and art and design key personnel, and all the regional promotion men. Album covers had to be improved; the whole look of the country line had to be streamlined. I sent my assistant, Ron Bledsoe, down to Nashville—his original home—to become Vice-President of Nashville operations. He was to take all burdens —except for A&R—off Billy Sherrill's shoulders. And Sherrill was made a Vice-President of Nashville A&R as a recognition of his achievements.

I pitched in as well, conducting the negotiations to get George Jones and Lynn Anderson. I also went after and signed Sonny James, who was just coming off a streak of about seventeen consecutive Number One country records. Then time had to be spent with three major Columbia artists from the Don Law era who had stayed outside the Billy Sherrill operation. I was worried that they might feel left out of things, and indeed one of them, Marty Robbins, left to go to Decca Records. I moved in at that point to shore up our relations and make sure that Johnny Cash and Ray Price also felt close to the company. During Country Music Week I met with Cash and Price at some length to make sure that all was well. I also met with artists that week at breakfasts, lunches, dinners and at the hospitality suites, and I MC'ed the shows Columbia hosted. I also spent time with Sherrill in rehearsals. Beyond that, Popovich and Alexenburg, who also came along on these trips, held things together. It can be a very severe problem if an important A&R man feels that the national heads of promotion don't understand his music; Alexenburg and Popovich not only understood it—they loved it.

It had also become clear that country music's chart influence was growing. New York City, for example, now has a full-time country station. Contemporary performers are also influenced by country writers, and the number of crossovers of songs from country to contemporary charts was growing. Columbia's position in Nashville, moreover, grew. During 1972 and 1973, we often had more than half of the hits on country's Top Twenty charts, thanks mainly to Billy Sherrill's prodigious talent.

Nashville, however, remains conservative. The buildings and fashions are more modern, but there is still reluctance to change. When Ray Price wanted to add strings to his backing, for example, there was tremendous resistance—similar to what happens when a jazz artist adds rock to his repertoire and is then drummed out of the hard-core purist fraternity as if he has "sold out." For a while, some country disc jockeys refused to play Ray's records. But he stuck to his new ideas—to his credit, I think—and even started wearing tuxedos; no more pictures in cowboy hats and boots. He wanted to change his image so strongly that he took it almost too far, picturing himself as a Las Vegas act. Nonetheless, his insistence on broadening his music helped to loosen things up in Nashville. Not *that* much, but enough to allow a few artists to try new ideas.

In the same vein, country music fans consistently resisted the advances of rock artists. A number of contemporary writers became quite enamored with country music during the late sixties; country-rock albums suddenly were "in"—to critics and some rock fans, that is. The country audience wasn't interested. The Byrds, The Flying Burrito Brothers and Poco all decided at one point that their music could attract large country audiences. They were wrong. The Byrds' country albums—*Sweetheart of the Rodeo, The Notorious Byrd Brothers*—got excellent reviews; but except for their hard-core fans, rock audiences were turned off and didn't buy these albums. A hoped-for country following never materialized. The Byrds performed during Country Music Week one year, for example, and got only polite applause. It *was* good music, but the average country fan simply resists rock. He is likely to be very put off by the performers themselves—long hair, bell-bottoms, suspicion of drugs, etc.—and so even the finest music may pass by him. Bob Dylan's *Nashville Skyline* album, for example, got relatively little air time on country stations.

# 5

During the period 1968 through 1972, Country Music Week's biggest moment for Columbia each year was the appearance of Johnny Cash. He was the industry's best-selling country singer—but when he came to Nashville each year, it was a free gig. He not only came at his own expense, but he brought his wife, June Carter, the entire Carter family, the Statler Brothers and Carl Perkins as well. His performance was spellbinding. Most artists limited their appearances to one or two numbers in these shows; Cash was the exception. His performance was a major event; the demand was so great that we eventually booked the municipal auditorium for it—and opened the doors to thousands for free.

Johnny was a culture hero as well as a recording star. When he walked into a room, all eyes turned toward him; it didn't matter who else was in the room. His presence was absolutely commanding. He dressed totally in black. He is tall and powerfully built, and when he walked in your direction, you automatically stepped out of his way. He had been through a number of difficult periods in his life when I met him—a broken marriage, temperamental ups and downs, drinking and drug-taking—but with June Carter he had changed profoundly, somehow finding the peace and understanding that allowed him to deal very maturely with the almost religious fervor of his admirers.

I had little contact with Cash initially, but followed his career closely when he went on television and his albums *Johnny Cash In Folsom Prison* and *Johnny Cash In San Quentin Prison* jumped to the top of both the pop and country charts. Cash somehow conveyed gentleness *and* power at the same time. He always gave autographs in crowds. He showed his fans a kindness and concern that added enormously to their love for him. Then I began getting disturbing reports; he was dissatisfied with Columbia. He wanted more advertising support. This was strange. Cash normally didn't complain about things like this; and we happened to be giving him great support. We'd spent tremendous amounts of money to advertise his albums in every kind of medium: country, middle-of-the-road and rock stations, as well as in *Rolling Stone* magazine and other underground newspapers. Cash appealed to every kind of music fan and we advertised everywhere.

I decided to talk to him. I arranged to meet him outside the Municipal Theatre one day during Country Music Week in 1971. When Johnny arrives at a theater, the fans crowd around as he makes his way slowly—always exuding this black-clad electricity and charisma—toward the dressing room. It is a small drama in itself. He finally saw me and came over to shake hands, calling me "Mr. Davis" as usual. Country artists have a tendency to be courtly and formal. I asked him repeatedly to call me Clive, for there was no lack of warmth between us; but I remained "Mr. Davis." So it was "Johnny" and "Mr. Davis" again. I asked if we might have a chat before the show began, and we went to his dressing room.

I laid it out directly: You've had a great relationship with the company, and it's been a wonderful time for everyone, I began. But I'm worried about reports I'm hearing. I don't think any problems *really* exist. We are behind you one hundred percent in advertising and promotion. Are you really unhappy, or am I getting bad information?

Johnny reacted with surprise and dismay. It was "terrible" to hear this, he said. He was "thrilled" with the company's efforts. He did not like his name used this way, and he began to wonder out loud how this was happening. It looked as though the problem might be Bob Johnston, who apparently was trying a little too hard to be Cash's "protector" against the company. Producers often—sometimes understandably—feel insecure about their relationships with artists, who can be very capricious. Johnston might have been trying to add strength to his influence with Cash by assuming a—false, as it turned out—protective role; a very irksome problem for a company.

Johnny ended the discussion quite simply. "I'm giving some thought to the question of producers," he said, "so let's talk again in December [this was October]. I don't feel I'll be with Bob Johnston much longer anyway." Indeed, by Christmas Johnny notified me that he wouldn't be using Johnston again.

Even though, as it turned out, we didn't have a serious problem with Cash, it occurred to me when I was hearing about his "complaints" that this sort of problem develops because of a lack of elementary communication. Artists who think they are not being supported enough are consistently unhappy. Dealing with this problem can take a great deal of time.

I finally solved it by having a copy of *every* advertisement, trade notice, radio ad, press release, or whatever, sent to the artist's manager when it appeared, complete with statistics showing how many papers or radio stations it appeared in or on. Nor was this information sent only to the manager; for managers sometimes keep these details from an artist when it suits their needs. The clips were sent *directly* to the artist as well. This eventually eliminated more than 90 percent of artists' complaints.

# Fourteen

## 1

Classical music caused me more than a few problems. Creatively, the landscape had been rather arid during the last decade; little major writing seemed to be emerging. And commercially, it was clear that classical sales had leveled off. This led to discussions that amounted in some cases to finger-pointing. Were the poor sales caused by record companies unjustly ignoring new works by modern composers—or was classical creativity simply at a low point?

At Columbia, it was never a question of *ignoring* the classics. We continued to seek out the best recording talent available. John McClure, Tom Frost, Tom Shepard and several other top in-house classical producers listened carefully to the new musical works and traveled throughout the world looking for new talent. We recorded the contemporary works of Cage, Carter, Riley, Subotnick, Stockhausen and Xenakis—as well as the performances of promising young virtuosos such as Anthony Newman, André Watts and Pinchas Zuckerman. We continued to record extensively the works of twentieth-century greats: Copland, Hindemith, Ives, Mahler and Stravinsky. And, naturally, the giant performing masters were well represented: Vladimir Horowitz, Rudolf Serkin, Isaac Stern, E. Power Biggs, Glenn Gould, the Budapest and Juilliard String Quartets and, of course, the New York Philharmonic, first with Leonard Bernstein and then with Pierre Boulez.

But with a limited amount of new music creating special excitement, and the endless repetition involved in recording the so-called classical "war-horses"—Bach, Handel, Beethoven, Mozart, Tchaikowsky, Chopin, etc.—the classical A&R department became at best a break-even operation.

By contrast, another form of music—contemporary rock—was changing with blinding speed. Much of the new music was also becoming a sophisticated new art form, drawing on folk, classical and jazz roots and creating new modes that would ultimately reach *every* kind of musical listener. The audience for popular music was suddenly spending more than a billion dollars annually on records, and this figure was growing meteorically. My responsibility as a record executive was obviously to involve myself deeply in this phenomenon.

Yet I also felt a considerable obligation to try to stimulate interest in the classics and to provide for the widest possible exposure of important new classical talents. With classical music in such a static period, it was not an easy role to play.

The severity of the problem was apparent early. Let's begin with the story of how we dropped the Philadelphia Orchestra.

The Orchestra's contract came up for renewal in 1967, and its reputation under Eugene Ormandy was substantial. It had an enormous catalog and its lush string sound was known worldwide. Only the New York Philharmonic under Leonard Bernstein could rival it in sales, and this was due primarily to Bernstein's personal fame. In the aggregate, the Philadelphia Orchestra sold greater numbers of albums because of its vast catalog.

The economics of classical music presented a problem for all record companies. RCA had the Boston Symphony Orchestra as well as the Boston Pops, and their sales were respectable. But symphony orchestras across the board were only marginally profitable. Besides the Philadelphia Orchestra and the New York Philharmonic, Columbia also had the Cleveland Orchestra under George Szell, whose recordings received mounds of critical acclaim while losing money. The Orchestra's records sold only five to ten thousand copies a release.

Now it costs from twenty-five to fifty thousand dollars to record a classical album. The losses on this can range from minor to substantial, especially if you add in advertising outlays. The New York Philharmonic's and the Philadelphia Orchestra's albums generally sold well over a long period of time; so you couldn't compute your profit-loss ratio in the first or second year as with a pop album. Yet, even if sales were calculated over a five-to ten-year period, most classical recordings failed to recoup their recording costs.

Columbia had a tremendous reputation in the classics. The company had inaugurated the Modern American Composer series, allowed Stravinsky to record everything he had ever written, and was very, very active in recording newer works, especially by Bernstein, whose twenty-year contract allowed him practically to dictate his own repertoire. During this time, in fact, he was so prolific that the company couldn't put everything he recorded into the market. We built up an enormous backlog of his records, in what is called "the can." The albums would be released whenever there was a dry spell. Columbia also had a large backlog of Philadelphia recordings, caused in part by the Philadelphia musicians' union contract which guaranteed orchestra members a specific annual income from recordings. It was considerably in excess of what the company was contractually required to record in orderly and commercially desirable fashion; so this led to a substantial accumulation of unreleased Philadelphia recordings.

The question of classical profits loomed large when I took over. No sophisticated study of the subject—meaning a truly separate P&L accounting—had ever been conducted at the company. The existing reports listed Broadway original cast albums as *part* of the Masterworks area of classical music, which meant that real profit and loss figures simply didn't exist. The feeling also gnawed at me that sales factors important during the previous ten years were no longer relevant. I had to look at the question more closely. With Mitch Miller's albums gone, Broadway dying and Streisand's, Williams's and Dylan's contracts up for grabs, could I have the *luxury* of a loss operation? The study was made; its results were eye-opening.

It was clearly evident, for one thing, that the lighter works we'd persuaded Ormandy and Bernstein to record during the previous decade were paying for nearly everything. Their Christmas albums had sold extremely well—usually from two hundred and fifty to five hundred thousand copies. A series of albums the Philadelphia Orchestra had recorded with the Mormon Tabernacle Choir also sold very well, often nicely into six figures. War-horse recordings sold consistently, fifty to a hundred thousand copies each. And finally, we could usually count on the really light classics: Gershwin's "Rhapsody In Blue," for example, and Ravel's "Bolero."

Beyond that, the introduction of stereophonic recordings had also greatly helped. Long-playing albums had originally been a tremendous stimulus to classical sales. And when stereo came in, the public flocked to the stores to buy their monaural repertoire again in stereo.

This was the background of the problem coming into the Philadelphia Orchestra negotiations. There were very few war-horses left to record. Not only had the Philadelphia recorded everything for which it was famous, but we had similar recordings on the market by the New York Philharmonic as well as by the Cleveland Orchestra. Bruno Walter had also left a great legacy of albums, often recorded by a select group of studio musicians called the Columbia Symphony Orchestra. All the basic Christmas material was recorded—and then some. You have the familiar two or three dozen Christmas songs, and that's it. This was also true with the important light classical works.

The only really new excitement lately was an awakening of interest in Mahler and Ives; not much was happening commercially with current works.

So the problem was acute, and no technological breakthrough like stereo albums was coming to the rescue. To further complicate matters, a number of foreign orchestras and conductors had gained American followings: the London Symphony, the Concertgebouw, Herbert Von Karajan, and others, all of whom were recording the same repertoire. I was looking for new horizons but they were difficult to find.

Armed with these facts I went into the Philadelphia Orchestra negotiations frankly longing for the luxury of previous years when the lighter classics and Christmas music had paid for the innovation and public service that gave Goddard Lieberson and Columbia an excellent reputation among classical musicians and critics. I hardly relished being the one to pull back. But times had changed and there was little room for luxuries. Still, I felt I would stretch as far as possible to recommend keeping the Orchestra.

In early 1966, Lieberson and I went to Philadelphia to meet with the Orchestra's imposing Board of Trustees. Lieberson was aware that the economics of classical recording was changing, so we both went down hoping for a realistic agreement that would help us cope with the business problems we expected to have over the next five years. Unfortunately, the trustees had an entirely different perspective.

As with most classical orchestra associations in recent years, the Philadelphia's finances had become shaky. They wanted more income, not less, and they demanded a two-million-dollar guaranty *plus* a substantial bonus. They were also required by the musicians' union to provide an additional guaranty of recording income for union members that was far beyond the previous one. And finally, the guaranty could come only from new recordings. The catalog royalties had to be additional payments not offset by the new guaranty.

Our faces fell nearly to the floor. The terms were impossibly out of reach. Worse yet, RCA had made an offer approaching their demands. They expected Columbia to follow suit. Seeing our expressions and deepening gloom, the trustees decided at least to explain how high the stakes were for them. The Ford Foundation had given the Philadelphia Orchestra Association a tremendous grant; but it was a "matching" one. The Foundation would double every dollar raised by the Orchestra—a golden opportunity. Understandably, they wanted to get all the money they could. And since RCA had showed avid interest in them, they didn't understand Columbia's shock.

We said that we'd study the matter and get back to them. Returning to New York, I met with Walter Dean, then head of Business Affairs; John McClure, Director of Columbia Masterworks A&R; and Peter Munves, Director of Classical Music Merchandising. Each of us wanted to keep the Orchestra. We thought losing it would cost us considerable prestige. Yet Dean—as he was required to do—kept pointing to the economic studies we'd just conducted. The loss would be tremendous, and the precedent set for classical recording contracts would be devastating.

McClure was the coolest appraiser of the problem. He had been Bernstein's A&R man for years, and of the two orchestras, he was closest to the New York Philharmonic. For some time there had been a subdued competition between America's two premier orchestras which extended to Bernstein and Ormandy themselves. Bernstein didn't feel it nearly so much as Ormandy, for Ormandy's luster had been eclipsed somewhat by the fast rise of the younger, more glamorous Philharmonic leader. Ormandy recognized Bernstein's talent, but he professed to be more respectful of Szell, the purer classicist.

McClure's talks with Ormandy and with Tom Frost, the A&R man for the Philadelphia, indicated that Ormandy now wanted to branch out into new areas. He intended to move toward other repertoires and depart from the Orchestra's romanticist roots. No one felt that this foray would be particularly successful. McClure was also very concerned that a major loss from the Philadelphia might lead to a curtailing of much of his other recording plans, and was the first to recommend that we not try to win a pyrrhic victory.

In any event, no one understood how RCA could afford to sign the Philadelphia at the amount being asked. The grass must have looked far greener than it truly was. RCA had to be wildly overestimating the Philadelphia's actual sales. Munves also pointed out that we had enough unreleased sides in the can to last for almost five years. We could easily fight RCA in an advertising battle, and with our existing vast Philadelphia catalog, plus a steady stream of new releases, we could maintain Columbia's image and link with the Philadelphia Sound for years.

The decision was making itself. The financial loss would just be too great. Yet I was still very reluctant to cut the cord without one last effort. Corporate management had to be consulted. The loss of the Orchestra would undoubtedly get a lot of publicity—and some adverse comments for the company—and management had to be alerted even though Lieberson had already given us the green light to pass.

I knew that we could not possibly justify the signing on an economic basis. But this was classical music and a contribution to culture. Economics should not be the sole determinant. Would Paley and Stanton consider the projected two-million-dollar deficit as a charitable contribution? I didn't have to wait long to find out. The answer was immediately negative, and the Philadelphia Orchestra went to RCA—which proceeded to lose a tremendous amount of money on the deal. The loss, in fact, later contributed to RCA's dramatically pulling in its horns in regard to new classical recordings, and also to the dropping of a number of classical artists, including the Boston Symphony Orchestra. (The Boston went to Deutsche Grammophon, which in turn probably similarly overestimated sales of the Orchestra, again on the "grass is greener" concept.)

For RCA, Columbia or any other company, classical recording is generally a trouble spot today. Costs of recording have risen dramatically, and sales of new releases haven't kept pace. There are also low-price lines now—Nonesuch, Odyssey and Seraphim, for example—that offer consumers big bargains: their $3.49 list price is roughly half that of regular albums. And among regular classical releases, the Schwann catalog offers a tremendous variety of performances to choose from . . . for identical works. Sales of good repertoire are thus seriously diluted. An aficionado or connoisseur may appreciate the nuances of difference between conductors. The average collector won't care; he'll keep the sets he already has.

## 2

Obviously, not every decision was determined by profit-and-loss considerations. We willingly *lost* money on Vladimir Horowitz. Each of his albums cost Columbia in guaranty, recording and advertising expenses about a hundred thousand dollars; they generally recouped half that amount. But it *was* Horowitz, who is generally considered the greatest living pianist. Only Artur Rubinstein challenges him—and the legend surrounding Horowitz is greater. In movies, Garbo had the mystique. In rock music, Dylan has it. In classical music, it's Horowitz. We decided that the business loss was more than offset by the musical contribution and accompanying prestige.

In 1967 Horowitz and his wife, Wanda, who is the daughter of Arturo Toscanini, sent word that they'd like to spend an evening with Janet and me. I called Mrs. Horowitz to ask what they'd like to do and where. She had no ready answer, so I suggested making music part of the evening. She replied that Horowitz loved black music and loved to watch discotheque dancing when done well. I was shocked; it wasn't exactly my image of his preferences. But she insisted that he'd enjoy this, so I arranged to meet them at the Dom, a small discotheque in the East Village that catered mostly to a black crowd. Mrs. Horowitz's sister was with them, as was Bob Altshuler, head of Publicity and Press for Columbia, and his wife, Barbara. I had expected someone quite stiff and somber, but Horowitz's classically thin and angular face was buoyant. His eyes darted happily about him as we walked in.

The owners knew that we were coming, but no one else in the crowd of dancers recognized him, which was fine with him. The Supremes and The Temptations rocked out of a jukebox, and Horowitz had a marvelous time watching everyone frug and boogaloo. When a particular couple *really* got going, he broke into smiles and laughter and made sure that we were all watching as well. He was in excellent spirits during the entire evening, a far cry from the aloofness that was his trademark.

In business dealings, though, Horowitz lived up to his reputation. He remained in the background and everything was handled by Mrs. Horowitz. If Horowitz gave a concert in Boston, *she* called to say that a particular store had no album covers in the window supporting the concert. She also asked for, and usually got, specific promotional commitments with each new album release. And if you wanted to discuss other business matters, you called Wanda, not her husband.

I once initiated such a call. This time I wanted to meet directly with the maestro; I was troubled by the repertoire he'd been recording. We didn't have great commercial expectations from him, but I felt that he wasn't reaching even the audiences he was *capable* of stirring. We wanted him to do a piano concerto with a major orchestra. Horowitz had been flirting with the thought, but he wouldn't be pinned down to anything specific.

I wanted to try, so Janet and I joined the Horowitzes at their Manhattan brownstone for cocktails. Horowitz wore a handsome dressing gown that night, and he and Wanda listened intently to my arguments—which were almost purely commercial. A concerto album would sell two or three times better than the sonata albums, I said, and would generate enormous interest. Horowitz shrewdly ducked the issue by saying that he was closest to Ormandy and the Philadelphia Orchestra, but since they were now under contract to RCA, an album with them would be impossible. I suggested Bernstein, but Horowitz remained politely impassive. I then mentioned George Szell and the Cleveland Orchestra. He said this was a possibility. He promised not to rule out concertos; indeed, he'd give the idea serious thought. But I didn't think I was making any great headway that night—and, in fact, I wasn't. He never did any concertos for Columbia.

Paradoxically, after years of avoiding live audiences, Horowitz had made a highly publicized return to the stage and resumed recording with zest and enthusiasm—but he still refused to perform the concertos, live or on record, which would assure a commercial momentum. And it was not that he and Mrs. Horowitz weren't commercially minded. Contract negotiations were usually long and hard-fought. We ended up paying a tremendous amount to keep him without guarantees of any cooperation from him on our repertoire suggestions. He was Horowitz, take him or leave him. We took him.

# 3

One concession Horowitz made to the public was a televised performance. The concert was taped at Carnegie Hall before an invited audience. A few months later, Janet and I were asked to join Mr. and Mrs. Horowitz to watch the actual television show. It was a Sunday night, and Mike Dann, the colorful, outspoken CBS Vice-President of Programming, was along with his wife, with music critic Howard Taubman and Mrs. Taubman also sitting in. Dann had been responsible for putting Horowitz on the network, and in commercial terms it was a noble decision, since good ratings in evening prime time depend on mass appeal and numbers much larger than classical music devotees can bring.

We met in a television viewing room at CBS and sat in lounge chairs to watch the program. I couldn't help but watch Horowitz watching Horowitz. No one talked, but it was fascinating to see his long, thin, expressive fingers move from being clasped under his chin, to tapping the chair, to playing imaginary notes in sequence with what was being shown on the screen. The performance was an incredible display of virtuosity, and the televised close-ups of Horowitz's hands were brilliant. As if it were an opening night, we left to have dinner at L'Aiglon, a French restaurant, and await the reviews.

Horowitz showed still another side during dinner—patience. In performance or rehearsal, he is a perfectionist, demanding and unrelenting in pursuit of excellence. He can be cutting and harsh when he sees—or thinks he sees—incompetence in others. Yet he had boyish enthusiasm when something delighted him, and he could show warm appreciation for favors. This night he deeply appreciated Dann's having gone out on a limb to put him on television. In one night, he had been seen by more people than he could ever play for in live concerts in a lifetime.

So he put up with a rather overzealous Dann performance. Dann at that time was the most successful executive in television. He later left to go to the Children's Television Workshop, which produces "Sesame Street," but for now he was the man who had guided CBS to number one ratings consistently over the years— a passionate goal of his at the time. He spoke loudly, with great animation, and seemed to say everything that was on his mind, without any editing. He could be witty—and brutally frank seconds later. Horowitz was taken aback by this. It was occasionally amusing, but mostly painful, to watch Dann attempt to deal with Horowitz in his down-to-earth way. Dann miscalculated the tone to be set that evening, preferring not to show obeisance to Horowitz's lofty achievements, but rather to treat him familiarly, as if bantering with a close friend. At one point he told Horowitz that his brown suit was passé and old-fashioned, way out of style. At another, he pointed out that the program would probably get swamped in the ratings competition and suggested that Horowitz —who was oddly worried about ratings—needed psychoanalysis if he didn't appreciate the number of people who *did* see him. He even teased that a lobotomy might be in order.

This type of jesting frequently goes down easily among friends. Tonight, as Horowitz nervously awaited the reviews, it was out of place. Dann's television mannerisms mystified Horowitz, who didn't know whether to be grossly offended or not. He couldn't *believe* what he was hearing. He kept looking at Wanda for instructions and she kept repeating, "Volodya, don't pay attention to him. He's not serious. He's a good man who has done us a good turn." Horowitz took the lead from this, twitching nervously and smiling occasionally, patiently sitting it out. It happened that Dann really meant well. He was genuinely fond of Horowitz and was trying very hard to lighten any tension, but he failed totally to recognize the contrast between their styles—the one back-slapping, hail-fellow-well-met, armed to the teeth with jokes, repartee and sarcasm; the other guarded, sensitive, somewhat paranoid and suspicious. It was fascinating—and awkward. Fortunately, the night ended with great reviews and warm toasts.

# 4

There remains the problem of *selling* classical records. In some ways, the future is promising. To me the answer lies in closing the gap between classical devotees and the serious fans of rock. I believe it can be done. Now that rock music innovators are including long guitar and keyboard passages in their albums, it becomes plausible for a sophisticated pop music fan to get into classical repertoire as well. More and more rock musicians are borrowing from the classics and presenting it palatably and acceptably to youth.

And if an album crosses into both markets, the results are staggering. One example was *Switched-On Bach*. This album brought the electronic excitement of the Moog synthesizer to the beauty of Bach. It was a stunning fusion of old and new by Walter Carlos, a brilliant young experimenter who had mastered the instrument to perfection. *Switched-On Bach* was a major breakthrough for Columbia.

I had supported John McClure's efforts to explore the works of modern composers and musicians in electronic music. McClure was fascinated by this and plunged in wholeheartedly. But he eventually came to believe that his other obligation, that of continuously *re-exploring* the classics, was nonproductive, even boring. (In fact, his taste began veering more and more toward young avant-garde rock musicians—The Velvet Underground, for example.) It finally became hard to get him excited about the next Stern, the next Serkin or even the next Horowitz album. He clearly appreciated each man's genius, but he missed the spark of dealing with the unexpected. Bluntly put, this was dangerous; for these three plus Bernstein and the Philharmonic were the heart of our classical roster. True, we were trying to bring along the careers of Watts, Zuckerman and Newman, but this involved long-term career-building; the sales of their albums, despite glowing reviews, hovered between five and ten thousand copies, almost always losing money.

I appreciated McClure's desire to try something different, but I felt that we had to be involved in a two-pronged struggle. If we couldn't afford to keep the Philadelphia Orchestra, which was an *emotional* blow, we at least had to try to stimulate interest in the classics.

When we appraised the entire picture, it was apparent that unless the company agreed to finance a substantial deficit, the outlook was bleak. We clearly had to stimulate new thinking, new ideas, new creativity; we had to encourage the work of young musical minds and we had to reach today's rock audience, whose attention to music—but primarily contemporary music—had zoomed.

In the past, popular music had consisted mostly of repetitive messages about love and lost love. But now a dramatic change had taken place; the music had become enormously complex. Bright young intellects could get into popular music and be challenged. Classical music, however, seemed to belong to another era and was being ignored by most of the youth. I felt that we had to bring these people to the classics, the war-horses, the best of serious music. Once introduced, I knew they'd become involved.

McClure and his staff worked hard recording such composers as Cage, Riley and Stockhausen, for example, and holding special campaigns and month-long promotions for electronic music. Nothing seemed to help. Reviewers applauded our efforts, but sales totaled about five thousand copies an album, or less, and not much enthusiasm was generated.

Then came the breakthrough of *Switched-On Bach*. The album got enormous press coverage. Here was something fresh and new, and the public responded. It sold to all ages. FM radio embraced the album; and, surprisingly, so did middle-of-the-road stations.

We launched a major advertising campaign, covering not only established media like *The New York Times* and *High Fidelity* magazine, but also *Rolling Stone,* the underground papers, and FM rock and classical radio stations. *Switched-On Bach* became one of the best-selling classical albums of all time, its sales approaching one million units.

Well, this showed us something. It was true that the novelty of the concept helped, but it *was* Bach's music, given to the public straight. Instead of the average sale of ten thousand copies, we'd reached a hundred times that amount. We were encouraged, as was the industry, and many companies rushed out Moog synthesizer albums—classical, rock, ballads, whatever they could think of. The imitations didn't fare well. For the genius of Carlos was as vital as the use of the synthesizer. As always, the public and the reviewers distinguished easily between art and pale imitations. Over the next few years, they bought only Carlos albums in any kind of real numbers.

Unfortunately, this was only a start. The real answer hadn't arrived. We knew that the public could be reached by something new and exciting, but new writing had to be encouraged as well, for traditional classical music lovers still regarded electronic music as gimmicky and uninteresting.

Concert-hall efforts to showcase new music, moreover, were badly received. I sat through several concerts in which large numbers of season subscribers walked *out* during an extended electronic performance. They wanted no part of it. The gap between classics lovers, who want their music straight, and followers of contemporary rock and modern electronics would not be easily closed. It had *seemed* to me that electronics could be used to link the two worlds. But the human element was missing. I felt that young people were ready to move on and absorb other kinds of music, including that of Beethoven, Bach and Handel. They were wrong in rejecting classical music as the product of another generation irrelevant to them. It was a case of being so absorbed with events around them that they had become deaf to what their musical heritage offered. I felt that the man who could best deal with this problem was Leonard Bernstein, and I turned to him.

The time was right. It was 1971, Bernstein had semiretired from the New York Philharmonic, and he was searching for new challenges. For the moment, he was most interested in opera, which he'd recently had a triumphant European tour conducting. Buoyed by the crowds and by extensive worldwide media coverage, he served notice on Columbia that he was going to record a substantial number of operas.

This didn't strike joy in our hearts. For years we'd stayed *out* of opera. Except for albums of arias by Richard Tucker or Eileen Farrell, we'd done little in that area, largely because of high costs and low sales. The cost of recording an opera in recent years had ranged from a minimum of seventy-five thousand dollars to sums frequently in excess of a hundred thousand. What's more, in order to record in that range, you had to work in Europe, where you were not faced with American Federation of Musicians pay scales. So opera was very expensive; each album contained as many as three LPs, plus texts and other packaging. As a result, an opera album usually cost between fifteen and twenty dollars. The cost to consumers, combined with the relatively limited repertoire, meant limited sales.

Bernstein first recorded *Falstaff*. The reviews were excellent; we launched a heavy advertising campaign, looking for some measure of the commercial importance of Bernstein's name here. Sadly, we found out: the album sold less than ten thousand copies in the U.S.; about the same number in foreign countries.

It had seemed to me that opera was primarily a singer's medium, even though a conductor could clearly make a big contribution, and his presence could lend excitement to the production. It had cost us more than one hundred thousand dollars to record and promote the *Falstaff* album; we lost a lot of money. Bernstein, moreover, was said to be displeased with the company's promotional efforts—not enough, he said.

In reality, we had spent a tremendous amount of money on advertising, to no avail—and now I heard that Bernstein wanted to do *Der Rosenkavalier* next. I didn't want to commit Columbia to this. I felt that we at least needed to test-market a war-horse— *Carmen* or *Madame Butterfly*—before we went further with operas that happened to catch Bernstein's fancy. If *that* didn't sell, then we'd give him a "selective" release to go to another company for his operas. We simply didn't want to lose a hundred thousand dollars each time he wanted to make an album. Culture was just not being enriched commensurately.

Bernstein was immovable; he insisted on *Der Rosenkavalier*. Schuyler Chapin, who now directs the Metropolitan Opera, was Bernstein's manager at the time and acted as spokesman for him. Schuyler and I knew each other well from the days when he used to head classical A&R for Columbia. We were good friends, but our perspectives differed here and we had several spirited conversations about the role of a record company. Bernstein had a contract which allowed him to designate repertoire, and he felt that Columbia was obligated to go along with whatever he wanted to do. He was, after all, an outstanding musician—that much we all could agree on. Nonetheless, monetary considerations were not as boring to us as to Bernstein. I felt that we at least had a right to find out how *much* these projects were going to lose by testing Bernstein's commercial success with a war-horse.

Yet Bernstein was saying that he didn't care about the *Falstaff* results. He wanted to do *Der Rosenkavalier* and other operas after that, and he wanted Columbia's support . . . not just its consent. And he was said to be miffed that he was getting any flack *at all* from the company.

I decided that the time had come for me to talk frankly with Bernstein. I had long wanted to urge him to take a leading role in fusing classical and contemporary music. This had to be a more exciting and fruitful contribution for him to make to music than the recording of still another version of a much-recorded opera. The time to talk, I felt, was *now,* before problems got entirely out of hand. I asked for an appointment at his Park Avenue apartment.

Bernstein was tired from rehearsals the afternoon John McClure and I arrived to meet with him and Schuyler Chapin, but we ended up speaking for several hours. I argued my case against his spending more of his valuable time recording already oft-recorded operas. Bernstein was not inclined to hear this. Occasionally he looked quite upset. He was clearly unaccustomed to having a record executive challenge his views.

I wasn't making much headway, so I moved on to my major point—that Bernstein was uniquely qualified to reach young people and bridge the gap between classical music and rock. A few years earlier, he had devoted an entire hour of a television special to singing the praises of certain rock artists. Youth appreciated the endorsement by this towering figure of music. I knew that he had visited the Fillmore East several times, and admired several groups, especially The Who. I offered to make my services available—arranging meetings and so forth—for any classical-rock work he might be willing to try.

Gradually Bernstein realized that I hadn't dropped by just to complain about money. I was quite blunt: he could have a release to record any operas he liked *if* he would just give us a chance to test-market a war-horse. We resolved the issue (I thought); he agreed to try a production of *Carmen.* On the question of his involvement in contemporary music, he said that he was interested but felt that this would require too great a change in his life-style . . . for he never went into anything half-heartedly. *If* he did it, it would involve going nightly to recording studios and throwing himself intensely into the world of rock and youth culture. He felt that this was just too arduous for him at this point in his career.

I didn't push it; I was pleased enough that I'd gotten him

even thinking about something other than opera. As a postscript to the opera issue we recorded *Der Rosenkavalier*. As with *Falstaff*, sales were less than ten thousand, and we lost another hundred thousand dollars. Bernstein eventually did *Carmen*—but he decided to record it in New York, which meant paying the expensive union scale. The album would have cost more than two hundred thousand dollars to produce, so we decided to pass. He was given a release, however, to take it to Deutsche Grammophon. As we expected, the album lost money.

I don't like sounding hard-nosed. I admit that business considerations affect recording decisions. I accept the fact that this kind of thing can give a man poor marks in the culture department. Everything *doesn't* have to pay for itself. But if you are willing to release albums that lose money, you should either balance them with profitable ones or believe that the loss was worth taking for the sake of music. To record the best of the new virtuosos was worthwhile. To record the best of the new avant-garde serious works was necessary, indeed an obligation. But to record a work that had been recorded several times before had to be weighed against economic considerations, and each decision had to be made *ad hoc*. Would corporate management consider any part of this as a contribution to charity? After we dropped the Philadelphia Orchestra, the answer was pretty clear that it would not.

About a year after my talk with Bernstein, his *Mass* was scheduled to premiere in Washington. Our relationship was rather distant, and I had hoped to make the opening night as a gesture to him; Janet and I planned to fly in and shorten our planned visit to St. John and Puerto Rico. Unfortunately, she had a false alarm with her pregnancy and we missed our flight. I soon received word that Bernstein was terribly offended. He always expected the fullest support from the company; on a foreign tour, he wanted Columbia representatives everywhere he played for promotion and advertising assistance. I felt that he had a right to this—that he had a right to expect me at the Washington premiere—and I was sorry to miss it.

Matters got worse because business kept making it impossible for me to get to Washington for a subsequent performance. There was no sound reason for missing it, and it was easy to misinterpret my absence . . . for the *Mass*'s critical reception was tumultuously mixed. I saw Mrs. Bernstein at a New York Philharmonic concert and apologized profusely, telling her about Janet's illness, etc., etc. She acknowledged my excuses rather coolly. I then wrote a note of apology to Bernstein, and what I received in return pleased me greatly. Bernstein replied, thanking me for my concern, but, most important, he said that he had keenly felt my absence because it had been our talk at his house that had influenced his thinking while he was writing the *Mass;* the whole idea of the *Mass,* he said, was stimulated by the concept of fusing the classical and contemporary musical worlds.

When the *Mass* finally opened in New York in June of 1972, Janet and I hosted a party at Lincoln Center to celebrate the event for the benefit of the New York Library for the Performing Arts at Lincoln Center. Janet suggested serving a natural foods banquet, and this novel idea generated an enormous amount of press coverage for the occasion. I hoped that the New York opening and the party following it made up for any unintentional slight that Bernstein had felt.

# 5

There was one more time that I tried to build a bridge between young people and the classics. It was the beginning of 1973 and Radio City Music Hall had lately opened its doors for midnight concerts, booking acts such as James Taylor, David Bowie and West, Bruce & Laing as a way to make extra revenue. It seemed to me that its great stage had room for classical music as well.

The hall's acoustics were good, and it could seat more than five thousand people. For the concert, I scheduled E. Power Biggs, the brilliant organist, and the innovative harpsichord-conductor Anthony Newman. We also planned to put the "Monster Pianos" onstage—ten grand pianos whose sound together is booming and spectacular.

It was a bastardized concept, but the idea was to explore as many new musical avenues as possible, and—most important—fill the hall with young people who might not venture into, say, Lincoln Center. There was never a question of diluting the music. Each of the artists was to choose his own repertoire and perform it as he wished. We planned to have some fun with the staging, but the idea was to have this add to, rather than dilute, the music.

We hired Joshua White, a director who once ran the light show at the Fillmore East, to stage and direct the program, and we looked for the best sound assistance possible. Radio City's stage is incredibly adaptable, with movable levels, turntables, separate sections and a rising orchestra pit. We had Biggs playing Bach on the Music Hall's famous organ, Newman emerging from the orchestra pit after that with his chamber ensemble, and the Monster Pianos whirling around on stage platforms in a "Stars and Stripes" finale with flags waving. The concert was great fun, offered exceptionally fine music—and the hall was jammed. Some tickets for orchestra seats were scalped at from fifteen to twenty-five dollars.

It became impossible to make generalizations about the audience. Since the show started at midnight, I thought the late hour in midtown Manhattan might scare away middle-aged music lovers. As it turned out, almost every age group was represented. As usual, the young people were the loudest.

During my opening remarks, I misjudged their volatility rather badly. It was a Columbia concert whose profits would go to charity, and I felt it meaningful to explain *why* we were doing this. But when I got onstage, I realized that the audience would be hard to handle. As I read off the names of the performers, someone shouted: "We can read the program!" Then I blundered into the nexus of the problem by saying that Columbia's intent was to "bring serious music to the masses." The phrase was booed. I suddenly realized that I wasn't talking to a Philharmonic audience. The Fillmore would be a better analogy. My talk soon led to alternate cheers and boos, and I realized that I was caught in the classic Fillmore situation—the audience repeatedly applauding or booing the MC.

I finally referred to the Fillmore, saying how "nostalgic" it was to be back in front of an enthusiastic audience again. This drew the loudest cheer of all. Not wanting to push my luck, I made a quick retreat, staying offstage until the end, when I thanked everyone for coming.

The concert was a big success. We received offers to put on the same show at the Hollywood Bowl, the Miami Convention Center and Forest Hills Stadium. But, unfortunately, it wasn't easy to do this. I tried to organize a similar show at Los Angeles' Ahmanson Theatre in May of 1973, but we couldn't include Biggs on the program. The organ he needed couldn't be brought onto the stage. So I tried a new variation—mixing rock and classical musicians on the same program. We had Anthony Newman and a small chamber ensemble appear with John McLaughlin and The Mahavishnu Orchestra, and Loudon Wainwright III. Classical, progressive rock and folk music—each of the highest caliber. The common denominator was quality, and the program got a great response and glittering reviews.

But the problem for the future is that these combinations are hard to arrange except in unusual cases. People generally want their music—whatever their taste—straight. In the end, the concerts have to be viewed as special events that demonstrated musical fusion without firmly fixing it in the public mind. Encouragingly, however, classical sales have risen in the last year. I fully believe it is the result of the growing sophistication of contemporary audiences. They are better prepared to enjoy the classics. The task now is to stimulate this even further. Eventually the gap must, and will, close.

# Fifteen

## 1

Among Columbia artists, the two who came closest to being personal friends of mine were Paul Simon and Arthur Garfunkel. They were already on the label when I took over, and our friendship developed slowly, sometimes with difficulty.

Producer Tom Wilson had signed them in 1964. They had recorded an album, *Wednesday Morning, 3 A.M.*, which got little or no attention. But a year after the album's release, one of its cuts, *"The Sound of Silence,"* was programmed out of the blue by a Boston disc jockey who loved it and wanted to test public reaction. Students at campuses such as Harvard, Tufts and Boston University immediately began requesting it. Our local promotion man picked this up and reported it to New York. After repeated listening we decided that the record required some instrumental backing to be a real hit. So Wilson went into the studio and did the necessary overdubbing. Neither Artie nor Paul was available: Paul was in England and Artie was studying for a master's degree at Columbia.

The record was then re-released as a single—and it resoundingly launched the extraordinary careers of Simon & Garfunkel. By this time I had A&R reporting to me and I took particular interest in the fatalistic nature of all this. If that disc jockey hadn't experimented with a song from an unknown, year-old album, Simon & Garfunkel probably would not exist today in music. They had already separated. But when the news reached Paul in England that the single was exploding across the country, he came back and, in December, 1965, he and Artie rushed into the studio to record the album *The Sound of Silence,* which included the overdubbed hit version of the title song. There followed a succession of hits, including "Homeward Bound," "I Am A Rock" and "Scarborough Fair," and by 1967 they were established artists selling several hundred thousand copies of each album.

We related easily at first. They had both gone through public schools in Queens and were bright and articulate. I always had the feeling that we could be close—quite apart from our business relationships. But business always managed to get in the way. One example involved the film score for *The Graduate.* Paul had been asked by Mike Nichols, the film's director, to write the motion picture score. When I heard about the project I felt that there was real potential for a best-selling soundtrack album. Soundtracks do not always do well; their success often depends more on the extent of the movie's appeal than on the quality of the music itself. Still, when Embassy Motion Pictures asked if we wanted the soundtrack rights, I grabbed them; the movie had all the ingredients of a big box-office hit.

Then Mike Nichols decided to use little or nothing of Paul's new material. Apart from about a minute of a new song, "Mrs. Robinson"—named after the character played by Anne Bancroft—he chose four cuts from the earlier Simon & Garfunkel albums, the two best-known being "The Sound of Silence" and "Scarborough Fair." When I asked Paul if he thought there was enough material in the movie for an album, he said no. I was extremely disappointed, for I felt the movie would do very well.

When it came out the reviews, of course, were superb. I called Paul again—"Are you *sure* there's not enough material?" I asked. "This could be an absolutely giant album."

No, Paul said again.

But I couldn't get it off my mind. I sent Ed Kleban, an A&R man in charge of soundtrack and Broadway show albums, to see the movie. "There just isn't enough music," he said afterward. "You can't come out with an album that has only fifteen or eighteen minutes of songs from older albums on it."

"Well, it's a damn shame," I said, and brooded further about it. Columbia's profits were then shaky. I needed a blockbuster album to replace Mitch Miller and the Broadway show albums.

This was no passing academic question; one good album that year could make or break the year's bottom line. A simple hit-movie theme—the theme from *Exodus* or *Never On Sunday,* for example —can take an album of routine background music to the top of the charts, where it will stay for months.

The problem continued to gnaw at me, and one day, right in the middle of an afternoon's work, I left to see the film myself. Inside the theater, I suddenly realized that all I had been told about was the fifteen minutes of Paul Simon music. No one had mentioned that composer Dave Grusin had written background music for the film as well. There was *plenty* of music to fill out the album. Grusin's music was standard background material, the kind of music in every other soundtrack album. So why not this one? Besides, people who buy soundtrack albums are entirely different from regular record consumers. Mostly, they want to re-identify with a film they really liked. It was already clear to me that *The Graduate* would be one of the major box-office films of all time; it made obvious sense to release an album.

I called Mort Lewis, Paul and Artie's manager, and argued my case. He said that Paul did *not* want the album released; Artie agreed. They felt that a Simon & Garfunkel album should have eleven strong cuts on it; anything less would insult their fans. Besides, they were working on the *Bookends* album, and they didn't want any soundtrack album to interfere with its sales. I argued that the soundtrack album would reach a vast number of moviegoers rather than just Simon & Garfunkel fans; many wouldn't have even *heard* of them. A whole new audience would open up to them, far larger than the half million or so who had bought each of their previous three albums.

I asked to speak to Paul. I told him my reasons and assured him that the album would be packaged as a movie soundtrack. I said that the album's cover would use a scene from the film, that the album title would clearly state this was the official motion picture *soundtrack* rather than a specific Simon & Garfunkel album. Something like: "Mike Nichols directs . . . starring Anne Bancroft and Dustin Hoffman . . ." with a credit saying "Songs by Paul Simon, performed by Simon & Garfunkel." I added that the album's hoped-for success would *not* cause me to push back the release of *Bookends,* which was to contain the complete version of what looked to be a smash single, "Mrs. Robinson."

Paul felt very strongly about this. "We've been working on

the *Bookends* album a long time, we love it, and we think it's a major creative breakthrough," he said. "We don't want to wait six months to release it just because of your commercial problems."

I repeated that *Bookends* would be released right on top of the *Graduate* soundtrack album. I loved the idea of this from a career point of view. "These albums together," I said, "could really make you superstars. If *both* hit the top of the charts, you'll have undreamed-of commercial success, a breakthrough that will firmly establish you."

The rest, of course, is history. Paul and Artie agreed reluctantly to its release in the spring of 1968, and sales of the soundtrack album, coupled with *Bookends,* took them over the top of five million units. Simon & Garfunkel became household names all over the world.

Unfortunately, Paul and Arthur were fairly indifferent to the *Graduate* album's smash success; they harbored negative feelings about Columbia that lasted almost two years. Disputes kept cropping up. We charged an extra dollar for *Bookends,* for example; it had a large poster inside and I was trying to establish further the concept of variable pricing. They opposed this. They were concerned about the consumers, which was laudable. I was concerned about the increasing cost of recording and a shrinking margin of profits, which cast me in the villain's role. Soon after, the renegotiation of their contract put us on opposite sides of the fence again. They were now on top of the rock world and felt that they deserved a much better royalty deal than when they signed as total unknowns.

I didn't disagree but I was smarting from their coolness. I had pushed for the *Graduate* album and it had paid off handsomely; when that album and *Bookends* went to the top of the trade charts, my predictions of their superstardom came true. An album that reaches Number One creates a star. For two albums to reach the top at the same time creates a superstar. For all the usual human reasons, I felt that I deserved their thanks; nothing happened.

So feelings on *both* sides clouded the negotiations, delaying them longer than was really necessary. The matter was finally resolved by giving them the higher royalty and giving us an extension of the contract.

My relationship with the two of them still needed improvement. I began to try harder. I related to both of them on emotional as well as music levels, and I knew that the barriers could be broken down. What's more, I loved their music; at home I played their albums more than any others for pure enjoyment. I started inviting Paul to lunch and he began to open up slowly, partly because some difficulties were developing in the Simon and Garfunkel relationship as a result of Artie's extended stay in Mexico making the Mike Nichols movie *Catch-22*.

The *Bridge Over Troubled Water* album, which was well over a year in the making, was finally completed in 1970, and Paul and Artie asked me to come to the studio to listen to the tapes. Paul's parents and his brother were there and it was a very special moment; the album was absolutely breathtaking. After we listened, and I told them how beautiful it was, they asked what I thought the single should be. "It just *has* to be 'Bridge Over Troubled Water,'" I said; they were surprised. It was not a typical single; they had assumed that I would suggest "Cecilia," a more up-tempo cut (which later became a hit also).

"We love 'Bridge,'" Artie said, "and we planned to make it the album's title song—but do you *really* think it could be the album's hit single?"

"I can't be absolutely positive," I said, "but this is one time to go for a home run. It is the age of rock and this is a ballad—and a long one at that—but *if* it hits, it could become a classic." I wanted to release it as a single simultaneously with the album and avoid even the slightest chance of another record breaking out first. The market response might have dictated "Cecilia" or "El Condor Pasa," but they would be just hits, not a shot at an all-time standard. The rest, again, is history. The *Bridge* album had the biggest worldwide sales of all time, selling about nine million copies—approached only in recent years by Carole King's *Tapestry* album. It won more Grammys than any other album had ever received, and Simon & Garfunkel were carried still further along on a wave of huge success.

Our relationship had settled down by now and we had become friends. Artie was traveling a lot at the time, but when he was in town we would talk and I'd bring him up to date on what was happening in music. Paul and I had lunch often, and once he touchingly said, "I think our lives are going to be interwoven at some point. I may not always be a recording artist. I just know we will be more closely involved in some way."

# 2

Then trouble developed between Paul and Artie. It began, as I've noted, when Artie's role in *Catch-22* unavoidably held up the recording of *Bridge Over Troubled Water*. Paul becomes very impatient once he finishes writing all the songs for an album. He wants to go into the studio immediately. Artie had taken the *Catch-22* role as much to kill time as for any other reason—but without realizing that Mike Nichols would take a year to finish the picture. The original Nichols estimate was a few months, but once you commit yourself to a film, you can't leave. Money was hardly the question. Artie made around seventy-five thousand dollars for his role in *Catch-22;* he made about a million dollars from *Bridge*. But he couldn't leave the set in Mexico, and Paul felt quite burdened. Then, too, their approach to album production was painfully slow, requiring enormous teamwork—laying down one track at a time, then deciding *together* whether they were happy with it. For this to work, you have to be perfectly compatible in taste, and this was becoming an increasing problem with them. So somewhere between his impatience with Artie's movie-making, and a feeling that he wanted more exclusive control over the songs he'd written, Paul decided they should part company.

One day he called and asked to see me. "Before others find out," he said, "I want you to know I've decided to split with Artie. I don't think we'll be recording together again." I was *very* much taken aback. I knew that there were problems, but I didn't think *this* was the solution. Simon & Garfunkel were an institution; they were among the two or three top artists in the world. And now, once again, a winning group at the absolute peak of its success wanted to split! But, as usual, there was really nothing I could do. You can't legislate love between a married couple, and you can't make two artists stay together.

It is a theme I can't help but repeat: an *institution* is far more important commercially than its component parts. I remember thinking how stupid it seemed for The Mamas and the Papas to break up at the height of their career. Each member thought that he or she could be bigger than the group, a misguided idea. This always seemed so obvious—I couldn't understand why Paul felt forced to take this risk. I had hoped it would be different with him and Artie; they'd grown up together, they seemed to me like brothers.

I warned Paul that he would have to work for a long time even to attempt to reach the level of success that Simon & Garfunkel enjoyed. No matter how well each of the Beatles has done individually—and they have done exceptionally well—no one of them has achieved the kind of success the group did. I believed that Paul's individual career would have the same problem. This upset him a great deal, though I didn't realize it at the time; a year later I read an interview in *Rolling Stone* in which he said that he'd wanted *total* support from me—and that my theories about individuals and institutions disappointed him. I can understand his feelings; yet for my part, I could not have feigned enthusiasm. I didn't want Simon & Garfunkel to break up.

It is to the enormous credit of both men that their careers have continued to prosper and grow. Paul's subsequent albums have received tremendous critical praise. His *There Goes Rhymin' Simon* album was nominated for the Grammy Award for best album of 1973 and sold over a million units. Artie was at first hesitant to record. He felt pressure to do something, but for a while he didn't know which direction to take. We stayed in touch, and I kept encouraging him to do an album of other people's material. He resisted this, misconstruing it to mean that I wanted him to "cover" hit songs, like Johnny Mathis or Andy Williams. That wasn't my thinking at all; I wanted him to sift through the best of current writing—and also have songs written for him—to put together a very personal album. Composers and music publishers will go great distances for you because of your name, I argued; you'll have the pick, if you want, of writers like James Taylor, Carole King, Paul Williams and Jimmy Webb.

Artie continued to equivocate. For a while he wanted to combine classical and contemporary music; next he talked of church music, and then of Greek music. At each turn, I tried to push him as far as possible in the direction of contemporary writers. The others were fine concepts, but they were very eclectic and unlikely to reach any sizable audience. Finally he came around and went to San Francisco to record the album with Roy Halee, the brilliant engineer-producer who had worked on all the other Simon &

Garfunkel albums, making an invaluable contribution to each of them. I listened to a few cuts at one point, and I thought the album was shaping up beautifully. But, as I expected, Artie's perfectionist tendencies had emerged strongly; he took more than a year to record the album. At one point he even called to hold *my* hand.

"Look," he said, "I just want you to know that I haven't lost my perspective. The album is taking a long time, but I'm fully in control." Rather than directly bring up the cost of studio time, he backed into it. "How many copies will I have to sell for Columbia to recoup its investment?" he asked. I figured about two hundred to two hundred and fifty thousand, and he said: "Don't worry about a thing. It's in the bag." That was like Artie. He knew that I must have been very concerned about the wildly mounting studio costs, but in view of his past contributions and our relationship, I wasn't bringing it up. He appreciated that; so he dealt with it in his own way.

His prediction was correct. The costs of *Angel Clare*—more than two hundred thousand dollars—were recouped. In fact, sales of the album were close to the million-unit mark by the spring of 1974, a major winner for him.

# 3

Paul finished his first album in 1972, and, as usual, I met him at the studio—this time with a few of his good friends: Charles Grodin, the actor who starred in *The Heartbreak Kid;* Zohra Lampert, the actress; and Michael Tannen, his lawyer, business advisor and closest friend—to hear the tracks. Paul and I spoke afterward and decided that the first single should be "Mother and Child Reunion" and the second, "Me and Julio Down By The Schoolyard."

This would be the follow-up album to *Bridge,* and we realized that it would attract a great deal of attention; we wanted everything to go smoothly. Paul felt more comfortable about doing the initial press interviews in England and then the rest of Europe. He was a giant star there—the *Bridge Over Troubled Water* album had sold more than a million copies in

England alone—and we knew that the coverage would be tremendous. I planned to be there at the same time to make it easier. Obviously, questions would be asked about the split-up, and I knew that Paul would be candid; that's his style. But I didn't want him to be so blunt that he and Artie would never be able to get back together again.

For I believed—and still believe—that they will record together again. They will undoubtedly continue to pursue their own individual careers, but every so often the special magic they create will be heard again. It happened in 1972 at a special fund-raising concert for McGovern at Madison Square Garden. Three great "groups" were reunited for a cause they strongly supported: the brilliant comedy team of Elaine May and Mike Nichols; the group that crossed all barriers of folk and rock music, Peter, Paul & Mary; and Simon & Garfunkel. Nichols and May started the evening off. Although they were a little rusty in their timing, they showed the eighteen thousand people who jammed the Garden— most of whom were young and had never seen them before—how their comedy had created a whole new dimension in humor. They were devastatingly funny. Peter, Paul & Mary came next. I was moved listening to them breathe their special meaning into Dylan's "Blowin' In The Wind" and seeing them charm the audience with "Puff (The Magic Dragon)" and then bring them to their feet with "This Land Is Your Land." Then, after Dionne Warwicke had showed everyone why she is such a unique interpreter of the great Bacharach and David hits, Simon & Garfunkel came onstage.

I loved watching them amble on, Garfunkel striking that awkward, boyish stance at the microphone and Simon shuffling back and forth and then from side to side, grinning and waving to the crowd, which was standing up shouting greetings to these two troubadors who had brought so much good music to them. And then they started to sing—"Mrs. Robinson," "Emily Whenever I May Find Her," "The Boxer," "The 59th Street Bridge Song (Feelin' Groovy)," "America," "The Sound of Silence," "Cecilia," "Mother and Child Reunion," "Me and Julio," "Homeward Bound" and, of course, "Bridge Over Troubled Water." It was staggering. The audience responded with wave after wave of applause. All in all, a beautiful evening, ending with a party I arranged for them in the glass-enclosed penthouse of the New York Hilton Hotel.

But things didn't change. Paul still planned to record his next album alone, and we met one day to discuss it. His first album had sold a million—great for anyone else . . . but not satisfactory to Paul. With typical self-appraisal, he asked where he had gone wrong. I assured him that the album was a smashing success. The only way it could have done better would have been if he had toured, giving performances in major cities behind the album's release, or if the single had become a major copyright in the "Bridge Over Troubled Water" or "The Sound of Silence" tradition. "Me and Julio" and "Mother and Child Reunion" were big hits, but they weren't the ballad kind of hit which is recorded by many *other* artists, thereby providing an extra kick to album sales.

Paul agreed to tour behind the *Rhymin' Simon* album. For a long time he had been against giving any more concerts—saying how wearing it was to tour. We had discussed the subject when his first solo album was coming out, but he was adamantly against it. When we were in England for the press interviews, however, he began to change his mind. We went to a Cat Stevens concert with Michael Tannen, who was in England helping Paul coordinate his affairs, and Barry Krost, Cat Stevens's manager, had reserved the Royal Box for us; we were joined there by Prince Rupert Loewenstein, the business advisor to The Rolling Stones; Penelope Tree, the famed society model; and her beau, photographer David Bailey. Paul and I sat in the first row and I watched him reacting to the stares from the audience down below. I could see his adrenalin rise during the concert as the performance built in intensity. He was getting excited. I had an idea; I debated with myself whether to ask Barry to have Cat Stevens introduce Paul from the audience—maybe he'd even play a number or two. I thought that it would be great for Paul to be on a stage again after such a long absence. The publicity would be tremendous. But would he mind? He had said that his performing days were over. Did I dare encourage it? Would Cat Stevens mind sharing the spotlight? I decided against it.

After the concert, I asked Barry what he thought of the idea. Would he have been upset? "Hell, no," he said. "It would have provided great electricity and made the evening even more of an event." Then I asked Paul, "Suppose Cat had introduced you to the audience and then asked you to join him onstage. What would you have done?" His answer: "I had three numbers all picked out." It was clear that Paul would tour again.

The question of which single to release first from *Rhymin' Simon* was discussed at length. Paul said that he thought "American Tune" would be the best single. I disagreed. I didn't think it would take off that easily and I suggested "Kodachrome." "My God," said Paul, *"you're* the one who talks so often about the importance of a ballad hit! This is a quality song with strong lyrics. It could be another 'Bridge Over Troubled Water.' " The lyrics *were* strong; but I didn't hear a strong enough melody line. "If it's going to be a hit," I said, "it will break out of the album anyway. But up front it's a questionable choice. Since you haven't really toured yet, your solo image still isn't fully established; it's better for you to release a safer and more obvious single."

"Kodachrome" was a much surer thing. I urged him to pick it first.

He said he'd think about it. By the next day, he agreed. As a result, *There Goes Rhymin' Simon* got off to a tremendous start. It picked up further steam when a second single, "Loves Me Like A Rock," was released after AM stations had begun to request it heavily. That single went gold, selling over a million copies. Paul toured fairly extensively, building a great show around his awesome list of classic standards. Then *Rolling Stone* delighted Paul by choosing "American Tune" as the song of the year. Its quality was finally recognized.

All this has further solidified Paul's position as one of America's top writer-performers. If he continues to work and perform with his current momentum, he clearly will become an institution all by himself.

# 4

I seem to be writing a lot about arguments with Columbia's artists, and this distorts the picture somewhat. For my memories are flooded with long periods of bliss and good times, the fantastic highs of artists' careers suddenly exploding, and the warm relationships with artists and managers that continue to this date. My *love* of the business dominates all my memories. When things went well —which they did most of the time—they really went well; when times were tough, it could be pretty dramatic.

Which brings me to Miles Davis. When I took over the Presidency of Columbia, he was one of the company's mainstays. His albums *Sketches of Spain, Kind of Blue* and *Porgy and Bess* were landmarks. But his sales in recent years had fallen off; he sold between forty and fifty thousand albums now—he'd once sold more than a hundred thousand, sometimes a hundred and fifty thousand. In the process of becoming the star of the jazz world, he'd acquired some expensive habits: exotic cars, beautiful women, high-fashion clothes, unusual homes. He'd also gotten in the habit of calling Columbia regularly for advances.

I decided to subsidize him. I felt that he contributed to Columbia's jazz and progressive music roster just as Vladimir Horowitz contributed to our classical list. It eventually got to be a problem, however. Fifty thousand albums barely takes you out of red ink. We began to give Miles additional money each time he recorded an album; we weren't making any money at all.

Miles nonetheless called constantly to ask for more. He has a raspy, low voice—a fiery whisper that conveys heat over the telephone while you are straining to find out how much money he wants. He is spellbinding, and he can talk. After a while, the money business got to be sort of a joke. For Miles called often— sometimes urgently—and I had to figure out each time if he was serious. Walter Dean got some of his calls, too—fortunately—and handled them well; sometimes he spent *hours* on the phone listening to that hoarse, almost demonic voice and dodging its monetary thrusts.

Then one day Miles called me to complain about his record sales. He was tired of low sales, and angry about it. Blood, Sweat & Tears and Chicago had borrowed enormously from him—and sold millions. These young *white* artists—he was in a rather militant frame of mind—were cashing in while he was struggling from advance to advance. If you stop calling me a *jazz* man, he said at one point, and just sell me alongside these other people, I'll sell more.

In part, I agreed with him; the younger rock musicians were borrowing freely from Miles by fusing jazz and rock. The other part of the problem was his alone. He had been playing only in small jazz clubs. I suggested that he play the Fillmore—or places like it—if he wanted to reach a larger audience and raise sales. Youth was ready for Miles Davis, but he had to play where they went for their music.

Miles became very upset. He wasn't going to play for "those fucking long-haired white kids." He would be "ripped off"; Bill Graham wouldn't pay him enough *money*. The audiences would be prejudiced because he was black. And furthermore, if the head of Columbia was espousing this, he wanted off the "fucking label." And he hung up on me.

Then I got a telegram saying that he would make no more recordings for Columbia; he wanted off the label *now*.

I was both disturbed and amused by this; it wasn't his first outburst, but it was by far the most explosive to date. Miles's manager called the next day. Wow, Miles was really heated up! What in the world had I said to him? I told him what had happened and added that I was *still* convinced we had the same objective. Young audiences were getting into sophisticated fusions of jazz and rock; they could easily get into Miles—but they had to be exposed to him. The way to do it was for him to play the Fillmore. I added that I had nothing to apologize for; I wasn't giving Miles his release. If he was willing to try this—and I thought it would benefit his record sales enormously—I'd be glad to help. Bill Graham was a good friend of mine; I knew something could be worked out.

A few months went by. Then Miles called again. He'd gotten a little hot under the collar, he said; he'd play the Fillmore if I could get him a decent amount of money and the right circumstances. Around this time, I'd gone to a Laura Nyro concert at Princeton University and she told me afterward that she'd been a Miles Davis fan since childhood. She'd love to play with Miles in any engagement I could arrange. I decided that the two would fit together perfectly and mentioned this to David Geffen, who made the necessary arrangements. They were given equal billing; Miles opened the show and Laura closed it.

A week before the Fillmore East concert I had to go to California on business; a package arrived at my hotel one day containing black and gray striped flared pants, a black and gray striped vest and a long-sleeved black silk shirt. A note from Miles asked if I would wear the outfit to the first performance. "I want you to look special," Miles wrote.

I was very touched. It wasn't a typical outfit for me, but everyone needs a change of style now and then; and so I took it to a clothing store for a fitting. Miles played a beautiful set that night, and he was terribly pleased to see me in the outfit. We posed for pictures, which eventually appeared on the cover of *Cashbox*. After that, Miles toured with Santana and played rock halls across the country. His next album, *Bitches Brew,* sold over four hundred thousand units. Young people suddenly caught on to him, and his albums thereafter regularly sold in six figures—giving him a completely revitalized career.

Miles didn't stop calling, of course; nor was our new relationship free of trouble. During even our warmest periods, he occasionally poked at the company in press interviews. He would say that he was being treated very well by Columbia—so well you'd almost think he had blond hair and blue eyes. "I'm the company nigger, but I'm doing okay." Then he would complain in *Ebony* or *Jet* that Columbia didn't have enough "really black" artists—which was probably true at the time, but I was hardly pleased to have the problem aired.

I'd tell him that I wouldn't sign black artists just to fill a quota. We had The Chambers Brothers, Sly, Mahalia Jackson and O.C. Smith, among others, and we were trying to get Stevie Wonder or James Brown at sensible prices—but we couldn't. They had other contracts. So I'd keep saying to Miles: if you've got a grievance, tell me *privately*. We are working hard for you; why create trouble? Miles's eyes always sparkled when we talked about this. He liked being a gadfly and I expect he rather enjoyed my exasperation. "Don't pay attention to that," he'd say. "Sometimes you've got to say what people expect of you."

Miles played the Fillmore many times. The audiences didn't always know how to deal with him. For there are no breaks when he performs. His sets are long, extended productions lasting from thirty minutes to a full hour. When he finishes a solo passage, he sort of stalks around the stage or gets up and walks off for a few minutes. He has a sense of arrogance about him that speaks out to an audience. During the first Fillmore concert, some of Laura's girlish fans had trouble getting into him. Miles makes no concession to his audience, of course, whether at the Fillmore or Philharmonic Hall. He's unique and charismatic, one of the more brilliant musicians of our time.

Miles has also gotten much more musically productive. When we met, he felt underpaid and he was producing relatively few albums. After that, we had trouble slowing him down. He started recording three albums a year, sometimes right on top of each other. He would call Bruce Lundvall, Bob Altshuler (another jazz aficionado), or myself and play long passages. Then he'd want *that* album released, despite his backlog. If we had just had a release in December, he'd record an album in January and want it out immediately. And we'd protest, saying that the December one needed time for sales and exposure. Then he'd call in March telling us to forget the January album—he had a new one.

At no time did Miles ever fully recoup his advances. Yet our relationship remained warm because I dealt with his financial problems on the assumption that he was good for Columbia in the long run, both on commercial and cultural levels. He demonstrated his appreciation in his own way. At one point, in 1971, I asked him to attend a Waldorf-Astoria luncheon where I was to receive the Anti-Defamation League's Man of the Year award. It was not a typical scene for Miles, but he viewed it as a personal responsibility and sat with me, Paul Simon, Andre Kostelanetz and others on the dais. In May of 1973 he rearranged his schedule on my behalf to make an important charity appearance. Our relationship, in short, bounced all over the musical scale. I am grateful for *all* the experiences.

# Sixteen

## 1

I had no *average* working day. The music business comes at you like bullets: sudden, fast, explosive, hot. I arrived at the office between nine and nine-thirty and usually called my dining room for cornflakes and coffee. Then I got into the work. The first hour involved catching up with the previous day's leftovers, which for openers meant a dozen or more unanswered telephone calls. Let's say the previous day had brought fifty—not an unusually large number; I might have gotten back to thirty-five people. Fifteen to go.

Telephone calls are the lifeline of any business. I worked on the assumption that you—or someone you designate—*must* return calls. Someone has to take care of it that day, or within one or two working days. I could be compulsive about it. Sloppiness here has hurt more than one career. I gave each caller no more than four or five minutes, and then things would start to happen. My secretary might start passing me messages, or reminding me of an appointment, or whatever. I also got to know who the chronic telephone people were—callers who wouldn't get *off*. For them, I was "halfway out the door" or "behind in my appointments."

I also had involuntary mechanisms. My staff people knew that they had about five minutes to talk, and that was it. Then my mind usually began moving beyond whatever issue was at hand; my words became . . . distracted. On *my* end, I was going up the wall watching the phones light up and hearing them ring again and again as the minutes passed. Five minutes was the limit.

The mail arrived on my desk about ten-fifteen. This consumed thirty-five to forty minutes; I answered or dealt with each piece immediately unless it required detailed thought. In that case, I saved it for the day's end. Mail arrived throughout the day, perhaps four or five more times; my secretary brought it in each time and took whatever dictation was necessary. I also read sales figures whenever they came in; this was a peculiar habit. I could never *stop* reading them, impractical and time-consuming as it was. When they came in, which was daily, I dropped everything else.

There were always tapes to listen to. I played them in the morning over cornflakes, at lunch if I could steal half an hour alone, and often late at night. I also came into the office every Saturday to do this. The tapes and acetates poured in like floodwater: new singles, audition tapes, album acetates. Each tape was elaborately screened before it reached me so that my time would not be wasted; that still left enough of them in my office each week to cause a prodigious clutter. Some managers, in addition, could get an artist in front of me—or a tape to my desk—without going through the usual screening (Steve Paul or Todd Schiffman and Larry Larson, for example); most people had to tread a labyrinthian set of corridors. There simply weren't enough hours in the day for me to listen to everything.

Meetings and luncheons took up considerable portions of each day. Monday began with an advertising meeting, which involved going over the week's trade ads, the albums we were promoting and judgments about upcoming campaigns. I also went to an Epic singles meeting in the afternoon. That lasted from two thirty until four, sometimes longer. People at the Monday advertising and singles meetings were burdened by the fact that I had spent much of the weekend reading . . . and thinking. I usually had a lot of questions in my head and wanted to know something about practically every key record in circulation. The top national promotion men also came in Monday so that we could go over selected records and review how they were being worked. We'd also run through the Top Forty radio charts to see how our records were doing, and then make a variety of decisions: stop working this record, work that one harder, try this technique, and so on.

Columbia's singles meeting was held on Wednesday. I lunched with my key operating heads each Thursday for about two and a half hours, which meant a free and rapid-fire exchange of concerns from all corners of the company. Several days a week I ate at my desk in order to talk at length with executives such as Walter Dean or Elliot Goldman. I had also to attend three corporate CBS meetings each month: the Board of Directors meeting, the "Operating Committee" meeting for group presidents, and Development Committee meetings.

The rest of the nine-to-six day was filled with smaller, impromptu meetings. A staggering number of people always seemed lined up to get into my office. I might see three different managers during an average workday, sometimes starting with breakfast. Artists also dropped by constantly to talk about their careers. In that case, if the matter was less than urgent, I walked out of my office and talked to them in the hallway. A hallway meeting lasts five to ten minutes; if the artist gets into your office, even just to say "hello," it takes half an hour. Beyond impromptu meetings with executives, A&R men and managers, there were auditions, sudden crises and an endless parade of things to sign, scrutinize or make judgments about.

Toward six o'clock, the day's tempo changed a bit. I scheduled auditions for about five-thirty, and they took place about twice a week. Every four weeks or so, I'd also have to audition a Broadway property. The composer and the lyricist would come in to play the score; it became very time-consuming. After a while I started reading the script *first;* if I didn't like it, the audition of the score didn't take place. If the book is weak, the score usually won't be able to save it.

After six-thirty, I met with my immediate aides for more relaxed discussions of the day's issues; we usually worked on the more complicated problems during that time. I had three shifts of secretaries. One arrived at nine in the morning for the mail and early phone calls; my regular secretary, Octavia Bennett, came in at nine-thirty and stayed until about six-thirty; and an evening girl came in at six and stayed until I finished up at eight-thirty or nine o'clock. I did my dictating and quieter thinking at this time of day—but soon word spread that I tended to be in the office late and I began to be inundated with calls, particularly from the West Coast. About that time of day, Walter Dean, Elliot Goldman and Larry Harris usually came in to bring me up to date on crucial contract negotiations. Ron Alexenburg and Steve Popovich would arrive after that to talk about key singles and how they'd done that day.

Then I went home. Dinner with Janet and the children—if I didn't have an audition or a business dinner scheduled—lasted about half an hour, after which I got to my heavier reading. This involved trade papers, sales charts, corporate reports, five-year planning studies, monthly statements, technical reports (quadraphonic research, for example) and *Rolling Stone*. Eventually I arranged to have the trade papers—which came out on Mondays—delivered to my home on the weekends. This weekend reading sometimes spilled into Monday and Tuesday—and on Wednesday *Variety* came out. I also read the biweekly promotion reports from all forty promotion men, the sales reports from the sixteen sales managers and the four regional directors' reports. I didn't *have* to do this, but I was compulsive; no matter how many times I tried to stop— or berated myself for this inefficiency—I still kept reading them. They gave me a tremendous feel for the company's inner and far-flung workings; I often wrote comments on them, congratulating a promotion man in Minneapolis or Florida for making a particularly telling point. I wanted these people to *know* that I was reading their reports, that I knew what they were into; I assumed that this had a therapeutic effect—possibly a motivating one as well, since they always knew that I was "watching."

The job involved at least 90 percent of my waking hours every day except Sunday, which was always reserved for my family (though I sneaked some light trade reading into that day as well). There seemed no other way to do it well. The demands were huge, and they left little time for real relaxation. I usually had two or three club dates each week, and for at least two years I'd rush home on Thursdays to dress for the Philharmonic so that we could make use of our season subscription tickets. The job was mostly a matter of knowing how to keep twenty or thirty balls in the air at one time; I tried not to show it if I felt harassed or worried about a particular business problem. People who worked with me could tell, but I rarely showed this face to the public. People were constantly amazed that I could keep on top of so much work—and so many constant mini-crises. But the fact was that I didn't mind the tension; I am a habitual worker.

Admittedly, this got to be rather harrowing. Apart from reading *The New York Times* in the morning, an occasional book, and

*Time* magazine each week, I had little contact with the rest of the world. My life became almost totally involved with music. I tried to give all I could to my growing family—my son, Mitchell, was born in July, 1970, and Douglas was born in March, 1972. I got up earlier in the morning to spend time with them and, even if I had nighttime auditions, I came home to have dinner with Janet and my two older children, Fred and Lauren. But it was a difficult juggling act.

Many people looked upon me as some sort of machine. My output was enormous, and various department heads expected me to buzz in and out of their fiefdoms at a moment's notice. I'd suddenly want a particular piece of information, or I'd hear something on the radio, or I'd see something in the sales charts that interested me . . . or . . . or . . . it all seemed tense and hectic to many of my employees, but actually it was just my way of doing business. Action, movement, questions-and-answers, crisp ideas—no time for schmoozing. It was never cold; just fast and to the point. People were often surprised to see me in a social context; I'd be relaxed and—I like to think—gregarious. I wasn't *testing* people on the job; my standards were my own, not ones I was setting for others. I set a pace, but it was one for *me,* as well as them to follow.

# 2

Prominence, whether in rock music or politics, invites publicity problems. Let's begin with the day Terry Knight, then manager of Grand Funk Railroad, called me and wanted to go to lunch. It was early 1972.

Terry was an extremely imaginative promoter. Grand Funk was enjoying substantial commercial success, the result in part of Terry's use of Times Square billboards and heavy, heavy trade and consumer advertising. Musically, they were drawing mixed notices; but Knight had persuaded Capitol that they could pull in huge audiences if promoted correctly. And he was right; despite critical put-downs, he propelled Grand Funk to the front ranks of rock groups. I was deep into my talent-raiding campaign when he called. We agreed to meet at a small French restaurant on Manhattan's Upper West Side to avoid rumors.

Terry arrived with his attorney, Howard Beldock. We had a very pleasant lunch spiced with industry gossip and interesting observations about current albums and artists. I had been a little apprehensive because Terry was known for histrionic behavior; when he wanted something from Capitol, I heard that he stormed and raged until he got it. It happened that many of his unorthodox promotion schemes worked—amazingly well. He soon became looked upon as an expert in the field of large-scale, off-beat promotion. So I was rather surprised to find him a charming and (seemingly) open person.

We eventually turned to business; even then he was pleasant. Terry said he'd "given thought" to the contract he wanted for Grand Funk, but he had to go to a recording and editing session now. Howard would give me the details at my office. Back at the building, Howard and I began a preliminary mating dance. Grand Funk, said Howard, was getting better and better; the group had yet to scratch the surface of its potential. They were getting bigger and bigger. In other words, Howard wanted a lot of money.

He asked for eight million dollars.

I was stunned. I had done my homework before meeting Terry and Howard for lunch; Grand Funk had one or two albums that had sold over a million copies—but they weren't the nation's top-selling group. A recent album had sold about seven hundred thousand albums. An eight-million-dollar guaranty was ridiculous!

"I can't make a counteroffer to that," I told him. "The amount is so absurd that I don't even want it used as a reference point in negotiations. I suggest you talk to other companies—perhaps to Capitol as well—and test their reactions. I don't think anyone will offer you that kind of money. When you get down to a more realistic level, we can start talking, *if* you're so inclined."

Howard still wanted a counteroffer; I declined. We were worlds apart, I said, and I didn't want to polarize things further.

Five weeks later, I read in *Rolling Stone* that I'd *offered* eight million dollars for Grand Funk Railroad's contract.

I'd been had. It was an absolutely foul trick, for that "eight million dollars" would inevitably come to haunt me. No retraction in *Rolling Stone* could change that. It didn't matter that the item was pure hype. Every important artist under contract to—or

—269—

negotiating with—Columbia would use it as a standard of reference.

My anger now centered on *Rolling Stone*. The magazine has made some extremely important contributions to music and journalism; I always made it required reading for my staff, and I never miss an issue. But *Rolling Stone* also seemed constantly suspicious of success, it constantly loved to needle establishment artists (the Streisand article; the Neil Diamond Winter Garden review) and the bigger record companies (its appropriate put-down of "The Man Can't Bust Our Music," for example). I always took those barbs badly; I realized that they shouldn't bother me, but they got under my skin.

The Grand Funk problem was different. No one at *Rolling Stone* had bothered to check it out. This was extremely irresponsible reporting; it threatened to cause me a lot of trouble. I finally called up *Rolling Stone* editor Jann Wenner and said, "My God, how could you print this! It's totally wrong. I expect this occasionally from the trades, but not from *you*."

Jann gave me lame excuses. Calls had been placed, and not answered—or someone had talked to our West Coast office . . . or something. Jann admitted that the magnitude of the story should have involved calling my office, and he agreed to print a retraction. Unfortunately, it was not conspicuous when it came out and had considerably less impact, of course, than the inaccurate item, which was in the widely read "Random Notes" column.

The most astounding thing of all was Terry Knight's response. He contacted me afterward saying that he had *thought* we were meeting confidentially. He was *amazed* that I would talk to *Rolling Stone*. I didn't bother to answer. I was flabbergasted, but there was no point in prolonging the quarrel.

The more serious question was *Rolling Stone*'s role. I'd always supported them, however piqued I might be at individual articles or "Random Notes" items. The paper was good for music; its documentation of the revolution in contemporary rock and the social and cultural context of this growth had been superb. It was sometimes guilty of overenthusiasm—if not hard-eyed zeal—and sometimes got a bit puffy with self-importance. Nonetheless, it had played an invaluable role in changing the consciousness of this country, and not just among music fans.

I'd always gone to considerable lengths to cooperate with *Rolling Stone*. When they needed advertising support, they got it. Financial subsidies? They got them. Jann told me at one point they were near bankruptcy and asked if they could have a year's advertising money *in advance*. They got it. And once, when Jann wanted some expertise on mail-order advertising, I turned the problem over to our staff and for a while, *Rolling Stone*'s advertising people worked in *our* building. They came to me another time for suggestions on financial consultants; I sent them to a firm that had done work for Columbia and stayed on the case for a while.

Our relationship was close, and at one point Jann asked me to be present when Columbia University gave *Rolling Stone* the Columbia Journalism Award. I was the only nonfamily member in attendance. There also was a period when he asked me to help with *Rolling Stone*'s distribution. He felt that the paper would profit from display in record stores; so Columbia's distribution force made the arrangements. From a journalistic point of view, this may be considered too cozy a relationship between a newspaper and one of its major advertisers. But I offered my aid only because I believed that the paper was good for music. It never seemed to stop them *at all* from shooting arrows into our corporate hide.

The hide wasn't so thick. I always took it personally when the paper made a snide comment about Columbia or took one of its artists to task. Despite my anger I recognized that *Rolling Stone* did this as a service of sorts to its allegedly anti-establishment readership. I occasionally wondered how they could accept consulting and advertising assistance from Columbia—and then poke fun at us . . . or say downright nasty things. Then I'd cool down and realize that this was part of the game. Jann knew his readership, and his loyalty obviously had to be to them. Nice notices for Columbia made him vulnerable to charges of "selling out." I began to realize that he blasted us occasionally just to protect himself against this kind of problem. Also, we were so successful that we could withstand the barbs and still come up strong.

Despite our differences, I always took my hat off to Jann. He has created a journal which meets an important need within the music community and among the public at large. He has high journalistic standards, and since his early, somewhat missionary days of making "rock consciousness" accessible for all, he has transformed the journal into a platform for other interests while still maintaining a watchful eye over the music business. His contribution to contemporary journalism is, I think, substantial.

# 3

One more big-money press story. The villain this time is *Billboard*. A few years earlier, we had been negotiating a contract extension with Chicago (offering a higher royalty rate immediately for a new five-year signing rather than wait for the earlier contract to run out and risk competitive bidding), and everything was going well. The deal was signed sewing them up for five more years, and a new royalty rate of less than 10 percent of retail was agreed upon.

Next week *Billboard* ran a giant front-page headline saying that I'd re-signed Chicago for *ten million dollars.*

It *had* to be a crazy mistake. The story was not attributed to a source; on *Billboard*'s authority, readers were invited to believe that Columbia had just advanced Chicago ten million dollars for their new contract. I called Jimmy Guercio and asked what in the *world* was happening.

He pleaded innocence. I read the article to him over the phone. "My God," he said, "the group is going to call *me* and ask where the money is. I never talked to *Billboard* at all."

"Who did?" I shot back. He didn't know.

I spent some time trying to track down the source of the article, finally narrowing things down to Chicago's attorneys. A now-deceased *Billboard* writer, Mike Gross, apparently had talked to the law firm, and then pulled out his adding machine and figured out—based on Chicago's track record—that the deal over five years might ultimately be worth ten million. That's fine; except that a world of difference exists between Columbia guaranteeing that Chicago will make that and what Chicago might earn from actual sales of its records.

Again, it was the problem of precedent. I'm delighted if a group makes millions off its contract. False reports of advance guaranties, however, can run the price of competitive bidding up to the sky. Also, artists currently on your label can get very upset over your making such a deal with someone else. As with the *Rolling Stone* incident, *Billboard* could have called me. I decided not to comment, fearing that it would be awkward to get into the habit of publicly confirming and denying trade stories of various deals. They printed a vague retraction at my request, but I never revealed the precise facts of the contract. This would have opened up the question of guaranties for other artists on the label, and I didn't want to do that either.

# 4

Other problems during this period transcended questions of money. For example, Mike Curb, the architect of that attempt to con me out of signing Chicago, tried around this time to get some mileage out of the drug problem. He was now President of MGM Records, aspiring to be "entertainment chairman" for the Nixon administration, and was leader of a group called The Mike Curb Congregation, which performed occasionally at the White House but most frequently in Las Vegas.

When Mike took over MGM, he looked at his roster and astutely saw that MGM's efforts in the contemporary music field were almost embarrassing. His own personal taste leaned more toward MOR and Top Forty artists. He was smart enough to realize that he would have to work in that direction rather than try to compete with Warners, Columbia and A&M for the underground acts that could develop FM—and hopefully AM—audiences.

Curb then had an eye-catching promotional idea. In order to make his company a mecca for middle-of-the-road artists and audiences, he announced that MGM was dropping all artists from its roster who had *anything* to do with drugs—through their lyrics or in other ways. It was an interesting idea, and in many ways hard to fault; for record companies *do* have a responsibility to be careful about drug propaganda. But Curb's motives were not solely a matter of noble ethics.

He didn't, for example, take Eric Burden off the label, for Eric was making money. As it happened, Eric was rather insulted by this. He joked about taking out some trade ads saying, "Look, I smoke marijuana. Why are they keeping me?"

I reacted very strongly to Curb's announcement. I thought that it was a really hypocritical stance at the industry's expense.

In reality, it painted an inaccurate picture of the rest of us. I was President of the Record Industry Association of America at the time, so I issued a statement mentioning the *repeated* efforts of the industry to take strong stands against drug use and lyrics encouraging such use. I also took public issue with Curb's rationale for making the cuts.

I've always felt that a record company must be responsible when it gets into areas involving censorship. We are not here to judge artists' personal lives. No book publisher would refuse to sign a Tennessee Williams or a Eugene O'Neill because of drinking or personal problems; nor would they censor such a writer because his work contained discussions of alcohol or unconventional sexual appetites. Musicians, like writers, are creative people who should be judged according to their artistic output, nothing else. The industry was probably naive about certain veiled references in rock lyrics during the mid-sixties, and a few songs undoubtedly slipped by. But as soon as the problem surfaced, record companies acted swiftly and responsibly—cooperating with the White House and law enforcement agencies, which were also attempting to deal with it. Propaganda encouraging the use of drugs should be stopped. That's self-evident, with all the tragic waste of human lives and talent we have seen all around us. But what Mike Curb was doing at the time was primarily clearing his roster of deadwood; it's terribly unfortunate that he had to do it at the industry's expense.

I had had a similar—but not identical—problem when Bob Dylan recorded his "George Jackson" single, the one that contained the lyrics that said that George wouldn't "take shit" from anyone. Why should Dylan be any less free than the writer of a book to express himself? The responsibility of the record company in this situation is to warn the radio station—not censor the artist. The station then has its own decision about what it will or will not air.

We also had to face the question of whether we could record the word "fuck." "Fuck" appears in books and movies, and on the stage; why not on records? Ironically, it also has no trouble appearing on *some* kinds of records, the recording of the play *Who's Afraid of Virginia Woolf?*, for example. As noted earlier, I chose a NARM convention to make my point on the subject.

The issue seems very obvious to me. It should not be confused with the separate responsibility radio stations have in the use of the public airwaves. You might not be able to show *Serpico* or *Mean Streets* on television, but you don't censor their release as films. Either we care *fully* about art and freedom of expression, or we have no business making records (or publishing books, or creating films). There is little room for compromise here.

# 5

Few men have meant as much to the contemporary rock scene as Bill Graham. First he established his pioneering Fillmore auditorium in San Francisco, and then expanded by opening another landmark music institution in New York—his Fillmore East theater, called "Carnegie Hall for the Hip" at one point by *Time* magazine. His influence has been substantial on everyone associated with music—the industry, the performers, the public.

Bill and I get on very well. He is a volatile, emotional, sentimental, aggressive and sensitive man all at the same time—a classic study in contrasts. He handled rock music's growing pains during the late sixties, including its share of nonprofessionalism, very well. He demanded a lot from his performers, and when they listened, he gave them very good advice. He'd also helped me in many ways, touting me on to Santana and It's A Beautiful Day. And when it came to booking Columbia acts at the Fillmore, our relations were excellent.

Bill was a fighter, going back to his early days as an actor, writer and even waiter in the Catskills. He'd worked very hard all his life, and he set professional standards that were very, very high. He had to. The rock world was filled with young people who had virtually no experience with show business; they might decide not to play a gig for personal, emotional—or simply obstructive—reasons, and Bill had to cope with this. He could be sympathetic or volcanic, whichever the occasion required. He orchestrated the San Francisco and New York Fillmores with considerable skill. From the managers to the ushers to the lighting and stage help, he hired a unique breed of organized, disciplined and efficient flower children. The atmosphere they created for music was unique to the world of theater.

But during the summer of 1971, Bill decided he'd had enough.

He was flying back and forth between New York and San Francisco constantly, and the pace was killing him. He decided that he'd had his fill of the unpredictable performers, tension, booking problems, unruly audiences and general chaos. So he quit, walking out of the Fillmore with a highly emotional tirade against rock music. There were too many negative factors, he said again and again; Joplin and Hendrix had died, other performers wanted far too much money for their gigs, it was all too much of a hassle. Besides, no *really* great performers were breaking through; and all the mediocre talents had the worst kind of pretensions.

Rock, he implied, was dying.

I considered this a very destructive idea, also inaccurate. It led immediately to all sorts of writing and commentary, and the articles always seemed to be headlined "Is Rock Dying?" followed by a conclusion that it more or less was. I disagreed, and I felt after a while that I had to say something. It was true that fewer performers were breaking through—but for good reason: lack of room at the top. So many artists had broken through in the late sixties that they were jostling each other on and off the charts. Many very mature and talented people had emerged; and they had staying power. This made it considerably harder for new artists to break through. It took enormous talent and originality to get *anyone's* attention these days.

Graham had raised a cultural problem as well. A lot of people were *looking* for rock to die: the Nixon administration, people who disapproved of its loud noise, people upset by the killing at Altamont, parents who thought rock lyrics contained propaganda for drugs and debauchery. Antirock hysteria sometimes got out of hand.

The problem, however, was real. It seemed to me that Bill's emotional—though sincerely felt—outburst could do great harm. I issued a statement of my own attempting to refute this idea; but it got considerably less publicity than Bill's original outburst. My purpose, at any rate, was to put the matter in perspective. Rock until then had been identified primarily with the raucous, hard-driving sounds that first came out of San Francisco. At times it *was* ear-splitting, and to some extent it drove a lot of other, quieter performers off the stage. At the time of Bill's statement, however, rock was being absorbed into a broader musical revolution. Individual writer-performers were emerging: James Taylor, Carole King, Elton John, Joni Mitchell. Other showcases were rising to take the Fillmore's place, including Carnegie Hall and Avery Fisher (formerly Philharmonic) Hall in New York.

Rock was not dying at all; the ear-splitting sounds had simply moved over to let other forms join in. Jazz artists were moving into the medium, black music was crossing over to white charts, country stations were appearing in northern cities. Barriers were breaking down, and diffuse forms of popular music were sweeping everything before them. People might argue that hard "rock" was gone; so what was next? A lot of *little* things, all borrowing their intensity and message from the musical revolution of the late sixties. And many of the important artists of that era were maturing, staying on the scene to make more and more sophisticated music.

Call it "consolidation." Call it "contemporary" music. Whatever the name, rock was hardly dying; it was simply taking its rightful place among contemporary forms—and justly taking credit among knowledgeable music people as a groundbreaking musical experience. Contemporary music became even stronger than it was in the heyday of the Fillmore. For a while, highly amplified electronic music threatened to obliterate everything around it, but it became part of the greater revolution of *all* contemporary music. I got tired of listening to complaints about the death of rock, and so, to demonstrate the vitality of music today, I arranged for a festival of contemporary music to be held in Los Angeles in the spring of 1973. We booked the Ahmanson Theatre in the Dorothy Chandler Pavillion and turned the proceeds over to charity for what proved to be a glittering week. First we mixed folk and rock music with classical by joining Loudon Wainwright III, Anthony Newman and Friends and The Mahavishnu Orchestra on the same program. It was a beautiful evening for the sophisticated music lover. Subsequent evenings demonstrated the strength of each category of music. The critics raved about the performances— Earth, Wind & Fire, Miles Davis and Ramsey Lewis for fans of progressive music; The Staple Singers, Billy Paul and Johnny Nash for R&B and Top Forty fans; Johnny Cash, Lynn Anderson and Charlie Rich for country music followers; Johnny Mathis, Peter Nero and Maxine Weldon, a new artist, for the MOR crowd; Loggins & Messina, Dr. Hook & the Medicine Show and New Riders of the Purple Sage for the rock contingent. Rock wasn't dying; it had simply joined the larger family of contemporary music, a welcome addition indeed.

# Seventeen

## 1

I never related well to the corporate structure, its hierarchy and bureaucracy. For one thing, I had no real "business" sense before I became Columbia's chief operating officer. I was a lawyer, and knew little of the dynamics of corporate business.

I never really acquired that sense. When you sit on top of the mountain it's fairly easy to avoid bureaucratic problems. Decisions are made by you, a few top advisers and several key operating contributors. You know that crucial things are happening down the line—merchandising, advertising, packaging—and you provide support for them. But on a day-to-day basis, the company is run by about a dozen people.

The only time I really felt Columbia's size was at the company's annual convention. I'd walk into a hall and suddenly see more than a thousand people—and these were only employees with a fair degree of responsibility—representing Columbia operations all around the world. It was breathtaking! This massive group would go through three or four days of intensive meetings, strategy sessions and the showcasing of artists, and I would, for a few days, get a feeling for the tremendous, far-flung nature of the operation.

This was not the case at all during the rest of the year. On the Records Division's floors, the flow of energy was channeled through a small group of people—everything was split-second timing, one crisis and deal after another. There was enormous esprit de corps and camaraderie; the bywords, however, were speed, efficiency—and taste. We looked at other companies and saw them lose artists because of their inability to make decisions. I wanted Columbia, by contrast, to operate as independently and hungrily as the smallest record company. This feeling—one that I encouraged and reveled in—separated Columbia considerably from the rest of CBS. We dressed differently, kept different hours and often lived by night.

Partly as a result of this, Columbia came to be known as very much my company. I was highly visible to the outside world—mostly because I was involved in practically every deal that Columbia made. This was in keeping with an industry trend for successfully run companies: the presidents were taking an increasingly greater role in creative matters. At times, however, my being singled out was unfair to my key colleagues. In their respective posts, they were easily among the industry's best people; it wasn't a case of my emerging from a mediocre, lackluster company and keeping it afloat alone. We had a first-rate organization—but when you are elbow-deep in the creative wars, you do get the lion's share of attention, which unfortunately left my associates somewhat in the background.

It was only after I left Columbia that I really thought about my job and the role I was called upon to play in music. For music is indeed a vital part of society. Until the sixties, it meant mostly entertainment, but now it has come to mean considerably more. It is now a platform for new ideas as well as an entertainment medium. It can provoke and stimulate thought; and artists are often spokesmen for cultural trends. Music, in fact, has become deeply enmeshed in the lives of millions of people, particularly the generation of the last decade. For we no longer sell records limited just to ballads of love and lost love. Frank Sinatra and Dinah Shore have moved over to make room for Paul McCartney and Carole King. Gershwin, Cole Porter and Rodgers and Hammerstein were, of course, marvelous composers and consummate musical poets. But Dylan, The Beatles and Paul Simon have added still another dimension to music. They have pierced more deeply into the human psyche and dealt with its frustrations and the problems of our times; our society is a richer place as a result.

As a music executive, I knew I was dealing with artists capable of having considerable cultural impact. My role was to provide—and to some extent create—a forum for them. Their music affected people's lives. I in turn was a transmitter of their talent. My goal was to find the largest possible audience for the artists in a way that didn't compromise their creativity.

# 2

I always felt enormous enthusiasm and pride in my work; no day at Columbia, in fact, passed without some kind of special excitement. For music is special. It has an exhilarating effect on me. When I hear a song I like, a *feeling* overcomes me; I feel uplifted, more together. Even the exhausting efforts required to keep Columbia's momentum going seemed more fun than work. Sometimes, late at night during a particularly difficult deal, I felt that I had used the energy of several lifetimes. But I did it willingly. And I loved every minute of it.

The pressure to keep Columbia's profits rising so astronomically took its toll. I had to keep "discovering" new artists or "attracting" major talent almost as if I were feeding an assembly line. And no one at the corporate CBS level seemed to have the foggiest notion that this might be a difficult, possibly even superhuman task. Their interest was clear: maintain last year's pace, plus 10 percent. Yet I deluded myself into creating a definite schism of worlds. In my world of *music* I was happy. Competitors offering millions of dollars couldn't buy me. My loyalty, devotion and life were dedicated to the creativity of the artists whom we recorded and to the men around me.

During April of 1973, I became aware that Columbia was conducting an internal audit stemming from questions raised by Federal prosecutors concerning the activities of David Wynshaw, head of Artist Relations. As a result of this audit, I was asked to fire Wynshaw, and I did.

I was concerned since I personally had relied upon Wynshaw tremendously to ease a number of my administrative burdens. He had become expert at the job of artist relations and, through that, he had become extremely efficient at booking hotels and flights and arranging all special business meetings for the Records Division since the early 1960s—before I moved to the business side.

After I became President he continued to take care of the arrangements for all dinners and showcasings of artists at any convention in which we were participating. Also, I more and more turned to him to handle many personal chores. It allowed me to concentrate 100 percent on the creative and business matters at the company that were consuming twelve to eighteen hours of my day.

I knew that the scope of the internal audit had been broadened, after Wynshaw's firing, to encompass the activities of all Columbia's executives, including my own. I had in fact talked on several occasions about these activities and about David Wynshaw with Arthur Taylor, the new CBS President who had taken office about eight months earlier, and CBS attorneys. After those discussions it didn't appear to me that a serious problem existed insofar as I was concerned. I was subsequently elected to the Board of Directors at the Annual Meeting of CBS stockholders that was held in April.

As it happened I asked myself during those weeks whether I *wanted* to stay at Columbia. I had offers to go other places. The uneasiness welling up within the company was beginning to be palpable. But it was also a busy time for me. We were in the midst of planning the music festival at Los Angeles' Ahmanson Theatre, for example—a complex task involving more than twenty artists and six different shows, plus arrangements to have the event filmed for the upcoming Columbia convention.

I was also involved in finalizing the negotiations for the Dylan contract (which, after I left, Columbia decided not to sign) and concluding a campaign to woo Billy Joel—this time right out of the hands of Atlantic Records. When I went to Los Angeles for nine days, to host the week at the Ahmanson and to meet with Billy Joel, I had to push the company investigation out of my mind.

I returned to New York from Los Angeles a week before Memorial Day. Again I felt the unrest at Columbia, and it seemed to be getting worse. But it made sense simply to concentrate on my work; my rather singleminded devotion to the Records Group over the years had left me largely without corporate sources of information. I could only wait.

I came to the office on the Tuesday after the Memorial Day weekend, May 29, and went into my usual routine: cornflakes at my desk, forty-five minutes with the morning mail, a meeting with the Advertising Department. I then met with Michael Levy, a business manager for several English producers, with whom Columbia was discussing a Jimmy Guercio-style deal for two of his clients.

Levy and I had finished up and moved into small talk when my intercom buzzed. CBS President Arthur Taylor's secretary came on.

"Mr. Davis," she said, "could you come up to see Mr. Taylor?"

When the President's secretary calls, she usually tells you when your presence is requested, say, at four o'clock, or whenever. If she doesn't set a time, it means *now*. I finished up with Levy and walked to the elevator.

I felt a little apprehensive. A sudden call to the President's office makes you wonder.

Taylor's office is on the thirty-fifth floor. He had two lawyers with him—and the meeting lasted about two minutes. It was calculated to last no more. I don't remember the exact words he said—perhaps I've blocked them—but the intent was clear. I was being told to leave the company.

"I'm in shock," I said, perhaps more than once. It was all I could think of.

"We'd like you to return to your office," Taylor continued, "and take whatever you'd like to take with you, and leave immediately."

That was it. That was the end of my love affair with Columbia Records. It was numbing; it seemed incredibly cold-blooded. I couldn't *believe* it. But that was it. There was nothing left to say. I turned on my heel and walked out of the office.

At the door, I was met by two CBS security men and served with the company's civil complaint against me, alleging ninety-four thousand dollars' worth of expense-account violations during my six years as President. The security men fell into step with me, and we took the elevator down to my eleventh-floor office.

Something in a man's life—or mind—tends, even at the worst moments, to put things in perspective. A week earlier, my thirteen-year-old cousin, Stephan John, had died of cancer. He was the grandson of my Aunt Jeanette, who had been like a mother to me after my parents died; she and I had visited him in the hospital for nearly three months, agonizedly watching this small boy literally *waste* away. My family and I had visited him nearly every night during the previous week, and when his death came, it was an extremely sad and difficult period for all of us.

Somehow the vision of Stephan's suffering held my emotions in check as I rode down the elevator and walked into my office for the last time. I kept thinking that *my* pain was insignificant compared to his; and I was still too . . . numb to realize what was happening to me. In the office, I took my checkbook, a few papers and other personal effects and loaded them into my attaché case. I told my secretary, Octavia, the news, and left quietly without seeing anyone else.

Taylor had said that I could take my company limousine home. When I arrived at my apartment, I was told that Janet was at my son and daughter's school; I sent my chauffeur to try to find her. Thirty minutes later, my housekeeper took a call from CBS saying that the chauffeur had been gone too long. They wanted him back. A cold chill went through me.

The telephone rang all afternoon. I was surprised at how fast the news had traveled. But I answered none of the calls, leaving my housekeeper to take messages. Beyond that, the afternoon seems mostly a blur. Friends, family members and a number of people from Columbia and the industry came over and, in effect, sat *shiva* with me. Janet returned an hour after I got home (the chauffeur hadn't been able to locate her) and we talked . . . and sat around . . . and talked some more. I spent most of the afternoon, in fact, sitting . . . and thinking . . . and dealing with my shock and disbelief—and pain and despair and deeply wounded feelings.

I reached my lowest point emotionally while watching the reporting of my dismissal on the six o'clock news. Somehow all those fresh media images finally brought me to tears after the numbing experience of the morning. And this wasn't the end of it. The media reaction seemed to me like a series of explosions. First the nighttime television news; then the papers the following morning. And the following week—the news magazines. Not to mention the trade papers, the gossip columns and the endless follow-up stories. The really upsetting part was the speculation, most of it horribly inaccurate, that appeared. Some of it was favorable—articles saying that I was the victim of a power play within CBS, or of corporate jealousies, or political problems, or whatever; and the widespread opinion that the expense-account charges were absurd in light of the tens of millions I'd made for

Columbia and the millions I would have received had I gone elsewhere. But some of it seemed malicious. This was the hardest of all to take.

I remained totally stunned by CBS's actions. Sadly, I could only speculate about why they did what they did. For Taylor and CBS's attorneys had known the complete facts behind each of the specific allegations in the complaint for a month and a half before my firing. Indeed, I had *volunteered* many of the facts, and despite statements made by them later, it had been made clear to me that if a difference of opinion existed, a financial settlement would be the solution. And as I've noted, I had been reelected to the CBS Board of Directors in the interim period.

What apparently had been their strong fear, bordering on obsession, was that Wynshaw might be involved with one Pasquale Falcone, a man who had been indicted for a drug conspiracy by a Federal Grand Jury in Newark. The prosecuting attorneys were the Federal Strike Force Against Organized Crime. No one at CBS knew whether Wynshaw was involved with Falcone in any serious way. But it was a legitimate major worry. CBS is a public company licensed by the Federal government to conduct its giant broadcasting business.

Actually, Falcone's only business connection with Columbia Records was that he had been a manager of one Columbia artist: O. C. Smith. He didn't manage Smith when Smith was signed to Columbia but he became Smith's manager a few years later. Falcone never really seemed to be involved commercially in records. I knew who he was but I never had any dealings with him at all. Smith had only one big hit and a couple of modest ones. He was not a major performer. Although I liked him, he just never warranted any special participation of mine.

CBS's attorneys had asked me if I knew any more about Falcone and Wynshaw. I did not. At one point they expressed apprehension, ostensibly for me, that since I had relied on Wynshaw to handle a series of personal matters for me, I might—notwithstanding my lack of knowledge—get indirectly tied to his troubles. After all, my name was better known and would provide more attractive headlines.

I had no idea whatsover about the nature of Wynshaw's outside activities—or troubles. I was tremendously upset and concerned that I might be connected to them, whatever they were.

It had never occurred to me that Wynshaw was anything but a selfless person totally dedicated to making my life free to handle the business of the company. If I left my office at 8 or 9 P.M., he'd always be there. If at 10 P.M., there'd be a message where he'd be having dinner in case I needed him. If a close relative were in the hospital and I was out of town, he'd visit and pay respects "for me." I continually said that to keep the creative momentum going for Columbia took up every waking hour of every day and that if I didn't have a Wynshaw, I'd have to invent one. I was shocked by the thought that he might have been secretly duping me for years.

On the basis of what I know, my best guess is that at some point CBS must have gotten word from someone—erroneously as it turned out—that Wynshaw was going to be indicted imminently, and be possibly linked to Falcone. This must have precipitated a state of panic which caused them to fire me. It must have been felt that the risk was too great that somehow I might get dragged in because of the history of my reliance on Wynshaw. It didn't matter that I never dealt with Falcone or that I didn't know anything about him. I was a member of the Board, and CBS as an institution must be kept unsullied at any cost. The stakes were high and if I had to be sacrificed, well, so be it.

As it later turned out, Wynshaw apparently did not become implicated in the trial in which Falcone was eventually convicted and the Strike Force Against Organized Crime moved out of the picture. But then the U. S. Attorney's Office in Newark moved in. Now, payola and "drugola" were to be the subjects for scrutiny. If there was smoke, where was the fire?

Despite repeated public denials by CBS, speculation ran high that payola or drugs were involved in the company. The CBS civil complaint against me seemed to the armchair analyst to be a smokescreen. My income and bonuses for the year 1973 alone would have totaled over three hundred thousand dollars. The complaint—rumors had it—just couldn't be the whole story. CBS's own actions had precipitated this uproar, and the consequences had been badly misgauged. They apparently became very disturbed about the press's new field day but that didn't make matters easier for me. If they were mired in the mess too, I wasn't thrilled with or comforted by the companionship. It was my name that kept getting prominently mentioned in the press and even though I was not being linked by anyone, including CBS, with Falcone, payola or drugs, I was the starting reference point for each article.

The worst problem of all was staying silent. My lawyer, Vincent L. Broderick, forbade comment on *anything;* this was tremendously frustrating. Press and industry gossip abounded; flatly inaccurate stories would appear, and I could do nothing about them. "No comment" was Broderick's invariable instruction—it was excruciating. The tension became almost unbearable. To see my reputation threatened after years of achievement was a crushing blow. I was able to sustain myself only through the love of my wife, family and friends and the incredible outpouring of support from artists, managers, countless executives of other companies and my devoted colleagues at Columbia itself.

In the meantime, CBS, worried that it might be accused of being negligent, had instituted its own investigation. Its outside counsel, Cravath, Swaine & Moore, a firm of well over one hundred lawyers, set up a special unit for the purpose and swarmed all over the records division, everywhere it had an office throughout the country. They would learn far more than I could ever know from my vantage point about the existence of payola.

The intensive investigation continued for several months. Information began filtering out to several people that the investigators were coming up clean. Then the investigators stopped investigating. I eagerly waited for the report to be made public. But no statement was issued. It was safest to be noncommittal. They weren't worried about me. The past contributions were over. To them, they owed me nothing.

At last their findings *had* to be made public. All record companies were required to file a report on the question of the existence of payola and drugs with the Senate Subcommittee on Patents, Trademarks and Copyrights. The CBS report finally stated its investigators had found "no evidence" of payola or drugs in Columbia's operations. Of course, the investigation would continue—leave a door safely open—but nothing had turned up after several months.

I waited for the newspapers to cover this, but any stories printed were buried. The earlier speculation was much more dramatic news. No doctrine of equal time or space here.

Naturally, the New Jersey investigation would continue. The press reported that the whole industry was receiving scrutiny. It would take a month, or a year or more. So my dilemma was whether I should write this book. Despite my scars, my lawyers forbade me to write about the details of the CBS complaint against me and the allegations described in it. There might be disappointment and criticism because the legal issues could not be dealt with more extensively. But, after serious evaluation, I decided that the reason for writing this book had nothing to do with seeking vindication through a unilateral outpouring.

My purpose instead is to see that my first eight years in music will not have been wasted.

The period during which I led Columbia Records was unique. It spanned a revolution, a massive musical change, a cultural explosion. The wars of competition between companies and negotiations with artists took place during an incredible growth in public awareness of music and what it offers to everyone. Recording personalities became the subjects of intense media interest all over the world; youth gravitated to its musical heroes, not blindly, as did the swooners of yesteryear, but with discrimination, taste and intelligence as well as emotion. Popular music for the first time reached the masses with lyrics that could affect society, culture and the times in which we live.

These were exciting years. A whole new generation of record executives took over at or about the same time and lived through them. My colleagues from those days—Mo Ostin, Joe Smith, Ahmet and Nesuhi Ertegun, Jerry Wexler, Jerry Moss and others—are still actively devoting themselves to the continuation of the saga. I had an interruption. I felt, therefore, that it was up to me to attempt to chronicle these times from my rather unique vantage point. My memory was fresh. God knows I had the time.

And so in September, 1973, I sat down to unravel this period of my life. The work lasted about six months, between taping and rewrites with James Willwerth, and it was not always easy. For one thing I kept reading press stories that I was about to take over this or that company, make a variety of deals or do other extraordinary things. I was mentioned, for example, as the upcoming President of a new Sony, USA, record company; of a new American Express-owned record company; and of RCA Records. Other stories said that I was forming a new company with Bob Dylan, The Beatles and Simon & Garfunkel. Most of these stories were printed as *fact*. I never understood this; nobody bothered to check with *me* about them.

I did pursue discussions for a few months with Chris Black-well, who made me a very generous offer of a partnership in his American operations for Island Records. This involved his contributing several million dollars' worth of capital to set up an operation to supplement the American rights to his catalog. Ironically, I never saw a word about this in the press.

The endless press speculation, nonetheless, created a lot of pressure. Offers came in to take over various record companies; so did feelers from other industries. I wondered how *soon* I should get back into the business. Immediately? In a few months? Would the offers still be on the table a year later?

I decided for the time being to pursue only the Island offer. The advantage was that the deal couldn't be finalized until 1974, for Island was tied up with Capitol Records until June of that year. This was a very powerful inducement, since it gave me time to do this book—which I now had even greater reason to write. For a whole new set of amazing circumstances was being put in motion by Columbia.

**3**

Stories and interviews now emanating from CBS were clearly part of a calculated campaign to rewrite history at Columbia Records—almost as though I'd never existed.

Suddenly, there was nothing special or unusual about the unprecedented growth that had occurred. Forget the boasting to Wall Street analysts for the last six years—nothing much had changed. After all, said Goddard Lieberson, Columbia was important in rock before Davis was there. "The rock era began with me," he was reported in *The New York Times* to have said. The rest of the industry laughed, but it hurt . . . deeply. The general press and the national magazines had no real expertise, so they printed whatever was told to them. Bob Altshuler had a new publicity mission and he apparently pursued it with vigor: The King is dead. Long live the King!

Lieberson, truly a master politician, wrote me a personal letter saying, in effect, Clive, please don't believe what you read in the papers; I'm not saying these things at all. And then the stories kept coming—in *Time, Newsweek, The New York Times, Billboard, Cashbox, Record World, Variety*—all carrying CBS's rewrite of history. Were all the interviewers stupid or hard of hearing? Each time an article appeared, I received dozens of calls from well-wishers who all said that Goddard's interviews were resulting mostly in chuckles and groans in the corridors—even at Columbia. But they still hurt.

I knew and understood that CBS had a job to do. It could not allow the business community to think that Columbia Records would fall apart without me. For that matter, I still wanted Columbia to do well; too much of me was still there, I cared about too many people inside that building—and too many artists signed to the company—to want a holocaust to follow my departure.

But I was totally unprepared for the onslaught of revisionism to come.

For example, artists could no longer mention me in their liner notes; neither simple appreciation for my past efforts nor, God forbid, a dedication was allowed. My name couldn't be mentioned at the Columbia convention held the following July in San Francisco; I was told that Bill Graham didn't act as MC one night because he said that in so doing he'd have to pay tribute to me. The films taken at the Ahmanson Theatre—the featured entertainment of the convention—were edited to eliminate every single shot of me. This was quite a feat, since I had hosted the shows. It was all so transparent as to be laughable—*and* painful. They were obviously concerned that any one of these things might set off a demonstration. But did their fear of that justify such extremism?

To me it was just plain absurd. The new management could have created so much more good will and credibility for itself by simply acknowledging my contributions during the previous eight years and admitting that *they* now had to pitch in and fill the void. But the party line was that there was no void to fill. Sly potshots were taken at past "major talent acquisition" deals. Emphasis, they said, had to be placed on new discoveries. This really got to me, because it was just pure grandstanding; for this is an obvious truth of the business—the need for new blood. The fact, however, was that—although I had always placed prime emphasis on new talent—the Columbia "assembly line" desperately needed those major acquisitions.

They raised eyebrows at the Neil Diamond deal—until it

paid off handsomely with Neil's *Jonathan Livingston Seagull* album. The incremental profits from that one album—the soundtrack of a flop movie, no less—would recoup more than one-fourth of the entire five-year guaranty. Then they became silent. They moved next from Diamond to Dylan.

The Dylan contract, which had been fully negotiated, was immediately scotched when I left. The price, Lieberson said, was too high. Then Bob had a hit with his single, "Knockin' On Heaven's Door." Now they began scrambling to make amends with Dylan's attorney. But it was too late; Bob was ready to sign with Asylum Records. So the message was that Dylan had been a "no-profit" deal. It was nonsense. Dylan contributed substantial revenues to Elektra/Asylum with his *Planet Waves* album and will provide even more with his Live album with The Band. In fact, realizing their error, Columbia unsuccessfully rushed in to offer a much higher royalty for the Live album than Geffen had paid on his "no-profit" deal. It is now very apparent that Columbia will spare nothing to bring Dylan back into the fold. They finally understand that they need Dylan and have no choice but to lure him with an outstanding royalty not only on new albums but also on his extensive catalog. It's been an expensive lesson, indeed.

Contradictions seemed to occur every week. In a *Time* magazine interview, Lieberson said that he wanted to turn the record industry back to a time when deals were more sensible. The price of talent had gotten out of hand, and Columbia was going to stay out of those wars.

Then his executives went out and offered a multimillion-dollar deal to Helen Reddy and talked about offering the moon to Elton John.

Next comes the problem of new artists. To really maintain momentum, Columbia must develop at least four to six major artists a year of the magnitude of Loggins & Messina, Earth, Wind & Fire or Edgar Winter. So I began to see announcements that *looked* as if new deals were being made. In fact, *I'd* made them. Dave Mason, Billy Joel, then a deal with Steve Paul's Blue Sky Records that brought in Rick Derringer—all these suddenly emerged in the trade papers with new stories and picture-taking. I could hardly wait for the "signing" of Pink Floyd!

Watching this from the sidelines was sometimes amusing—but mostly very sad. Was *this* the company I'd given so much of my life to? I could hardly recognize it. My friends urged me not to fret; no one was fooled by Columbia's massive press barrage, they said. "Just wait it out. Our hearts are with you." Yet it was deeply painful to confront one's puppet status as the institutional guns powered away. I just watched—and wrote some more of the book.

The momentum I had established at Columbia was continuing—and I was proud of that and of my colleagues who stayed on. Columbia's biggest gold-record year, indeed, was 1973, and the first quarter of 1974 was their biggest in history—and I felt good. More of the artists I had brought into the company were exploding as 1974 continued. Earth, Wind & Fire had become a giant group; Edgar Winter had burst into stardom; Kris Kristofferson and Mac Davis finally achieved the recognition each deserved. The Isley Brothers had sold unprecedented numbers of albums; Mott the Hoople became major headliners; The O'Jays and MFSB became firm Gamble and Huff bonanzas; Liza Minnelli was confirmed as a recording star; Chicago, Loggins & Messina and Johnny Winter remained as big as ever; the brilliance of Herbie Hancock and of Weather Report finally reached a mass audience; and Billy Joel began to stake his claim.

And on and on. It all confirmed my faith in the organization I had helped to build and in the men I had worked with so closely. Our lives may go separate ways in the future, but we *did* share something very special—no matter what the party line at Columbia ever may be. It was a wonderful, exciting, pride-filled time. I will always remember it; I hope they will too.

April, 1974

# Index

*Dynamite!* [handwritten marginal note]